Issues in Recreation
and Leisure

Issues in Recreation and Leisure

Ethical Decision Making

Donald J. McLean
and
Daniel G. Yoder

**HUMAN
KINETICS**

Library of Congress Cataloging-in-Publication Data

McLean, Donald J., 1959-
  Issues in recreation and leisure : ethical decision making / Donald J. McLean and Daniel G. Yoder.
     p. cm.
  Includes bibliographical references and index.
  ISBN 0-7360-4399-3 (softcover)
  1. Leisure--Philosophy. 2. Recreation--Philosophy. I. Yoder, Daniel G., 1952- II. Title.
  GV14.M36 2005
  790'.01--dc22
                                        2005006623

ISBN: 0-7360-4399-3

The Web addresses cited in this text were current as of April 2005, unless otherwise noted.

Acquisitions Editor: Gayle Kassing, PhD; **Developmental Editor:** Ray Vallese; **Assistant Editor:** Derek Campbell; **Copyeditor:** Alisha Jeddeloh; **Proofreader:** Joanna Hatzopoulos Portman; **Indexer:** Sharon Duffy; **Permission Manager:** Dalene Reeder; **Graphic Designer:** Nancy Rasmus; **Graphic Artist:** Dawn Sills; **Photo Manager:** Kelly J. Huff; **Cover Designer:** Jack W. Davis; **Photographer (cover):** Comstock Royalty Free Images; **Photographer (interior):** Kelly J. Huff, except as otherwise noted; **Art Manager:** Kelly Hendren; **Illustrator:** Al Wilborn; **Printer:** Versa Press

Printed in the United States of America 10 9 8 7 6 5 4 3 2 1

Human Kinetics
Web site: www.HumanKinetics.com

United States: Human Kinetics
P.O. Box 5076
Champaign, IL 61825-5076
800-747-4457
e-mail: humank@hkusa.com

Canada: Human Kinetics
475 Devonshire Road Unit 100
Windsor, ON N8Y 2L5
800-465-7301 (in Canada only)
e-mail: orders@hkcanada.com

Europe: Human Kinetics
107 Bradford Road
Stanningley
Leeds LS28 6AT, United Kingdom
+44 (0) 113 255 5665
e-mail: hk@hkeurope.com

Australia: Human Kinetics
57A Price Avenue
Lower Mitcham, South Australia
5062
08 8277 1555
e-mail: liaw@hkaustralia.com

New Zealand: Human Kinetics
Division of Sports Distributors
NZ Ltd.
P.O. Box 300 226 Albany
North Shore City
Auckland
0064 9 448 1207
e-mail: info@humankinetics.co.nz

Contents

Part II Current Issues in Leisure Services

FIVE Community Recreation 71

SIX Commercial Recreation 91

SEVEN Therapeutic Recreation 111

EIGHT Outdoor Recreation 131

Preface

> Can you tell me, Socrates—is virtue something that can be taught? Or does it come by practice? Or is it neither teaching nor practice that gives it to a man but natural aptitude or something else?
>
> *Plato*

Since the time of the ancient Greeks, philosophers have debated whether it is possible to teach people to be ethical. It is the premise of this book that all individuals working in leisure services can improve their ability to deal with moral issues. The techniques of moral reasoning presented in these pages can help you make better ethical decisions, act fairly and consistently, and experience less personal and professional trauma. Our goal is not to present solutions to moral dilemmas but to enable leisure and recreation providers like yourself to systematically manage ethical issues. While intuitive understanding of right and wrong are important elements for making ethical decisions, all of us can benefit from learning a logical problem-solving method and then honing our newly acquired skills for resolving dilemmas. Indeed, traditional professions have increasingly recognized that fact and now require their members to receive formalized instruction in applied ethics. Leisure and recreation providers must not only do the same but also take a leadership role in promoting ethics in the workplace.

Teaching and learning applied ethics is a complex task requiring students and instructors to master a comprehensive understanding of how moral dilemmas can be justly resolved. In this book you will learn techniques and guidelines that you can use to develop sound approaches to ethical problem solving. Along with understanding techniques for dealing with dilemmas, you will also develop an appreciation of your own roles and responsibilities as a leisure and recreation provider. You will learn that your ability to resolve ethical dilemmas is enhanced when you are able to use your judgment to marry techniques of moral decision making to the broader values and service traditions unique to the leisure and recreation field.

The existing ethics-oriented literature in recreation and leisure studies has primarily focused on the macro issues of leisure values and lifestyles and the roles and status of leisure and recreation providers. Little effort has been given to exploring the micro issues of how these providers should implement their value systems on a daily basis to resolve actual ethical dilemmas. It is as though academics believe that by understanding the broad philosophic foundations of the leisure field, practitioners will intuitively know how to deal with moral dilemmas when they arise. We believe that this trickle down theory of moral knowledge is unlikely to provide much practical guidance unless it is complemented with training in applying moral theory to actual leisure and recreation dilemmas. It is perhaps wise to remind ourselves that the root of the word *ethics* means *habit,* and that Aristotle conceived moral reasoning as primarily a practical matter of learning good habits rather than a theoretical discipline focused on increasing one's knowledge of abstract concepts.

Most North American recreation, park, tourism, and sport management programs in higher education have similar curricula. Four years of leadership, programming, and administration classes cover the "what is" of the field. Then, a capstone class addresses prominent leisure-related issues, exposing students to the "what should be" of the field. This book is ideal for such classes as well as for upper-level undergraduate and graduate philosophy of leisure courses and professional ethics classes.

Features and Benefits

Several features of this book make it an ideal selection for a variety of recreation-related courses.

- This text carefully and concisely blends essential theoretical elements with practical applications in diverse situations, so students do not need two or three expensive and redundant books for the class.

- This book contributes to meeting multiple standards in the National Recreation and Park Association accreditation guidelines relating to ethical professional practice and service delivery.

- Each chapter begins with goals for what you should learn in that chapter and ends with discussion questions to help you better understand what you have learned.

- Numerous examples and vignettes illustrate how the principles can be applied. These illustrations correspond to different sectors in the field, including several situations you are likely to encounter in your own career.

- Ethical dilemmas are common themes in popular culture, especially movies. While some movies treat ethical situations superficially, others expose these individual and societal struggles. Throughout the book, Related Films sidebars encourage you to reflect on relevant films you may have already seen or inform you of movies that may help you develop a more comprehensive understanding of the particular situations.

- A three-step model for ethical decision making and acting, the crucial link between theory and practice, is thoroughly explored. Familiarity with the model is the first step in developing the habits that lead to ethical thought and action.

- Eight detailed case studies allow you to actually practice using the model. These cases are the result of the authors' experiences in a wide range of leisure service settings in the United States and Canada over the past 20 years. Questions at the end of each case study help you negotiate your way through what may seem like impossible dilemmas. These questions also give you the opportunity to reflect on the problem-solving process, perhaps even to customize the basic model that will work most effectively for you in your particular occupation.

- Each chapter contains Learning Activities that you can undertake in and outside of the class to enhance your understanding of important concepts.

- Finally, this textbook has been tested in classrooms since 2003. Both authors teach ethics classes, one at the undergraduate level and the other at the graduate level. Through classroom trial and error and a great deal of student feedback, we have refined the material, clarified key components, determined and then emphasized material that resonates with students, and eliminated material that is irrelevant or lackluster.

How to Use This Text

The format of the book provides flexibility for instructors to choose both the thematic areas they wish to teach and the depth to which they want to investigate a particular topic. This is especially important given the variations in park and recreation curricula in North America. Courses that meet 1 hour a week might use only the initial chapters and focus on one particular area of service delivery. This approach would be particularly advantageous for a course in professional ethics that is intended to target the needs of a particular group of students (e.g., professional ethics for therapeutic recreation students). A course that meets 2 hours a week might cover more, possibly all, the subfields of service delivery. Instructors of courses that meet 3 hours a week would be well served by using the entire book—the introductory chapters, subfield chapters, detailed case studies, and appendix. In addition, the way the book integrates literature from both leisure studies and applied ethics provides several supplemental sources for instructors to turn to should they want to investigate a particular ethical principle or debate in greater detail.

To most effectively serve students and instructors, the text is divided into three parts and an appendix. Throughout the course of the book and within each of the three parts, we progress from the general to the specific. This is consistent with our commitment to blending theory and application.

Part I

The first part of the book lays out several themes to build a solid foundation for the material that follows in parts II and III.

- Chapter 1 disputes the widespread belief that this field is little more than trivial pleasure pursuits. In reality, we are in a position to profoundly influence individuals and groups through our thinking and actions.

- Chapter 2 argues that the line between good and evil is not so easily discerned and acting ethically is not as easy as it may seem. Milgram's experiment is used to show the fine line between good and bad, while Kohlberg's theories of human development are examined to give insight into levels of ethical judgment. Rest's Defining Issues Test allows students to gauge their own moral development.

- Moral reasoning is the subject of chapter 3, and we offer three basic approaches to determining moral actions. The uses and limitations of consequence-based, rule-based, and virtue-based approaches to ethics are explained.

- Drawing upon the first three chapters, chapter 4 offers a logical model for ethical decision making and acting. Stage 1 helps students identify the moral dilemma, stage 2 addresses what is praiseworthy and what is blameworthy, and stage 3 helps students devise a moral action plan. A detailed example illustrates the key components of the model.

Part II

The second part of the book focuses on several prominent issues within well-established subfields of leisure services. Because new areas in leisure services develop every few years, this section does not attempt to be fully inclusive. We include chapters on community recreation and therapeutic recreation, for example, but we do not devote a chapter to correctional recreation that takes place in jails and prisons across North America. Although correctional recreation has its share of ethical dilemmas, including whether incarcerated individuals even have a right to recreation, this emerging subfield is so new that a lengthy treatment is not warranted at this time. In addition to pointing out key ethical topics, each chapter in this part considers the most common pitfalls that thwart the making of good ethical decisions in that particular subfield.

- Chapter 5 addresses ethical situations in community recreation and warns about naive legalism, or overreliance on the law.

- Chapter 6, devoted to commercial recreation, considers a wide variety of ethical quandaries that reflect the remarkable diversity of this subfield. The nature of commercial recreation also lends itself to a discussion of the seductive dangers of egoism.

- Chapter 7, on therapeutic recreation, considers special situations in that field and cautions about relying too much on codes of conduct.

- Chapter 8 addresses ethical dilemmas in outdoor recreation and points out that we must be willing to evaluate some of our long-held beliefs if we are to think and act ethically.

- Chapter 9 discusses issues in tourism and warns about the dangers of ethical relativism.

Part III

Part III brings together the previously discussed material, both theoretical and practical, as it looks toward the future.

- Chapter 10 addresses the topic of professionalism and its relationship to leisure services. After considering different definitions and qualities of professions, we examine the characteristics of leisure and recreation services. We ask readers two questions at the end of this chapter—first, if any or all leisure services subfields currently qualify as professions, and second, what the consequences and responsibilities might be for future personnel if the field is granted full professional status.

- The conclusion, chapter 11, is consistent with the rest of the book in that we offer no easy answers. Rather, we advise readers to thoughtfully and systematically resolve the issues they face in their field while considering themselves, other individuals, and society.

- Chapter 12 provides several detailed case studies for you to try out the decision-making model and refine your newly acquired knowledge in a safe environment. The case studies are the result of the authors' experiences and a thorough review of contemporary dilemmas in leisure services. The questions at the end of each case study are an extension of the problem-solving model offered in chapter 4. Although each set of questions is specific to the case study they follow, they follow a basic template. In this final chapter you will find stories about:

  - A nature center with several mounts of game animals
  - An employee who is less than honest on the water-quality reports at an aquatics facility
  - A dispute over who has the right to use a river in the western United States
  - A museum display about lynching
  - A college athlete who is also a stripper at a local bar
  - An agency director who is misusing grant funds
  - A struggle over who can do what on public trails
  - A girl who refuses to wear her team's jersey with the name of a local bar on it

When students of leisure and recreation sport services embark on their career, they should feel confident that they have the means to systematically resolve the ethical issues they will inevitably face in their professional life. A curriculum that includes courses specifically devoted to ethics provides students with such confidence and greatly enhances their chances of success. Ultimately, this book will assist and encourage faculty to help students from a wide range of disciplines improve their ability to function as ethically mature and competent human beings.

Acknowledgments

This book was written at a particularly difficult time for my family: my wife Sheila had been diagnosed with cancer in March of 2002. I cannot begin to express my appreciation for the support that family, friends, colleagues, and students have generously given to us. Their help has kept our daughter Jaime, Sheila, and me going forward with our lives. I would like to extend special thanks to my co-author Dan Yoder, who selflessly took on the lion's share of the writing for this book. I would also like to thank our editors, Gayle Kassing and Ray Vallese, for their patience and understanding. Sherie Brigham deserves thanks for her expert proofreading of the final text. Finally, I would like to give honorable mention to the alumni of my RPTA 399 and 515 classes. You served as both inspiration and guinea pig to what appears in the pages that follow. I wish all of you well in your journey through life.

—Don McLean

This book would not have been possible without the love and support of many individuals. First and foremost, thank you to my wonderful wife Sheryl, son Forrest, and daughter Kelsey. You were always there for me. My colleagues, especially department chair Nick DiGrino, gave me just the right amount of encouragement and assistance. Finally, thanks to all of the students I have been privileged to have in my classes. I will say it again—you really are the best and the brightest and humanity's greatest hope for a better future.

—Dan Yoder

Foundations

ONE

The Need for Ethics in Recreation and Leisure Services

Recreation and leisure services is a relatively new field that is an important part of postindustrial societies. While people have always engaged in play, it was not until the 20th century that a person could expect to earn a living by facilitating the fun of others. The rapid growth of organized leisure services makes the recreation field an exciting place to work. Every year, new forms of recreational activity are introduced as people seek novel and diverse experiences in their leisure time, which means new opportunities for employment are continually created. While the stereotypical career goal of a recreation major is to become a park ranger, students have an incredibly wide range of career options. They may find themselves working in hospitals, community centers, theme parks, museums, corporations, government agencies, nonprofit agencies—the list goes on and on. This range of opportunities makes it difficult to identify a single specific career within the recreation

Although leisure and recreation are pleasurable aspects of life, leisure service providers often encounter moral dilemmas.

sector. Perhaps it is best to think of people employed in leisure services as quality of life specialists. Such workers all use leisure and recreation as a way to help people live more enjoyable and fulfilling lives.

A primary attraction of leisure services employment is the prospect of doing rewarding work in pleasant, comfortable surroundings. Recreation providers are in the business of helping others achieve fulfilling leisure experiences. Such work typically occurs in settings of great natural beauty, such as a national park, or in facilities designed for enjoyment, such as a multipurpose recreation center. Recreation service providers can also often see the positive effects of their work on individuals, the community, and the natural environment. The park ranger knows her presence protects nature and educates the public. The superintendent of public recreation derives satisfaction from planning the building of a new aquatics facility that will serve lower-income families in an urban community. The therapeutic recreation specialist observes how the prescribed recreation activities have helped a disabled client become independent of caregivers. In short, leisure service providers usually find themselves in the enviable position of providing worthwhile services in an enjoyable work environment.

More Than Meets the Eye?

The pleasant work environment might suggest that ethical issues are rarely a problem for leisure service providers. But does this image match reality? Consider the following scenarios:

- A director of a city recreation department is concerned that an older building the city council has recently purchased for use as a recreation center may have asbestos contamination. The director would like to have the building tested, but the alderman who campaigned for the purchase of the building tells him that no testing is needed and the recreation center should open as soon as possible.

- A therapeutic recreation specialist working in a mental health facility suspects that a client is a pedophile. During treatment sessions the client makes frequent comments with sexual overtones regarding children. The therapist learns that the client will be participating in a church-sponsored camping trip for young children.

- The owner of a travel bureau has built a successful business by promoting specialty ecotourism packages to wealthy clients who are interested in visiting exotic environments and cultures. She reads an article concerning a tourist destination in Morocco that is both extremely popular with her clients and profitable for her business. The article chronicles the devastating effect of tourism on Berber culture in Morocco. In the village of Imilchil, an annual engagement ritual takes place in which thousands of young Berber men and women come together to find their life partners. At the end of the colorful 3-day festival several hundreds of young couples are married. Unfortunately, the Berbers are a private people and the presence of several hundred visitors has drastically reduced the number of young people attending the festival. In 2001, only four couples were married. Thanks to tourism, a significant part of this culture is rapidly disappearing.

- The superintendent of a state nature preserve receives a request from the local state representative to use the nature center and surrounding grounds for a family reunion. The preserve's policy is to rent the center only to groups engaging in outdoor education activities. The proposed reunion is purely a social event and the representative says he hopes to get a liquor license for it. Normally, the superintendent would deny such a request. However, he knows that this politician is a powerbroker who has a reputation for reducing state funding to agencies he regards as uncooperative.

• A commercial fitness club advertises itself as the "healthy-lifestyle experts." Yet many of the young patrons want the club to install tanning beds, which have been linked to skin cancer. Some have already indicated that they will consider switching to a competing club that has the beds. As one teenaged member said, "Skin cancer? That's what old farts get! Why waste my money here getting buff if I can't also get bronzed?"

Try to picture yourself as the decision maker in these situations. Think about how you would solve the problem presented in each example. Do you feel uncertain about what to do? Then undoubtedly you have noticed that none of them has a simple solution. In each instance, you must deal with an ethical dilemma with no easy way out. In fact, the word *dilemma* implies that a difficult choice must be made between two outcomes. For example, should the recreation director go ahead and open the youth facility? Or should he refuse to follow the alderman's instructions and delay use of the facility until it can be proven safe? What are the moral implications of choosing one course of action or the other? The director probably feels caught between a rock and a hard place, yet he has to make a decision.

Parks and recreation administrators must make decisions that ensure the use of parks and facilities by some does not unduly affect the use and satisfaction of others.

Ethical Responsibilities in Recreation and Leisure Services

The fact that we associate leisure and recreation with the more pleasurable aspects of life does not mean that they happen in a morally neutral environment. As providers of leisure services our actions and motivations are subject to moral scrutiny. Providing recreation is more than fun and games—it requires extensive interaction with others, including clients, coworkers, and the greater community. The ethical responsibilities of people working in leisure services derive in part from the fact that their actions affect the interests of those whom they come into contact with while carrying out their duties.

The power of leisure and recreation to affect people's lives can also be misused. We can probably all recall instances where others used recreation in negative ways. For example, it is likely that any child involved in minor sport leagues has witnessed adults yelling abusive, derogatory comments at the young athletes.

As well as affecting people's lives, leisure and recreation providers can also positively or negatively affect nonhuman things. Recreation agencies have stewardship responsibilities for natural and cultural resources that are used for leisure. National park officials, for example, have a duty to protect the natural environment while providing recreation opportunities for the public. Similarly, museum staff have curatorial responsibilities to preserve cultural artifacts while educating visitors. Leisure service providers therefore often are cast into conflicting roles: They must take care of significant public resources while also facilitating the public enjoyment of those resources. Balancing these interests is not simply an issue of managerial decision making, but often requires recreation providers to

Learning Activity: The Power of Leisure and Recreation to Affect People's Lives

- How have your leisure activities affected your own life?
- When you were growing up, did you join any clubs or sport teams?
- Were your experiences positive or negative?
- Do you think some of the things you now do for leisure were influenced by your experiences as a child?

confront the ethical implications of their actions. For example, should park visitors have access to a delicate ecosystem, even though opening the area to the public will reduce the native wildlife populations? This question cannot be answered simply by examining the facts or by employing complex business decision models; rather, managers must decide whether the loss of fauna is an ethically acceptable consequence.

Dealing With Ethical Issues Systematically

Thus far, we have seen strong evidence suggesting that leisure service providers have to deal with ethical issues on a continuing basis. It would therefore seem prudent for recreation students to prepare themselves for handling moral conundrums, just as they prepare themselves to solve typical management problems relating to the planning, programming, staffing, and financing of leisure services. However, many people think that morality is a gut issue—that is, they simply consult their feelings about right and wrong, good and bad. According to this view, ethical decision making cannot be approached like planning a budget or scheduling program activities. Instead, ethical decisions depend on the decision maker's intuition and judgment, and perhaps a good measure of luck. Hence, ethical issues are difficult because there are neither clear solutions nor standard problem-solving techniques.

But is it true that we cannot deal with ethical issues systematically? Do we have to simply fly by the seat of our pants and hope for the best when we encounter ethical issues? The purpose of this text is to demonstrate techniques for solving moral dilemmas. While emotions and intuition cannot be ignored in moral decision making, good judgment requires us to also employ our ability to reason. In addition, applying methods of moral reasoning to ethical dilemmas not only helps *us* decide what is right and wrong, it also helps *others* understand why we have chosen a particular course of action. People do have a gut reaction when they believe a moral misdeed may be occurring, so emotions are likely to be running high. Serious moral dilemmas typically have the unpleasant feature that someone, if not everyone, is going to be unhappy with your decision. You need to be able to justify your judgment call so that those who disagree with you at least have the opportunity to examine your reasons. While it is unlikely that opponents of the decision will be persuaded that it was the right choice, they will see that you were not acting arbitrarily but instead had a method and a rationale.

While strong emotions are common to ethical dilemmas, they must be managed for sound decision making and acting.

Goal of This Book

Our goal for this book is to teach you methods for solving ethical dilemmas you are likely to encounter in leisure services. While much of leisure studies literature deals with broad societal problems facing leisure services (e.g., constraints to leisure, problems of at-risk youth, leisure and gender issues), this text focuses on becoming proficient at resolving ethical dilemmas. Certainly, an understanding of ethical theories and issues relating to leisure services will help guide our justifications for dilemma solutions. However, we will only use ethical theories and leisure issues when they serve our primary goal: to practice solving realistic ethical dilemmas.

Case studies throughout the text will allow you to apply the techniques of ethical decision making that are explained in each chapter. Our intention is not to provide answers to the ethical dilemmas, but rather to help you develop your ability to systematically evaluate and resolve situations involving ethical issues in leisure services. You should not be concerned when your solutions to ethical dilemmas aren't always the same as those of your peers. As in most challenging situations, there is rarely only one correct solution. Instead, there are many solutions, some of which are more justifiable than others.

Conclusion

The journalist H.L. Mencken once quipped that "morality is the theory that every human act is either right or wrong, and that 99% of them are wrong" (www.brainyquote.com/quotes/quotes/h/hlmencke1557550.html). By saying that it is vital for leisure service providers to deal effectively with ethical issues, we are not suggesting that people's leisure choices need to be strictly policed. Surely a fundamental characteristic of the leisure experience is people's ability to choose those forms of recreation and leisure that they find intrinsically worthwhile and pleasurable. Yet by the same token, the moral boundaries of leisure cannot be without limits. The recreation and leisure choices that people make can have profound effects on other people and the natural environment. In your role as a leisure service provider, you have a special responsibility to recognize and effectively resolve moral dilemmas arising from people's leisure activities. As you read the chapters in this book and practice solving moral dilemmas, you will develop the abilities and confidence necessary for dealing with the many ethical issues and dilemmas that leisure service providers encounter.

QUESTIONS FOR DISCUSSION

1. Think of a time when you faced an ethical dilemma at work or in your personal life. Perhaps you felt pressure to do something you didn't think you should do. Ask yourself these questions:
    - How did you feel when you encountered the problem?
    - What did you do to solve the problem?
    - Was your solution to the problem effective?
    - Was your solution to the problem fair?

2. Think of a time when you had the opportunity to engage in a leisure activity that you thought was morally questionable.

- Did you go ahead and do the activity?
- If you didn't do the activity, what was it that stopped you?
- If you did do the activity, how did you feel afterward?

TWO

The Human Nature of Morality

GOALS

1. To recognize that morality is more complex than a battle between heroes and villains
2. To learn about the Milgram experiment and its implications for the human capacity to act unethically
3. To understand Kohlberg's theory of the stages of moral development

Learning how to solve ethical dilemmas might seem like taking lessons in etiquette—we think it is a problem only for those unfortunate few who are socially maladapted. We are no more likely to consider ourselves immoral than to imagine ourselves as uncouth boors. Bad manners and bad morals are problems that we prefer to notice in others.

But perhaps we are not as infallible as we would like to think. We have all experienced the embarrassment of making a social faux pas, and though we may be loath to admit it, we have all probably felt guilty about something we did. It isn't that we are mean or malevolent; we are nice, caring people who occasionally make mistakes. It seems reasonable to believe that most people are just like us—they mean well and usually do the right thing.

Given our belief that the majority of people are basically decent, we might conclude that ethics should focus on exposing and correcting the moral improprieties of a not-so-nice antisocial minority. Movies and television programs feed us a steady diet of morality tales in which the forces of good and evil come into conflict, with good triumphing in the end. The heroes and villains usually appear as caricatures cast according to the following rules: Heroes are personable, while villains are repulsive; heroes are physically attractive, while villains are deformed; and heroes are noble in motivation and care for others, while villains are devious and have malevolent intentions. We are so familiar with this dichotomy

Few, if any, of us are 100 percent pure and good. Few of us are entirely bad. Thus, we must pay constant attention to our decisions and actions.

Learning Activity: Good and Evil in Pop Culture

Most of us are familiar with the way movies and television depict good versus evil. Here are some questions to help you reflect on how popular culture may affect your views. Share and compare your views with those of your classmates.

1. Why do people watch professional wrestling matches when it is obvious that the participants are following a script?
2. Who are your favorite heroes and villains in animated movies, and why do you like (or like to hate) them?
3. Do you think the portrayal of doctors, lawyers, and police on prime-time dramas is realistic?

of good versus evil that the dialogue and plot of most movies and television shows are predictable. We know what the actors are going to say and do as the scenes unfold.

Milgram's Shocking Experiment

Pop culture's opposition between heroes and villains would seem to suggest that morality boils down to a battle between good and evil. But does this simplistic idea of good guys versus bad guys reflect real life? Social psychology research suggests otherwise. In the early 1960s, Stanley Milgram and his colleagues conducted an ingenious experiment to measure obedience to authority (Milgram 1974). Volunteers for the experiment were told that they would help teach other volunteers to remember pairs of words by using a special machine. The volunteer was to use the machine to administer increasing levels of electric shock to the learner each time the learner made an error in reciting a set of word pairs. A researcher stayed with the volunteer teacher to supervise the use of the machine.

Although the volunteer teachers believed they could shock the learner with the controls of the learning machine, this was not the case. The learner was actually a confederate of the research team who followed a scripted response to the teacher's actions. The experimenter instructed the teacher to increase the level of electric shock each time the learner made a mistake. The learner acted as though the shocks were becoming increasingly painful, to the point of being life threatening.

The results of the experiment were indeed shocking. Over half of the teachers administered what appeared to be a lethal level of shock to the learner. Although some volunteers refused to continue the experiment

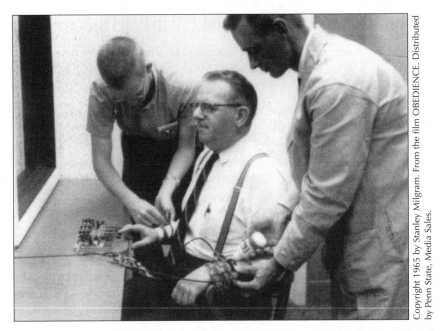

Milgram's experiment is evidence that human beings are capable of both good and evil.

once they thought they were harming the learner, the majority continued when the supervising experimenter insisted.

How could so many people be persuaded to commit acts that they believed were causing grievous harm to another person? Milgram cautions us that we should not jump to the conclusion that these volunteers were sadistic monsters who enjoyed attacking the learners. Instead, he emphasizes that the cooperating teachers typically objected to continuing the experiment, and often exhibited signs of distress and anguish. The results demanded a more complicated explanation than simply labeling the cooperating teachers as "bad guys." Instead, the results revealed a paradox: The cooperative teachers were concerned about the learner's well-being, yet they still obeyed the experimenter's commands. They knew that what they were doing was wrong, yet most were unable to defy the experimenter's instructions.

Unlike sadists, the cooperating volunteers' behavior is conflicted. True sadists would inflict shocks because they only care about their own pleasure. The cooperating volunteers, however, were concerned about the learner's safety and wanted to break off the experiment. Their moral sensibilities and their actions were therefore in conflict. While we may be dismayed at their actions, it would be unfair to think of them as individuals who delight in harming others.

Learning Activity: Do As You Are Told!

Watch the movie *Obedience* (Penn State Media Sales [1990], University Park, PA; originally produced as a motion picture in 1965), which depicts Milgram's experiment, and then answer the following questions.

1. Do you think you would have resisted the experimenter's commands?

2. Can you think of a situation where you felt pressured to do something you thought was wrong? Did you immediately refuse, initially cooperate and then refuse, reluctantly but fully cooperate, or enthusiastically and fully cooperate?

3. Why do you think you behaved the way you did?

And what about the volunteers who defied the experimenter and chose not to continue? Should we regard them as moral heroes? Again, the reality is more complicated. Milgram found that those who quit the experiment typically cooperated with the experimenter in the beginning. They exhibited many of the same symptoms of unease with increasing the electric shock before they finally refused to continue. Thus, the defiant volunteers might be classified as partial cooperators. Their behavior is certainly more admirable than the volunteers who complied with all of the experimenter's instructions, but in many ways they seemed to experience the same moral conflicts as the volunteers who thought they were administering the maximum level of shock. Ironically, although his remarkable experiment garnered Milgram much attention and notoriety, it also negatively impacted his career as an academician. Many colleagues criticized the obedience experiment as an ethical breach of experimental protocol that abused naive subjects. Yale University denied him tenure, and for a time he could not secure an academic position (Slater 2004).

The results of Milgram's experiment should serve as a warning that most people can be persuaded to commit highly unethical acts. Lest you think the experiment was too artificial to really measure people's responses to ethical dilemmas, perhaps a few historical examples will suffice.

• Have you seen photographs of mob lynchings that occurred in the United States from the Reconstruction period after the Civil War until well into the middle of the 20th century? Many of these photos capture not only grisly images of the victims but also the perpetrators and audience. In most cases they are smiling for the camera as though they were posing for a picture at a family gathering. Some of these photographs were even turned into postcards that people would mail to friends (Allen 2000).

- Adolf Eichmann, one of Hitler's key subordinates, was largely responsible for transporting deportees to the Nazi death camps that killed 6 million human beings. By many reports, however, he was a loving husband and father who cared deeply for his family. Eichmann often came home with presents and candy for his small children after a long day of fine-tuning the operation of the death camps (Arendt 1963).

- The Sand Creek Massacre, which took place in southeast Colorado in 1864, has been called the most horrific attack on Native Americans in North America. On a fateful November morning, approximately 700 U.S. soldiers attacked a village of over 550 Cheyenne and Arapahoe Indians, most of whom were women and children. Nearly all were killed. A few days after the raid, Colonel John M. Chivington, the leader of the attack, regaled cheering crowds in Denver with souvenirs of the so-called battle, including scalps and the genitalia of Native American women (Hoig 1961).

- In 1978, the world's largest mass suicide took place in Jonestown, Guyana. For several years, charismatic leader Jim Jones and his church had practiced what many churches preached. They started soup kitchens and helped the homeless. When someone was sick, members from the congregation visited to see if they could help. However, Jones also convinced his followers that it was good and right to drink fruit punch laced with cyanide. Of the 914 dead, 276 were children who had been given the poisonous drinks by their parents (Maaga 1998).

It is tempting to think that there must be something desperately wrong with societies that allow such atrocities to occur. Yet the pattern of apparently average people committing heinous acts is repeated across cultures and throughout history. Why is it that most people can be persuaded to commit unethical acts? Psychologists have conducted a great deal of research on the ability to act ethically. From his studies of the ethical decision-making ability of adolescent boys, Lawrence Kohlberg developed a way to classify moral development.

Kohlberg's Theory of Moral Development

In the 1960s, Havard psychologist Lawrence Kohlberg posited a six-stage theory of moral development. Kohlberg's stages are similar to Piaget's theory of the cognitive development of children. Like Piaget's theory, Kohlberg's theory holds that as children mature, their ability to reason has the potential to become more sophisticated. **Kohlberg's theory of**

moral development describes the six ascending levels of complexity in moral reasoning:

- **Stage 1.** The lowest stage of moral cognitive development is highly egoistic. Moral decision making at stage 1 is done only with regard to one's own self-interest. Like a young child who does not want to be punished, people operating at this level avoid unethical actions only because they are concerned about the retribution they might face.

- **Stage 2.** At this stage, morality is more sophisticated because the interests of others are recognized. People who operate at stage 2 see being ethical as a quid pro quo—we get along with someone else because neither of us wants to get hurt. Children initiate such behavior to work out the sharing of a favorite toy. Both would like to have the toy for themselves, but they share to avoid an unpleasant conflict.

- **Stage 3.** At this stage, morality is based on affiliation. Whereas cooperation in stage 2 is based on mutual self-interest, stage 3 operates on the basis of friendship. People at stage 3 behave ethically because they have established long-term relationships in which they care for others at a personal level. However, individuals outside of one's circle of friends do not receive the same consideration.

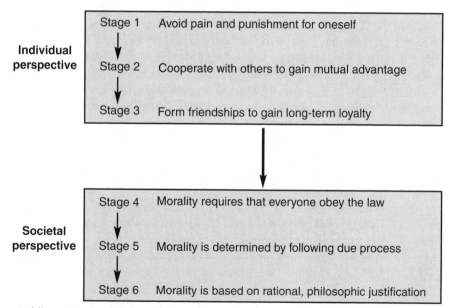

Kohlberg's six levels of moral development.

- **Stage 4.** This stage marks a conceptual watershed in moral cognition, as it requires one to understand ethical relationships according to abstract principles. People who abide by the law because they recognize that everyone benefits from avoiding anarchy are at stage 4. Their thinking is more abstract than in the earlier stages because they are willing to support ethical behavior on principle rather than on the basis of self-interest or personal affiliation. Those who often want to resolve ethical dilemmas by determining what the law says may be at stage 4.

- **Stage 5.** At this stage, morality builds upon the idea that everyone must follow the same moral rules, but it questions how those rules are created. Only those laws that are created through due process are justified. Stage 5 thus resembles the notion of procedural justice in that abstract moral rules are only justified when they are created in an appropriate manner. For example, an accepted idea in our society is that rules should be created by some sort of democratic process that give people a voice in their governance.

- **Stage 6.** This stage is the highest level of moral development, going beyond the requirement that moral rules be created by an appropriate process. Stage 6 requires providing philosophic justification to demonstrate that a moral rule is worthy of acceptance.

Kohlberg's hierarchy of moral development has two distinct phases. Moving from stage 1 to stage 3, people become less self-centered as they become more concerned with the well-being of those with whom they have personal relationships. Stages 4 to 6 represent the second phase of moral development, where personal relationships are no longer the only justification for acting ethically. At these higher stages people extend moral consideration to strangers. Abstract principles rather than personal affiliation determine right and wrong. Kohlberg believed that few people could operate at stage 6. His research led him to hypothesize that most people's moral deliberations occur at the lower stages of moral development.

Some researchers have criticized Kohlberg's work. For example, in the early 1980s, psychologist Carol Gilligan (1993) argued that Kohlberg's research is sexist and does not represent the moral development of women. Gilligan posited that women's morality is based on what she called a care ethic emphasizing interpersonal connections, while men's moral development centers on concepts of impersonal justice. However, while Gilligan's critique has generated much controversy, there is little empirical evidence to support her thesis that the moral deliberations of women and men are fundamentally different (Rest 1994).

Learning Activity: What's Your Stage?

At what stage of moral development do you think you deal with ethical issues?

- Are your reasons for doing the right thing motivated by fear of punishment?
- Are you mostly concerned with being nice to your friends?
- Are you mostly concerned with following the law?
- Is your sense of morality guided by deeply held principles that you have critically examined?

Think of a time when you faced a moral dilemma as an adolescent. How did you resolve the problem? Now, imagine how you would deal with the same dilemma as an adult. Would you make the same decision? Would your reasons for your decision be different?

Human vanity probably makes us think that we personally operate at the higher stages of moral development. After all, who wants to think of themselves as morally unsophisticated? Psychologist James Rest devised a test that helps measure an individual's level of moral development. Rest's **Defining Issues Test (DIT)** uses imaginary stories that describe an ethical problem. Respondents are presented with the scenario and then asked to rate the importance of a set of statements relating to the story's problem. Each statement is worded to reflect a particular stage of Kohlberg's theory of moral development.

Respondents tend to assign greater importance to statements that most closely express their level of moral development. For example, respondents who function primarily at stage 4 are probably attracted to statements that suggest moral problems should be resolved by appeals to the rule of law. Similarly, respondents who view moral issues primarily in terms of philosophic principles are likely to rate statements reflecting stage 6 as of highest importance.

Imagine yourself in the following situation. You have recently graduated from a university and have been hired as the director of a summer camp for boys. One of your first tasks is to hire a lead counselor. You have received several applications for the position, but one resume stands out from the rest. It is from John Green, a young man whom you know from your high school days. John is definitely the most qualified applicant. However, you also know that John is quite open about the fact the he is homosexual.

While you know that John would make an excellent employee, you also believe that the parents of some of the campers would strongly object to a homosexual man being in a leadership role for young boys. You are wondering whether you should hire a less qualified candidate who would also be less controversial.

Given his sexual orientation, you now face a moral dilemma of whether to hire John. Depending on the sophistication of your moral reasoning, you could make your decision based on the following rationales:

- If your primary worry is that your decision might negatively affect your career, then you are using stage 1 moral reasoning to resolve the dilemma.

- If you are concerned that your decision will result in loss of cooperation of the people you work with, then you are using stage 2 reasoning to resolve the dilemma.

- If you are afraid that you will lose the friendship of others because of your decision, then you are using stage 3 reasoning to resolve the dilemma.

© Bruce Coleman, Inc.

The director of this camp faces a dilemma about hiring a new lead counselor.

- If you believe you should obey whatever rules the agency has regarding a job candidate's sexual orientation, then you are using stage 4 reasoning to resolve the dilemma.

- If you think that the agency's rules regarding the hiring of homosexuals should be followed because they have been created through an open and democratic process, then you are using stage 5 reasoning to resolve the dilemma.

- If you think the agency's policies regarding the hiring of homosexuals are justified by ethical principles and concepts, then you are using stage 6 reasoning to resolve the dilemma.

Notice that your actual decision about whether to hire John is irrelevant to the stage of moral reasoning you are using. In other words, each stage of moral reasoning could provide reasons for both hiring or not hiring John. Moral sophistication does not guarantee one's ethical decisions will be superior to the decisions of someone else who operates at a lower stage. People with little to no formal training in ethics have made profoundly good moral choices. Conversely, highly educated people have done absolutely reprehensible things for complex reasons.

So, if complex reasoning does not guarantee ethically praiseworthy decisions, then does it matter whether leisure service providers are morally sophisticated? Absolutely! While complex moral reasoning does not ensure that you will act ethically, it does give you the ability to better understand the moral deliberations of others. For example, Denis is a person who reasons at a lower level of moral sophistication, say stage 3. He can make good ethical decisions, but he will not be able to understand the moral reasoning of Margaret, who bases her decisions on a stage 6 rationale. Denis determines right from wrong and good from bad on the basis of friendships and personal affiliations. He is motivated to treat his friends and associates fairly. But Denis would not understand why he should be as concerned about people whom he has never met. Margaret, who is a stage 6 thinker, might try to explain to Denis that both friends and strangers should be treated fairly because the concept of justice must necessarily apply to everyone, not just the people we like. However, Denis will likely be puzzled by Margaret's abstract reasoning. It is not that Denis thinks Margaret is immoral. Rather, he doesn't understand why he should give as much consideration to strangers as he would to friends.

In contrast to Denis' bewilderment with Margaret's "philosophizing about the importance of strangers," Margaret is able to understand Denis' point of view. She too has a natural inclination to want to give more help to friends than to strangers. So she knows where Denis is coming from. But she is also able to recognize that there are good reasons for applying the same moral standards to both strangers and friends. Her moral reasoning is more sophisticated, which means that she is able to understand Denis' rationale whereas Denis cannot understand hers.

Thus, there is an advantage to attaining a high level of sophistication in our moral reasoning abilities, as it puts us in the position of being able to understand and respond to moral deliberations of people who are operating at a lower stage. Of course, this explanation of the utility of moral sophistication is not meant to suggest that people like Denis are fated to be unsophisticated moral thinkers. In fact, Rest's research based on the Defining Issues Test strongly indicates that people can increase their powers of moral reasoning through education (Rest and Narvaez 1994). As people become more educated, they tend to gravitate toward statements that exemplify the higher stages of moral reasoning. Thus, college graduates tend to interpret moral issues in more theoretical terms than high school dropouts. While Rest found differences in DIT scores based on the academic discipline and individual studies (e.g., philosophy students were found to score higher on the DIT than business students), it is generally the case that education attainment is a reliable predictor of moral sophistication. Furthermore, age, culture, and gender do not significantly influence the effects of education on moral thinking.

Conclusion

As Milgram's experiment on obedience to authority showed, morality is more complex than a battle between heroes and villains. Nice, law-abiding people are capable of committing unethical, even heinous, acts if they are placed in situations where an authority figure is issuing commands. From research on the ability to act ethically, Kohlberg developed a six-stage theory of moral development that has six ascending levels of moral reasoning. He also found that by educating yourself about moral reasoning, you should be able to increase your ability to deal with moral issues in increasingly sophisticated ways. Of course, being able to distinguish at an intellectual level between what is ethical and unethical does not guarantee that a person will also *act* ethically when faced with a dilemma. However, knowing how to rationally judge and justify what we think is morally right and good is the first step we must take if we want to act as responsible, moral agents. We do not want to shoot first and justify later our solutions to moral dilemmas. When dealing with ethical issues, our reasons need to precede our actions. In chapter 3, you will learn three theories that you can use to help you apply your powers of reasoning to your ethical decision making—so read on!

QUESTIONS FOR DISCUSSION

1. A childhood rhyme says that little girls are made of "sugar and spice and everything nice," while little boys are made of "spiders and snails and puppy-dog tails." Do you think there is difference between the ways men and women resolve moral issues? Do you think one gender is inherently more moral than the other?

2. The Milgram experiment was performed in the 1960s. Do you think people today are as obedient to authority?

3. Knowing how people process moral dilemmas can be helpful in understanding why they resolve ethical issues in a particular way. At what stage of moral development would you expect the following groups to operate?

   • Children under 10 years of age
   • At-risk adolescents
   • Blue-collar retirees
   • Middle-aged, college-educated parents
   • Prison inmates

Ethical Theories

THREE

GOALS

1. To learn about consequence-based ethical justifications and their strengths and weaknesses in analyzing moral dilemmas

2. To learn about rule-based ethical justifications and their strengths and weaknesses in analyzing moral dilemmas

3. To learn about virtue-based ethical justifications and their strengths and weaknesses in analyzing moral dilemmas

We have seen that moral thinking can be derailed in a myriad of ways. Many fallacies of ethical reasoning short-circuit the dilemma-solving process by diverting our attention from the dilemma, casting the responsibility onto others, or reassuring us that the problem will sort itself out. In this chapter we will learn how to avoid such moral end runs by applying ethical theories when we evaluate and resolve dilemmas. It is possible to structure our thinking about morality so that we do not simply react to ethical dilemmas but instead thoughtfully and systematically try to solve them.

For centuries, philosophers wrestled with questions concerning ethical behavior, and they have said a great deal about theories of moral justification. For our purposes, it is acceptable to examine three basic systems of moral thinking:

- **Consequence-based ethics**
- **Rule-based ethics**
- **Virtue-based ethics**

Consequence-Based Ethics

Let's begin with moral justification that appeals to consequences. As children, our parents most likely forbade us to do certain things or else be punished. Our choice to obey our parents' wishes or not was spelled out in terms of consequences. Of course, not all consequences were bad. We also learned that certain behaviors brought rewards, or positive consequences. As we grew older, our ability to forecast the negative and positive consequences improved. We thus learned how to evaluate our choices based on the consequences that we believed would result.

So, does the ability to predict and evaluate the consequences of behavior help us determine what is ethical? Yes and no. Perhaps it would be more accurate to say that being able to predict and evaluate consequences lays the groundwork from which we can construct moral justifications for our actions.

Consider the following example. John, a freshman at a state university, is trying to choose a major. He decides to study accounting because his career research indicates that he will probably be able to command a high starting salary upon graduation. As an outdoor adventure enthusiast, John would ideally like to study recreation, but he thinks that white-water river operators don't earn enough money. So he chooses accounting, even though he doesn't really like working with numbers. John justifies his decision on the grounds that he is being prudent—that is, he's seeking what he thinks is in his best interest. Time will tell whether John has chosen

© Photodisc

Ethical dilemmas often involve competing interests.

wisely. He may find rewards in the standard of living an accounting career affords, or he may regret choosing money over work that he truly enjoys. Given the possible outcomes, we would not say John has made an ethical or unethical choice by choosing to study recreation or accounting. He is simply trying to do what's best for him, as we all do.

At this point, John's pursuit of his best interest has no moral implications. However, let's say John eventually becomes bored with his accounting career, so he returns to school to get a masters degree in recreation. Upon graduation he starts a white-water expedition company. John is now doing the work he loves, but he misses the disposable income that accounting gave him. To increase the profits of his new business, he decides to cut some corners by overloading the rafts, firing his experienced guides and hiring inexperienced ones at minimum wage, and merely repairing damaged equipment that should be replaced. John knows that these measures significantly reduce the safety of his clients, but he justifies his actions on the grounds that he is pursuing what's in his best interest, and besides, no one has been injured as a result.

Although John is aware of the consequences of his actions, he no longer is guided simply and innocently by self-interest; instead, he is acting with a selfish disregard for the interests of others. Because the possible consequences of his actions affect others negatively, John's behavior crosses the line between legitimate self-interest and unethical selfishness. When we judge the ethicality of the consequences resulting from our actions we must consider how our actions affect others. While it is legitimate to look out for our own self-interest, to be morally justified we must also give due consideration to how we affect others (Twardzik 1984).

The ability to be other-regarding when assessing the consequences of our actions is the basis of an ethical theory called **utilitarianism.** In this theory, the consequences of actions are judged by how much good they produce for others. Utilitarianism seeks the maximization of the good for the majority. Performing actions that result in the greatest good for the greatest number is the guiding principle for determining the right thing to do.

A utilitarian analysis of John's business practices suggests that his actions are not resulting in the greatest good for the greatest number. While John is happier because he has increased his income, others are less happy. The experienced guides who were fired have suffered a loss of livelihood, and the clients receive poorer service while being exposed to more risk. Of course, John might argue that the clients will not be upset as long as an accident does not happen. However, when determining the ethical status of John's choice to cut corners, we need to take into account the probability of many people being harmed if an accident does happen. Certainly, the clients would not be happy if they knew that John was risking their well-being to improve his own situation.

By focusing on attaining the greatest good for society over the individual, utilitarianism provides a powerful method for evaluating the moral status of our actions. Indeed, many public policy decisions are based on utilitarian principles. Part of the justification for national parks, for example, is that they provide multiple outdoor recreation benefits for current users and future generations. If natural wonders are destroyed so that land can be developed as industrial parks or housing tracks, society as a whole will be worse off.

Although utilitarianism is a useful principle for determining ethical behavior, it is not without its pitfalls. A standard criticism of utilitarian justifications is that they recommend actions that impose significant costs on minorities. Since utilitarianism seeks to maximize overall happiness in society, it is easy to imagine situations where the interests of a minority might be sacrificed for the benefit of the majority. The arena games of ancient Rome, which began in 264 b.c.e., were extremely popular public events, with venues such as the Colosseum drawing crowds in excess of 50,000 (Futrell 1997; Kyle 1998). Throngs of people derived immense pleasure from the bizarre, cruel spectacles that included gladiatorial combat, the hunting of exotic animals, and gruesome executions of criminals. Of course, those individuals in the arena, most of whom were victims, were not having *their* pleasure maximized. But overall, the pain and suffering of a few was far outweighed by the pleasure their deaths brought to thousands of Roman spectators. The games went on for hundreds of years and served as a foundation of Roman culture and society.

Since the games maximized societal pleasure, from a utilitarian standpoint the Romans were justified in their cruelty toward those unfortunate

Learning Activity: Consequence-Based Ethics

You are a young college student from the Midwest who is on spring break vacation at a tropical tourist destination. You purchase a ticket for a 3-hour boat tour on a small yacht. The boat encounters a storm and you and your six companions are shipwrecked on a deserted island. You hope to be rescued soon, but unfortunately there is only enough food and fresh water on the island to support four people for the next month. Three people must put back to sea on a flimsy raft to seek help. The remaining four people left on the island will have to survive on the barest of rations while they attempt to attract the attention of passing ships and airplanes. After much heated discussion, no one can agree who should stay and who should go on the raft. It is decided that a chief will be chosen by drawing straws, and that person will then use his or her best judgment to select who goes and who stays. You draw the short straw and are designated the chief. Your companions are the yacht's bumbling skipper and first mate, a know-it-all science professor, an eccentric millionaire and his wife, and a vain movie starlet. You want to maximize everyone's chances for survival, so whom do you pick, and why?

individuals who found themselves in the arena. Yet no one would say that the Romans should be praised for their behavior. Utilitarianism, therefore, is not an infallible method for determining ethical behavior.

Rule-Based Ethics

We have seen that utilitarianism can subject minorities to the tyranny of the majority. Therefore, we are in need of an ethical theory that can protect minority interests. **Deontological ethics** (rule-based ethics) focuses on the obligations of human beings to one another. Consider the following example. Sue is a coach of a grade school girls' soccer team. As with all sport teams, some of Sue's players are more gifted than others. If Sue fields the less skilled players only when the team already has a large lead, she minimizes their chances of losing. However, this results in unequal playing time for team members.

Some of the players and their parents would probably think this situation is unfair. How, they ask, are players going to improve if their field time is cut? Don't the less skilled girls have the same rights as their more talented teammates? Sue is torn between the parents' criticisms that she is being unfair to certain players and her desire for the team to succeed in competition.

The way Sue resolves this dilemma depends on how important it is for her to consider her obligations as a coach to each player. In essence, she has to ask herself if she should let all players participate equally as a point of principle or if she should favor the better players so as to maximize the team's chances of winning. Are the parents justified in saying that all the players have a right to equal playing time regardless of how it might affect the team's standing?

To make a rights-based claim means we believe that others have some duty or obligation toward us. Philosophers believe these duty-based claims come in two basic forms: **negative rights** and **positive rights.** Claims based on negative rights stipulate that other people have an obligation to refrain from certain actions. In the United States Declaration of Independence, the right to life, liberty, and the pursuit of happiness is a classic example of negative rights. The declaration expresses the political principle that the government must refrain from interfering with the freedoms of individuals unless not doing so would result in direct harm to others.

Claims based on positive rights take the idea of duties and obligations one step further. While claims based on negative rights prohibit us from certain actions toward others, claims based on positive rights require us to do certain things for others. For example, the United Nations (UN) charter states that people have a right to leisure. A possible interpretation of the UN charter is that it makes a claim based on negative rights, that people's leisure should not be suppressed. In colonial America, for example, the Puritans restricted many traditional leisure pastimes that were thought to be profane or to encourage idleness. As Gary Cross notes in his book on the history of leisure, "the New England colonies banned dice, bowls, cards and even smoking (except at dinner) as time wasters," and they "prohibited Sunday labor, travel or even recreation, including in Massachusetts, 'all unnecessary and unseasonable walking in the streets and fields'" (Cross 1990, 31). Given our much more liberal sensibilities toward leisure, most people in Western cultures would invoke a negative rights claim to leisure that would disallow such heavy-handed restrictions. But the fact that we are not actively preventing people from engaging in recreation activities does not necessarily mean that they will experience leisure. What good is the negative right to leisure if you are so desperately impoverished that you must spend all your time and effort just trying to survive? A positive rights claim to leisure would require us to ensure that all people have at least a minimum level of resources to exercise their negative right to engage in recreation and leisure experiences.

Rights-based ethics, a form of rule-based ethics, are justified on the basis that certain obligations and duties are owed to others because of their status. Human rights are conferred to human beings, civil rights are conferred to citizens, property owners rights are conferred to those who have title to physical assets, and so on. The basis for conferring rights typically derives from two justifications: status and obligation.

Conferring Rights by Status

Some rights claims naturally coincide with a particular status. For example, human rights are often said to be inalienable because they are conferred simply as a right of being a member of the human race. According to this view, there is no justification for violating basic human rights. We all have obligations and duties to one another by virtue of the fact that we are members of the same species.

Conferring Rights by Obligation

Other rights claims are based on the obligations that derive from civil society. These rights are conferred by social institutions. Civil rights sometimes overlap with human rights. Many laws against discrimination are grounded in the belief that people deserve to be treated equally. Yet, many laws are also based on one's membership in a group. For example, the right to vote might only be accorded those who possess citizenship, are of a certain age, or are not incarcerated. Thus, civil rights vary according to the values of the society in question.

Given that civil rights depend in part on societal values, traditions, and institutions, it is legitimate to question whether many such rights are arbitrary conventions. Philosophers have devoted a great deal of effort trying to base civil rights on a rational foundation. John Rawls, for example, has argued that our obligations to one another should reflect the principles of fairness and opportunity that we would all choose if none of us could know either our current position or our future success in life (Rawls 1971). Essentially, Rawls asks us to imagine what basic obligations we would agree to accord one another if we could not know our own personal advantages and disadvantages.

Using Rights to Solve Ethical Dilemmas

Returning to the example of the soccer coach, we might apply the concept of rights to help Sue resolve her dilemma. Sue might not be persuaded that giving some players less time on the field is a violation of their human rights. Being on the team, after all, is voluntary, and there are all sorts of people who do not have the chance to play because of their age, sex, location, social class, and so on. The opportunity to play on the team

© Human Kinetics

Ethical dilemmas often involve competing rights.

is just that—an opportunity, and as such, unequal playing time is not a violation of an inalienable human right.

However, the players' parents may claim their daughters' rights are violated if it is plausible to assume that by being a member of the team they are owed equal consideration. It is reasonable to suppose that equal playing time would be the guiding principle if none of the players knew how well they could play soccer before the season began. Of course, once the season is underway and the better players discover their talents, they may not want to follow the principle of equal play. However, their reluctance to give up their advantage does not render the principle of equal play irrelevant. It could be legitimately questioned whether gaining playing time because of personal talent goes against the principle of being a team player. The parents' objections to Sue giving the better team members more play time illustrates the point that team members have obligations to treat one another fairly, and that as the leader, Sue is remiss if she does not ensure that all the players have equal time on the field.

This example shows that providing moral justification for our actions on the basis of rights can be complex. We cannot dogmatically follow a single rule. Instead, we must ask ourselves about the obligations and

Learning Activity: Rule-Based Ethics

You have decided to stay on the island to await rescue with the professor and the millionaire and his wife. The skipper, first mate, and movie starlet set sail on the raft and are never heard from again. After a few weeks, the conditions of you and the remaining survivors are becoming desperate as food and water are running short. The millionaire and his wife, both elderly, approach you on the beach one day holding a piece of paper. They don't think they can last much longer, and they want to give you a will that they had been holding on to for a long time. Their previous will had left their combined fortunes to a wonderful charity that helps sick children. However, they are having second thoughts and now want to leave all their money to their only son. They sign the new will in front of you and ask, if you are rescued, that you do everything you can to ensure that their Billy gets all the money. However, you have also learned from them that Billy is a crook, cheat, and compulsive gambler who cares for no one but himself. Sadly, the millionaire and his wife die the next day. Should you rip up the new will that gives all the money to Billy?

duties we have to others. We must also identify which duties take priority if rights claims come into conflict, as they frequently do. Legislation and legal rulings regarding people's rights can give some guidance as to the importance we should assign various rights claims, and in many circumstances we have to use our own judgment. The responsibility to use our moral judgment or conscience leads us to the third system of ethical reasoning: virtue ethics.

Virtue-Based Ethics

It would be more accurate to label virtue ethics as an approach to ethical reasoning rather than a system. Consequence- and rule-based ethical theories use our powers of reasoning by asking us to calculate the best outcome or determine the most important principle. Ethical theories based on consequences or duties therefore appeal to our intellect and logic. In contrast, virtue-based theories focus on character rather than cognitive abilities. Resolving moral dilemmas by virtue ethics depends on the type of person we are or the role we play.

Throughout our lives we assume many roles—child, sibling, student, worker, parent, senior citizen, grandparent, and so on—and our success or failure in life is determined in large part by how well we fulfill these roles. The behaviors and attitudes that make up our individual character help determine the ways we adapt to the demands of our various life roles.

According to virtue ethics, when confronted with an ethical dilemma we ask ourselves what a person of our standing or character should do when faced with such a problem.

For example, we typically hold adults to a higher level of moral responsibility than children. We expect adults to act more thoughtfully and to use better judgment than children. Irresponsibility in adults is taken as a sign of a weakness or character flaw. Similarly, in our work lives we set standards for our behavior based on the roles we assume. Presumably, the higher up an organizational ladder we climb and the greater status we achieve, the higher the expectations for our behavior. These expectations can even extend beyond the immediate workplace. People employed in professional occupations are typically expected to avoid leisure behaviors that might bring their professional reputation into question. For example, many people would think it unacceptable for kindergarten teachers to be patrons of strip clubs, or for clergy to gamble at casinos. While such activities might be legal, they are out of character for the roles that these professionals have assumed.

Virtue Ethics and Leisure Service Delivery

Virtue-based ethics has a long tradition in moral philosophy. Interestingly, its origins in Western culture are closely connected to the ancient Greek conception of leisure (Hemingway 1988). The ancient Greeks were strong proponents of virtue ethics, as they were deeply concerned with the question of how to live a good life. Their word for virtue, *arête*, meant "excellence." The Greeks judged objects to be virtuous if they performed their function well. For example, a good knife would be one that was sharp and well balanced. People could also be judged as to whether they had virtue. According to Aristotle, virtue meant engaging in those activities that were the most godlike. In his view, philosophic contemplation was the greatest activity that people could aspire to. To attain a leisured state of contemplation also required training in worthwhile leisure activities. To live the contemplative life meant that one was trained in the life skills of being a good person.

In *The Republic*, Plato describes the education of the ideal citizen, comprised of lessons in music, gymnastics, mathematics, and philosophy (book II, 376c-e). It was Plato's belief that such "ennobling" leisure activities prepared elite citizens for a life of public service. Aristotle, who was Plato's pupil, adopted much of his master's teaching regarding the use of leisure to educate citizens in how to live a good life. Ennobling leisure activities were used to shape the behavior and disposition of individuals—in effect, leisure was used to mold character. For the ancient Greeks, then, there was an inseparable bond between having a virtuous character and leisure. The leisured individual had to be a person of good character and upbringing who had the proper disposition and habits. The emphasis the Greeks placed on character traits is further illustrated by the fact that their word for ethics, *ta ethika,* is derived from *ethos,* which refers to one's character or "habitual way of life" (Peters 1967, 66).

Today we can see remnants of the Greek idea of leisure in leisure programming that involves character-building activities. Religious groups, nonprofit organizations such as the YMCA, and programs for at-risk youth such as Outward Bound provide leisure that encourages positive character development. However, as leisure service providers we need to carefully distinguish between the quality of the activities we facilitate and the ethical status of the way we provide those activities. For example, while the ennobling leisure of the ancient Greeks was in itself admirable, the way the Greeks provided for leisure was morally questionable. As many commentators have noted, the Greeks based their leisured lifestyle on the exploitation of an underclass of slaves and females who provided the material necessities of life for the elite male citizens.

Leisure and recreation providers can use a virtue ethics approach to evaluate how ethically we deliver services. The first step is considering the characteristics that we believe someone in our position of responsibility should exhibit. For example, the professionalism and certification movement in leisure services can be interpreted not only as a way to improve the quality of services, but also to assure the public that practitioners are expected to adhere to high ethical standards to protect both the individual client and society. By adhering to a professional service model, leisure and recreation providers should thus ask themselves what their professional responsibilities require them to do when faced with ethical dilemmas. While practitioners may consult a set of rules (perhaps a code of ethics) or calculate the most desirable outcome (cost–benefit analysis), they can also ask whether their solutions to dilemmas are consistent with their expectations of themselves as not only professionals, but also as persons of integrity. They must ask themselves if they can live with their decisions, or in other words, if they are acting in good conscience.

While it may seem intuitively correct that one should be able to feel that one has acted in accordance with one's conscience when making moral decisions, a criticism of virtue ethics is that the sagacity of one's decisions depends on the quality of one's character. People who are ethically immature or have little regard for the interests of others might feel justified in their moral decision making. Even professionals may adopt morally unacceptable values and behaviors that do not serve the interests of the public.

Determining What Is Praiseworthy and Blameworthy

To avoid the charge that virtue ethics makes moral decisions arbitrary and self-serving, it is necessary to identify characteristics that are morally praiseworthy and develop effective methods for incorporating those worthy characteristics into professional practice. If ethics is indeed the practice of good habits, then we need to be able to distinguish good practices from bad. However, getting everyone to agree on which characteristics are virtues and which are vices would appear to be a daunting task. Different cultures have different ideas about what is noble. For example, taking risks in one society may be admired, while in another it may be regarded as imprudent. In addition, there can be disagreement within cultures as to what should count as virtuous. For every advocate who claims that a particular human endeavor is uplifting and ennobling there is a critic who argues that it is demeaning and debasing. Some berate Americans for not sticking to their diets, while others say they are obsessed with body image. Some champion youth sport as a way for young people to experience teamwork and build self-esteem, while others argue that it encourages them to be ruthlessly competitive and creates future psychological problems. And so it goes with every debate about what we think we should aspire to in our lives. Apparently, we cannot find much common ground for compiling an agreed-upon list of virtues and vices.

However, in his influential book *After Virtue,* philosopher Alasdair MacIntyre (1984) argues that certain characteristics distinguish virtuous actions from those that lack virtue. While MacIntyre agrees that there are many competing and conflicting lists of virtues and vices, he believes that all virtues share common characteristics. MacIntyre's method for defining the essential characteristics of virtues is complex and would require an extended commentary. However, for our purposes it is sufficient to examine part of his theory by referring to the following vignette he presents of a child playing a game:

> Consider the example of a highly intelligent seven-year-old child whom I wish to teach to play chess, although the child has no particular desire to learn the game. The child does however, have a very strong desire for candy and little chance of obtaining it. I therefore tell the child that if the child will play chess with me once a week I will give the child 50 cents worth of candy; moreover I tell the child that I will always play in such a way that it will be difficult, but not impossible for the child to win and that, if the child wins, the child will receive an extra 50 cents worth of candy. Thus motivated the child plays to win. Notice however that, so long as it is candy alone which provides the child

with a good reason for playing chess, the child has no reason not to cheat and every reason to cheat, provided he or she can do so successfully. But, so we may hope, there will come a time when the child will find in those goods specific to chess, in the achievement of a certain highly particular kind of analytic skill, strategic imagination and competitive intensity, as new set of reasons now not just for winning on a particular occasion, but for trying to excel in whatever way the game of chess demands. Now if the child cheats, he or she will be defeating not me, but himself or herself. (118)

MacIntyre uses this example to highlight the difference between doing something because of extrinsic motivation (getting candy) versus doing something because of intrinsic motivation (seeing how skillfully you can play chess). When chess is played for extrinsic reasons it is simply a means to a goal. Assuming we can avoid detection, it is rational to cheat since that makes achievement of the goal (candy, prize money, a trophy, prestige) more efficient and economical. Students who choose to plagiarize term papers or cheat on exams often use precisely this sort of instrumental thinking. Why waste time and effort learning a subject if all that really counts is getting an *A* on your transcript?

Motivations affect our behaviors and usually change over time.

Learning Activity: Virtue-Based Ethics

Only you and the professor are left alive on the island. You both are losing hope of being rescued. The professor tells you that the longer the two of you stay on the island, the more likely it is that you will both contract a fatal tropical illness. The next day, while the professor is sleeping, you find a crate that has floated up on the beach. In it are medical supplies, including vials of vaccines for the illnesses the professor warned you about. You cannot believe your good luck! However, there is only enough of the vaccines for one person. Do you tell the professor about your discovery?

Contrast this approach to achieving a goal to the idea of doing activities on the basis of intrinsic motivation. If we find playing a game of chess or writing a term paper to be an interesting challenge in itself, then we need to follow the rules so that we actually test our abilities and competence. Cheating in this context is a complete waste of time, as it robs us of the opportunity to see just how well we can do. Intrinsically motivated activities are virtuous because we must commit ourselves to doing the best that we can, whereas extrinsically motivated activities lack virtue because we are encouraged to seek the easiest path to our goals.

MacIntyre's example of the chess game demonstrates why our motivations for performing an action are important. Essentially, a common characteristic of all virtuous actions is that they are intrinsically motivated. It does not matter that different cultures have different ideas about what activities are virtuous, so long as their practices are motivated by intrinsic rather than extrinsic reasons. Of course, we still may question whether some types of intrinsically motivated practices are morally acceptable. But MacIntyre's definition at least narrows the field by excluding activities that are done for extrinsic motives. Judging ethical dilemmas from a virtue ethics standpoint forces us to ask ourselves whether we are being unduly influenced by external circumstances to the point where we betray the moral expectations that we have set for ourselves.

Which Approach Is Right?

We have seen that the three ethical systems, which are based on consequences, rules, and virtues, can help us analyze moral dilemmas. We have also seen that each system by itself is unable to satisfactorily resolve every moral dilemma. Consequence-based theories such as utilitarianism ignore the interests of minorities as long as overall happiness is maximized. For utilitarians, the end justifies the means. Rule-based theories protect the interests of minorities through the institution of rights-based claims.

However, determining our obligations to others can be a difficult task if we are to avoid being dogmatic, ineffective rule followers, and we may find that following rules can result in costly consequences. For deontologists, the means justify the ends, possibly at the expense of the majority. Virtue-based theories offer a third way to deal with moral dilemmas. Rather than appealing to our heads, virtue ethics asks us to consult our hearts. But while it seems intuitively correct that our moral judgments should be in accord with our conscience, others may think we are acting arbitrarily if their moral sensibilities differ from ours. Virtue ethics requires us to justify the standards of character by which our actions are guided.

Given these three ethical systems of addressing moral dilemmas, you are right if you wonder which system you should employ. Analysis by consequences, duties, and virtues for certain dilemmas may point to the same course of action, but it's also possible that conclusions may conflict. Since the three ethical systems interpret moral behavior in fundamentally different ways, you are likely to feel that you have no way of knowing which approach is best for a particular dilemma. Randomly choosing an ethical system to analyze a dilemma would seem both irrational and irresponsible.

So, what is the value of analysis by ethical systems if it cannot lead to conclusions by which we can feel certain of the rightness of our actions? For one, understanding moral reasoning via the three ethical systems helps us understand the moral reasoning of others and how they analyze dilemmas. One person might be primarily concerned about the consequences of a solution, another might be worried about whether proper procedures are being followed, while another might be bothered by his conscience. Given that leisure service professionals typically work with a diverse clientele, it is no small advantage to be able to understand the reasoning of others when it comes to problems of ethics.

To illustrate the point, imagine you are the supervisor of a private fitness facility. The dilemma you face is that two groups have requested the facility's large workout room at the same time for the same date. Both groups made their request on the same day last week and there are no other room options for the preferred time block. The fee for the use of the facility is not an issue for either group.

• Marge has requested the room for 20 women who want to work out in an exclusively female environment. She mentioned that many of the women are influential business leaders in the community, subtly implying that there were long- and short-term consequences of their using the facility.

• John has requested the room for 20 slightly disabled adults who also need their own program. He alluded to the fact that the disabled

It can be difficult to decide which ethical approach is best for a particular dilemma.

adults are often refused the opportunity to participate like everyone else. He has always advocated for society's responsibility to care for its less fortunate.

The owner of the fitness facility, your boss, always likes to do the right thing. Over the past few years she has made decisions that were not popular or politically correct. She explained to you on a couple of occasions that she thinks each person has a guiding light inside to help them make tough decisions. You have to make the best decision you can about this situation. However, it is likely that one group and maybe even your boss will not be thrilled with the decision. Knowing the motivations of each of the key players can help you explain yourself and your decision to them in terms that they can understand and appreciate.

Conclusion

Perhaps we should not be surprised that these three ethical systems do not in themselves resolve all ethical dilemmas. It is more productive to think of them as tools for analyzing a problem rather than as decision-making procedures. The ethical systems are only part of the decision-making process. They help us decide how to address a moral dilemma, but they are not sufficient for practical problem solving. Solving dilemmas is a complex process requiring us to correctly identify the dilemma, posit and evaluate possible solutions to resolve the dilemma, and then implement our solutions. By employing ethical theories based on consequences, duties, and virtues we are able to structure our decision-making process in a reasonable, rational way.

As Aristotle noted, the purpose of ethical reasoning is not simply to be able to intellectually distinguish the ethical from the unethical. Instead, the point of *knowing* what is ethical is so that we can then *act* ethically. In *The Nicomachean Ethics*, Aristotle states, "We are inquiring not in order to know what virtue is, but in order to become good, since otherwise our inquiry would have been of no use" (1103b, 28-29). Simply knowing right from wrong and good from bad is not sufficient for being ethical. We also need to know how to translate that knowledge into ethical action. In chapter 4, we will learn how to integrate ethical reasoning into a moral decision-making process and action plan.

QUESTIONS FOR DISCUSSION

1. Which of the three ethical theories (consequence-based ethics, rule-based ethics, and virtue ethics) would you use in the following situations?
   - Breaking off a personal relationship
   - Dealing with a coworker who continually violates your agency's policies
   - Working with at-risk youth who are misbehaving
2. What character traits do you think a leisure service provider should aspire to in the following branches of service delivery?
   - Municipal recreation
   - Therapeutic recreation
   - Commercial recreation
   - Outdoor recreation

Resolving Ethical Dilemmas

GOALS

1. To learn how to identify and define moral dilemmas

2. To learn how to analyze ethical dilemmas in order to determine what is morally praiseworthy and blameworthy

3. To learn how to create a moral action plan to resolve a moral dilemma

Thus far you have learned many things about ethical issues in leisure services. You know that you will be confronted with moral dilemmas during the course of your career. You know that there are varying levels of professional expectations depending on the branch of leisure services. You have learned that most people have trouble doing the right thing in situations where they feel they should obey an authority figure. You have been introduced to three ethical theories that you can use to analyze ethical issues. But can you satisfactorily resolve an ethical dilemma? In the pages that follow we offer a model for making ethical decisions and putting those decisions into action.

Notice that we say *resolve* ethical dilemmas rather than *solve* them. Solving problems suggests that there is only one right answer, such as solving a mathematics equation. Resolving problems, on the other hand, suggests that we seek to determine a satisfactory solution, and we may find that there is more than one ethical solution to a moral dilemma. Our project therefore is not to focus on what is true or false, but to figure out what is morally justifiable and what is not.

A Courtroom Analogy

Perhaps it's easier to understand how to systematically resolve ethical dilemmas if we draw an analogy to the criminal justice system. Determining guilt or innocence is a complex affair. Before a case goes to trial there must be some preliminary evidence to suggest a crime has been committed. The police gather evidence and identify suspects. The suspects are presumed innocent until proven guilty. The trial follows a series of procedures in which arguments for and against guilt are presented. A judge or jury renders a verdict of guilty or innocent based on the arguments presented. If a guilty verdict is rendered, then a sentence must be passed.

Some believe the legal process represents the institution of justice, some find it an entertaining theatre, and others view it as a conspiracy that oppresses the economically disadvantaged. However, all would agree that it involves a procedure or method for determining guilt or innocence and it determines the appropriate course of action (e.g., the accused is set free, fined, imprisoned, and so on). The outcome of a trial is never certain until the jury announces its verdict and the judge passes the sentence, and even if all procedures are faithfully followed, some may still believe that justice has not been done.

The process of resolving ethical dilemmas shares many of the same characteristics as the legal system.

- Moral problem solving is a method or procedure. The outcome of moral deliberations is unknown until you go through the process of

The method for resolving ethical dilemmas is similar to the criminal justice system, which is a method for determining guilt or innocence and the appropriate course of action.

resolving the dilemma. Just like a trial, we are not looking for one answer to the problem. Instead, we are trying to render a morally justifiable solution.

- The decision process in trials requires a finding of guilt or innocence, and mistrials result when juries cannot agree. Similarly, moral issues require decisions about what is praiseworthy or blameworthy. When dealing with ethical dilemmas we must be prepared to come to a verdict about what is good and bad, right and wrong.

- Like trials, ethical dilemmas arise out of unfortunate circumstances that happen to specific people at specific times in specific places. We do not ask for ethical dilemmas to come our way. Instead, they are generated by human interactions, just like crimes.

- Ethical dilemmas require us to respond in an appropriate and fair manner, in the same way that crimes require justice. We might be tempted to ignore ethical issues, but avoidance in itself constitutes a shirking of moral responsibility, just as not reporting a crime is unjust.

- Resolving ethical dilemmas requires the collection and evaluation of evidence, as in a trial.

- Resolving ethical dilemmas requires the application of moral principles and theories, just as judging criminal cases requires the use of legal principles and precedents.

- Resolving an ethical dilemma involves not only determining what is praiseworthy and blameworthy but also choosing a course of action that brings morally justified closure to the dilemma. As in a criminal proceeding, if punitive action is warranted, it must fit the crime. Excessive leniency or harshness when resolving an ethical dilemma only undermines the objective, which is to do the right thing.

These similarities might lead you to believe you will need the training of a lawyer to deal with moral issues in your workplace. While some basic knowledge of the legal system may be helpful, resolving moral dilemmas and prosecuting criminal cases are not the same thing. Two obvious differences include the following:

- Legal and illegal behavior is clearly defined in carefully written statutes and laws. Ethical transgressions are harder to identify because our understanding of moral behavior is largely implicit. Thus, a major challenge in dealing with ethical dilemmas is first being able to even recognize that a problem exists.

- The legal system has highly defined roles that delineate the extent of authority. For example, police must gather evidence, judges must act impartially, and defense lawyers must represent their clients to the best of their ability. However, resolving ethical dilemmas can require you to assume many roles. You may have to be the investigator, then the prosecutor, then the jury, and then the judge.

Given the complexities in dealing with ethical dilemmas, it is helpful to have a method or process to guide our moral deliberations and justify the actions that we take. We propose the following three-stage model as a way to structure the resolving of ethical dilemmas. Based largely on Rest's theory of moral behavior (1994), the ethical decision-making model described in this chapter is designed to assist users without dictating specific solutions.

Rest's four-component model is based on his research into the psychology of morality. He believes that successful moral decision making requires four distinct processes. First, an individual needs to be able to recognize an ethical problem when he or she is confronted by a dilemma. Rest refers to this ability as one's moral sensitivity. Second, once the individual is aware of the problem, he or she must be able to employ moral judgment

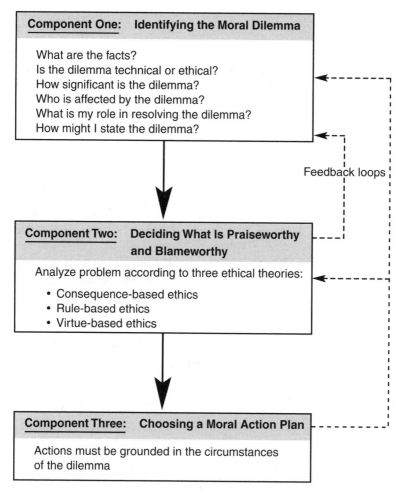

Three-stage model for resolving ethical dilemmas.

to distinguish the ethical from the unethical. Third, having determined the ethical course of action, he or she needs to prioritize ethical concerns over the nonethical values. For example, if it is determined that we are morally obligated to provide equal access to recreation facilities for people with disabilities, we cannot then refuse to reallocate funds from our budget on the grounds that it would be cost inefficient. Fourth, if we have identified the problem, subjected it to ethical evaluation, and prioritized ethical values over those that are nonethical, we still need to have the moral courage to implement our decision. As Rest notes, a "moral failure can occur because of deficiency in an component. All four components are determinants of moral action" (Rest 1994, 24).

Thus, Rest's model envisions moral decision making as a sort of chain or process that must be completed in sequence for ethically sound actions to take place. The three-stage model of moral decision making that we propose follows a similar pattern: First the ethical dilemma must be recognized, then it must be ethically evaluated, and finally a moral action plan needs to be constructed to put the ethically justified solution into effect.

Two Caveats

Before we delve into the problem-solving model, we must take note of two limitations. First, users of the model must acknowledge and control the powerful feelings that accompany ethical issues. Some authors advocate an unemotional, detached approach to making decisions. While such an approach may be possible when dealing with some purely technical matters, it is unrealistic to expect people to ignore natural human emotions when dealing with questions of right and wrong. Emotions may indeed hinder ethical decision making and behaviors, but at the same time, some emotions are essential to the problem-solving process. For example, indignation and anger often serve as triggers for exposing corruption among one's colleagues. It can also be argued that compassion must underlie all ethical decisions and actions. The model advocated here embraces and then carefully uses emotions to reach sound ethical decisions that lead to moral actions.

Second, as with any tool, regardless of whether it is a cement trowel, a computer, or a cognitive model, practice makes perfect. Initial efforts at solving ethical dilemmas using the model might be slow and clumsy. Decisions may turn out to be wrong and our actions may create more problems than we started with. But with diligence and practice, each of us can become better problem solvers and make sound ethical decisions followed by right actions.

Component One: Identifying the Moral Dilemma

We all have finite personal and institutional resources. Resolving ethical issues draws heavily on our mental, emotional, and physical capacities. At times it may require the organization we work for to commit some of its resources as well. Therefore, we need to be selective in the issues we take on. Just as the police cannot investigate every potential crime, we must prioritize the ethical dilemmas that we choose to resolve.

Ethical sensitivity is the ability to recognize significant ethical quandaries, and it activates the ethical decision-making process. Without a degree of ethical sensitivity, issues simply blow right past us. We are either oblivious to them or we lack the initiative to consider the problem. Of course, many of the problems we confront in the day-to-day provision of leisure services are managerial in nature, such as arranging meetings, creating budgets, preparing reports, and so on. While these tasks require us to employ our judgment and values to solve problems, they are unlikely to raise serious ethical problems. It is only when we encounter an unusually vexing or awkward situation that an ethical dilemma may arise.

When our gut signals to us that there may be something morally wrong with a situation, we need to assess whether we have encountered an ethical issue. We can ask the following questions to determine whether a serious ethical dilemma exists:

- What are the facts of the problem?
- Is it a technical or ethical problem?
- How significant is the problem?
- Who is affected by the problem?
- What is my role in resolving the problem?
- How might I explicitly state the ethical dilemma?

Let's examine how we can use these questions to help us identify whether we are facing a serious ethical dilemma. Like detectives at a potential crime scene, we will start by assessing the facts.

What Are the Facts?

At this early stage, you want to gather as much information about the potential dilemma as feasible. You don't want to jump the gun by accusing someone of immoral action when in fact they have done nothing wrong, nor do you want to ignore a serious ethical issue because your initial evaluation of the problem was incorrect. Getting the facts might involve not only finding out who said and did what to whom but also researching the moral implications of the problem. For example, an older recreation manager might think that sexual harassment only includes rape and therefore might view unwanted sexual overtures among employees as just playing around. If this manager learned that sexual harassment is also defined as inappropriate sexual gestures and words, he might change his attitude and no longer tolerate such behavior. Understanding the facts as much as you can may help you recognize significant ethical dilemmas.

Is It Technical or Ethical?

If the facts suggest that the situation is morally problematic, you can start to define the dilemma more precisely. A good strategy is to try to separate technical issues from moral issues. Some situations are obviously ethical in nature, such as whether to influence a government official in another country in an effort to secure a permit to build a beach resort. Other issues, however, may seem technical at first but actually contain underlying ethical elements. Consider the issue of whether to contract with a particular company for a marketing campaign to increase tourism to the beach resort. Perhaps the company has an impressive record of persuading tourists to visit new destinations, but it relies heavily on sexually suggestive images in its advertising. Should you hire the ad agency, even if its techniques include sexist stereotypes? At first glance it may seem like a smart business decision to contract with an agency that gets the job done, particularly when they do the dirty work and you reap the benefits. But you also might risk soiling your resort's reputation by hiring an agency that uses morally questionable methods.

How Significant Is the Problem?

Estimating the seriousness of an ethical issue can help us decide just how much of an emergency it represents. Situations involving ethical dilemmas can be incredibly complex, especially when more than one moral wrongdoing is occurring at the same time. Dealing with employees who are pocketing pens from work is probably not as important as dealing with employees who are stealing from the cash box. We therefore need to focus on identifying the primary ethical issue. Ranking the seriousness of ethical problems in a situation can help us determine which one most needs to be addressed.

Another technique for establishing the significance of a moral problem is to distinguish the causes of behavior from its symptoms. For example, suppose rangers at a national park are turning a blind eye to visitors who are negatively affecting environmentally fragile areas. Although the rangers do not like these activities, they have been told by park management that it is imperative to increase gate revenues, so enforcement of park regulations have been relaxed to try to avoid incidents that might annoy tourists. While the rangers' deliberate ignorance of the damaging activities may be blameworthy, the main source of the problem is the managers who appear to be placing revenue generation above environmental protection. Rather than focusing on the rangers' culpability, we need to trace the issue back to its source, which in this case originates with a decision by management.

Yet another way to assess significance is to ask ourselves what would happen if we were to ignore the problem and take no action. Would we feel guilty if we did not try to resolve the problem? Perhaps at this point we don't know what to do, but if we feel compelled to do something, then we are probably dealing with a significant moral dilemma. Conversely, if not dealing with an issue does not keep us awake at night, there is a chance it is less important.

Who Is Affected?

When trying to define ethical dilemmas, it is also helpful to consider who and what are affected by the problem. Given a particular situation, we can ask ourselves who we think the winners and losers would be. Many of the ethical dilemmas we face in leisure services involve conflicts between people, but the winners and losers can also be nonhuman, such as animals or the natural environment.

What Is My Role?

A final method that helps us define an ethical dilemma is to determine who is responsible for resolving a moral conundrum. Perhaps the best way to approach the issue of responsibility is to ask ourselves what role we can play to resolve the problem. Occasionally, we may find that matters are out of our hands. Suppose, for example, you are a varsity rowing coach. You take your crews to several regattas where you frequently observe the coach from another university verbally abusing her athletes. Your university has a coach's code of conduct that prohibits the mistreatment of athletes. As well, you strongly believe that it is unethical for coaches to use verbal aggression to encourage higher performance from athletes. However, you know that the university that the abusive coach works for has no such code, and in fact prides itself on having an aggressive, successful rowing program. You would like to stop the verbal abuse, but you know your options are quite limited. The coach and the athletes whom she is mistreating are from an institution that you are competing with. You have no formal authority over their rowing program, and you are likely to have very little influence over the coach or her athletes, who, though abused, are still going to perceive you as an opponent rather than an ally. Your alternatives may simply be to talk to your athletics director in the hope that she can pursue the problem by contacting the athletics director at the other university, or to lobby for a league rule against verbal abuse by coaches. In either case, your actions can only deal with the problem indirectly and may, in fact, prove ineffective because you simply lack enough power to correct the problem.

But usually we are not so powerless to deal with ethical issues that come our way. Job positions and titles typically give us both formal and informal authority and responsibility to fix problems. Even if we are not the primary decision makers in a situation, we may still have the ability to influence others to do the right thing, so we must clearly define our role as ethical problem solvers. As the saying goes, if you are not at least willing to be part of the solution, then you are probably part of the problem.

How Might I State the Dilemma?

Having asked the previous questions to identify an ethical dilemma, the final step is to explicitly state the dilemma by writing it down. Referring back to our courtroom analogy, we might think of the prosecutor charging someone with a crime. One of the basic rules of justice is that the charges

© David Sanders

Even the most thoughtful ethical decisions may leave some people unhappy.

must be clear and unambiguous. When dealing with ethical dilemmas, we should seek similar clarity by explicitly defining the moral quandary that we need to resolve. It helps if you accept the idea that most ethical dilemmas are just that—dilemmas. Philosophers sometimes speak of being on "the horns of dilemma," the uncomfortable spot where you may find yourself when dealing with ethical issues. Significant moral issues do not usually lend themselves to win–win solutions. You will most likely find yourself choosing between two unattractive courses of action. For example, do you report your coworker's affair with a client and get her fired, or do you cover for her even though your professional association prohibits such relationships? Should you allow the local chapter of the Ku Klux Klan to rent your recreation facility, or should you refuse them access while allowing other community groups to rent the facility? Should you avoid using volunteers because you fear that it will eventually lead to a reduction in funding for paid staff positions, or should you hire volunteers because you know that if you don't, many groups in the community will not receive services? And so it goes. Significant ethical dilemmas rarely go away of their own accord. Although they may make you feel uncomfortable, it is best to address them head-on by defining them explicitly. Do not worry if you are still uncertain about the essential ethical issue at this point. As you work through the process of resolving the situation, you can go back and sharpen your definition of the dilemma.

Component Two: Deciding What Is Praiseworthy and Blameworthy

Now that we have collected the facts and explicitly defined the ethical dilemma, we are ready to move on to analysis. This step of the process is similar to the courtroom trial: We need to arrange and examine the evidence so that we can determine what is praiseworthy and blameworthy. At this stage, the ethical theories discussed in chapter 3 can be very helpful. During the trial, the lawyers for the prosecution and defense attempt to construct the strongest arguments to win their case, giving the jury reasons to help them decide whether the accused is guilty or innocent. Similarly, when resolving an ethical dilemma we can educate ourselves by systematically analyzing the problem using the three ethical theories of consequence-based ethics, rule-based ethics, and virtue ethics. It doesn't matter which theory we begin with. The important thing is that we make a conscientious effort to apply each theory to the best of our ability, just as the lawyers in the courtroom try to construct the most compelling cases for the jury.

You might begin by considering the consequences that will result from choosing one or the other horn of the dilemma. Remember, significant ethical dilemmas create the unenviable position of having to choose between two courses of action, neither of which is particularly desirable. By comparing the possible outcomes of the two choices, perhaps we can weigh which course of action is the more ethically justified by determining which option creates the most good or causes the least harm.

But we must not stop there. We need to continue our "trial" by applying rule-based ethical theories to the dilemma, asking ourselves what duties will be upheld or violated depending on how we resolve the dilemma. We will probably find that both solutions to the dilemma require us to violate some obligations to uphold others, so we need to decide which obligations are the most important.

We can now move on to arguments based on virtue ethics. We might think of this phase of reasoning as the character witnesses who are called to testify in criminal proceedings. Using the virtue ethics approach, we need to consult our conscience about resolving the dilemma. Does one or the other solution enhance or detract from our integrity?

If we have done a good job playing the roles of the trial lawyers, we should have constructed a number of sound arguments for resolving the dilemma one way or the other. Now comes the tricky part. Having seen the evidence and heard the arguments, we now must play the role of the jury and come up with a decision. At this point we must weigh the arguments for resolving the dilemma one way or the other. We may find ourselves pulled in different directions if the conclusions we favor do not point toward the same resolution of the dilemma.

For example, we may find that one of our therapeutic recreation supervisors has been stealing some of the money that is designated for the agency's mentally disabled clients. Our head may tell us that not pressing charges and asking the offender to quietly resign would result in the best consequences for our organization, yet our heart may tell us we could not live with ourselves for letting the offender off easy. We may have to discern which aspect of the dilemma is most important: making sure the best consequences result, adhering to the duties and obligations at stake, or maintaining our personal integrity. While it is likely that we each naturally lean toward one ethical theory, to avoid being dogmatic we need to be open to the possibility that in some situations we may need to choose an alternative ethical theory to justify our resolution of a dilemma.

Gaining experience in solving ethical dilemmas can help us develop the flexibility to select the ethical theory that is most appropriate for the problem at hand. We might even go so far as to suggest that the ability to prioritize which ethical theory is most relevant according to the ethical dilemma we face is a mark of wisdom.

Component Three: Choosing a Moral Action Plan

We have now decided which alternative to the dilemma is the most ethically justified, but our work is only of academic interest unless we indicate how we are going to resolve the dilemma. Reaching a verdict in a trial does not complete the judicial process. If we found the accused guilty but imposed no sentence, justice would not be done. Similarly, when we are resolving ethical dilemmas, we need to devise a precise plan of action that maps out how we are going to do the right thing. It is not enough to simply assign praise and blame when we are dealing with ethical dilemmas. We also need a plan of action to set things right.

Just as a criminal sentence needs to be based on evidence presented during the trial phase, our moral action plan needs to be based on ethical analysis of the dilemma. If the judge's sentence is too lenient or harsh, then justice is not served. The sentence needs to match the circumstances of the crime. Similarly, moral action plans to resolve ethical dilemmas need to be grounded in the circumstances of the dilemma. After we have decided that someone has done something morally wrong, we need to tailor our corrective action to fit the seriousness of the moral transgression. In fact, it would be unethical for us to deliberately do otherwise.

Becoming proficient at resolving ethical dilemmas requires practice. When the stakes are high, reputations and livelihoods are often on the line. We would hate to make a mistake when judging people's moral behaviors and motivations. Fortunately, we can practice our techniques for resolving ethical dilemmas without running the risk of actually harming people. Law students learn how to conduct courtroom proceedings by engaging in mock trials. No one risks getting sent to prison as the students make mistakes in developing their courtroom techniques. You can practice your ability to deal with ethical dilemmas by actively role-playing scenarios that you might find yourself in. Let's use the following hypothetical situation in which three leisure service supervisors face an ethical dilemma. Each of these individuals responds differently to the same dilemma. As you read about the ways they choose to solve the dilemma, imagine how you would act in the same situation.

Applying the Model

Jon, Kelly, and Sonja all graduated from college a few years ago and began working in municipal recreation departments in large cities. All three were recently promoted to supervisor of large community recreation centers, and all three faced a similar ethical dilemma. Upon assuming responsibility for their respective recreation center, they gradually became suspicious that some of the employees were stealing supplies and other items from work. Things such as food for the snack bar and vending machines regularly came up short, and pieces of sport equipment were unaccounted for. While it was safe to assume that some of the items were stolen by the clientele, many of the thefts pointed toward the employees. Here is how each supervisor decided to resolve the problem.

Jon's Approach

Jon was always well liked by his employees. He was popular with his peers in high school and college, and his easygoing nature and ability to get along well with others helped him get promoted to the position of facility supervisor. When dealing with problems, Jon's motto was, "Keep on smiling." Jon did not want to confront the employees about his suspicions that some of them were stealing from the recreation center, so he asked the assistant supervisor about the problem. His assistant told him there probably was some employee theft, but it was a typical occurrence at the center. Although Jon was distressed by the fact that some employees were stealing, he thought it would be best if he simply monitored the situation. This would give him time to build relationships with his new employees. He reckoned that the problem would eventually resolve itself as the employees got to know him. He would set a positive example of honesty, friendship, and trust, which would discourage further thefts. Friends do not steal from friends, he reasoned.

As the months went by, Jon did make friends with his employees. They liked working for him. However, the thefts did not decrease. In fact, things were getting worse. Money was now disappearing from cashier receipts. One Monday morning the city administrator came to Jon's office. She told him that an audit of the recreation center's operation was commencing immediately, and that all records from the past year must be turned over to the finance department staff. After several weeks of investigation, the city administrator reported to the mayor that there was evidence of substantial employee theft at the recreation center. Although Jon was not accused of theft, the administrator said that he had turned a blind eye to the illegal activity some of his employees were engaging in. The report concluded that Jon had committed a serious breach in his responsibilities by not actively dealing with the theft issue. It was recommended that his contract to supervise the facility not be renewed. Jon was no longer smiling.

Kelly's Approach

Kelly was excited about her promotion to facility supervisor. She had enjoyed working as an activities programmer, but she had always wanted to move into a managerial position. She felt that she now had the chance to fully use her leadership skills. Kelly had done exceptionally well at her university. She had worked tirelessly at her studies, and she graduated magna cum laude with a grade point average of 3.8 out of 4.0. She also was involved in many volunteer activities and organizations. Kelly was an achiever who held herself and others to high standards.

When Kelly learned that some employees might be stealing from the recreation center, she was appalled. She decided to take immediate action. To avoid making false accusations, she knew she needed solid evidence. She decided to use the center's security cameras to catch the thieves in the act. After the staff left one evening, she stayed late to alter the position of some of the security cameras mounted on the ceiling. Three of the cameras normally pointed toward lounges in the building, but Kelly found she could twist the camera mounts so that they now pointed toward some of the employee work areas.

Sure enough, after several days of electronic surveillance, Kelly had videotape evidence of employees stealing. Several employees were seen helping themselves to bottled drinks and snacks stored behind the towel desk. Another employee was regularly letting her children use the photocopier. A longtime employee was seen putting one of the center's basketballs into his gym bag. Worst of all, the camera recorded a new employee stealing cash.

Just as a criminal sentence needs to be based on evidence presented during the trial, a moral action plan for resolving dilemmas needs to be based on ethical analysis of the dilemma.

Now that she had firm evidence of who was stealing, Kelly had to make some tough choices. Since she had studied business ethics at university, she used her understanding of ethical theories to guide her decisions. In her ethics class she had learned the concept of **fiduciary duty**—the responsibility of middle and upper management to oversee the effective and efficient use of the organization's money. She was also aware that a mission of the recreation department was to faithfully serve the leisure needs of the community, so she and her workers had an obligation to operate the recreation facility in the public's interest. But the employees seen on the videotape were stealing from the facility. Thus, not only were they thieves, they were also violating their duty to serve the best interests of the community.

Kelly decided that such behavior was intolerable. She fired all of the employees who were caught on the tape. She also decided to press criminal charges against the employee who stole the cash. With the guilty employees routed out, Kelly thought her problem was over. Even if some dishonest employees were still working at the recreation center, a stern message had been sent to anyone who wanted to steal.

Unfortunately, the termination of the employees only marked the beginning of other problems for Kelly. The employee whose children had used the photocopier was suing the recreation department for wrongful dismissal. The long-time employee who had been caught stealing the basketball committed suicide a few weeks after losing his job, and a lengthy article in the local newspaper described how he had taken the ball for his disabled son to play with. The remaining employees at the center seemed either nervous or excessively polite when Kelly spoke to them. And one weekend Kelly bumped into two of her employees at the local movie theater. After exchanging pleasantries, she thought she heard one of the employees whisper snide remarks about her as she walked away. Kelly felt hurt and confused—hadn't she done the right thing?

Sonja's Approach

Sonja had been working as the new facility supervisor for a couple of months when she began to suspect that there might be an employee theft problem. Food items for the center's vending machines were disappearing and cash receipts frequently did not add up. While she did not like dealing with employee discipline, she knew that she could not tolerate ongoing employee theft, so she decided to investigate the problem.

First, she asked the business manager to compare the staffing records to the instances when the cash receipts came up short. This comparison revealed that the thefts only occurred when a particular full-time staff member was on duty.

Sonja and the business manager decided to confront the staff member at the end of her shift. They asked him to come into Sonja's office and they counted the day's cash receipts. As expected, the amount was short $20. Sonja asked the staff member why money was missing. Looking uncomfortable, he said that there must have been a mistake in making change. The business manager then pointed out that a consistent pattern of cash shortages occurred when the employee collected payments from clients. Small amounts in the range of $10 to $20 were frequently missing, and there was never an overage. The business manager said that this was a serious matter as the total missing amount added up to several hundred dollars. At this point the employee blurted out he had been pocketing small amounts of money for about 2 years. He had been using the money to buy extra lottery tickets, especially when the jackpot was big. He said he always had planned to make a donation to the center if he won big. He begged Sonja not to fire him or summon the police.

Now that she knew the facts, Sonja had a difficult decision to make. She told the employee that he would be terminated immediately from the center because of the theft of funds. However, given the relatively small amount of money he stole, she declined to press criminal charges.

Having dealt with the missing cash, Sonja turned her attention to the disappearing food supplies. She noticed that food items seemed to go missing during the evening hours and weekends when the part-time staff was on duty. Many of the part-timers were students. Sonja decided she should start dropping by the center during her off-hours to see what was going on. On her third surprise visit, she observed several part-time employees helping themselves to snacks during their break.

The following week she called in the individuals whom she had observed taking the food. When told that they had been observed eating food from the supplies, the students expressed a mixture of surprise and regret. Several said they thought that helping themselves to a few snacks was simply one of the job's benefits, and as long as people weren't taking more than they needed for a snack at break, then it wasn't really a problem. Others had at first wondered if it was okay to help themselves to the food, but after they learned that it was a common practice, they didn't feel so guilty.

Sonja did not fire the part-time employees. Instead, she had a small refrigerator and microwave installed in the staff lounge. She held a staff meeting to announce that all employees should bring their own food to work or purchase snacks from the vending machines like everyone else. From now on, helping oneself to food or any other property of the center could result in dismissal and prosecution.

Later that week the city administrator asked Sonja why she had not fired the part-time employees who had been stealing food. Weren't they as guilty as the employee who stole the cash? Sonja disagreed. While both instances involved stealing the center's property, in her judgment the food theft involved mitigating circumstances. The filching of the food, though not right, was a generally accepted practice at the center, while the stealing of the cash was not. The part-time staff did not hide the fact that they were eating the food, whereas the full-time staff member concealed the fact that he was walking out the door with the center's money. The full-time staff member knew that what he was doing was illegal, while the part-time staff may not have realized that what they were doing was wrong. Therefore, Sonja reasoned that, unlike the full-time staff member, the part-timers deserved another chance. She clarified the rules regarding food and provided equipment to encourage the staff to bring their own food to work. After hearing Sonja's reasons for her actions, the business director approved of how Sonja had resolved the theft issue.

The Most Appropriate Response

The problem facing Jon, Kelly, and Sonja was the same—how to deal with the moral issue of employee theft. Each person had a different response to the problem. Jon's response was the least satisfactory of the three. Jon was uncomfortable with the idea that employees might be stealing, but he never came to grips with the ethical issue. His head-in-the-sand approach assumed that things would eventually work out, but they didn't. While it may be tempting to think that moral issues will solve themselves, the reality is that we commit a further wrong by choosing to ignore them. We cannot be responsible moral agents by turning a blind eye to ethical issues. Moral problems are created by people, and it takes conscientious effort to resolve them.

Kelly's response to the problem was more sophisticated than Jon's. Kelly explicitly recognized the moral dilemma of employee theft occurring under her watch. She used theories of ethical reasoning to determine that employee theft is morally intolerable, and she acted decisively to punish those who were at fault. Yet in some ways Kelly's response to the dilemma turned out to be even worse than Jon's. Whereas Jon was too passive in dealing with the ethical dilemma, Kelly was too headstrong. She relied exclusively on her ethical analysis of the wrongness of stealing to justify firing the employees who were engaging in theft. Her response to the problem was not tempered by considering what would be appropriate sanctions against the offending employees. Kelly's response was long on intellect but short on judgment.

Sonja's response was the most successful of the three. She addressed the ethical issues head-on, but she also tempered her corrective actions by using good judgment. Her objective was not simply to determine who was guilty of what, but also to produce a measured response that did justice to all who were involved in the dilemma. Sonja put a lot of effort into resolving the dilemma in a systematic manner. She gathered facts to determine that a dilemma existed. She clarified for herself what the dilemma was. She employed her knowledge of moral reasoning to help determine who was guilty of what. Then she tailored corrective actions to produce the most just solution for everyone who was affected by the dilemma.

Clearly, solving difficult ethical dilemmas is a complex process. To manage ethical dilemmas more effectively, use the worksheet at the end of this chapter. You can use it to analyze the sample ethical dilemmas in chapter 12. The worksheet is divided into three stages:

1. The first stage asks you to identify and state the ethical dilemma.
2. The second stage asks you to analyze the dilemma using the ethical theories you learned in chapter 3. The purpose of this analysis is to determine who or what is praiseworthy and blameworthy in the situation at hand.
3. The third stage asks you to describe how you will implement your resolution to the ethical dilemma. You want to praise those who have done right and apply corrective actions to fix what is wrong. You must translate the findings of your ethical analysis into a moral action plan, considering not only theoretical issues of what is right and wrong, but also practical issues of how to successfully implement the necessary corrective actions. Like a judge at the sentencing phase of a trial, you need to both explain and justify the actions you will take to resolve the ethical dilemma.

When working through ethical dilemmas, it is a good idea to compare solutions with your classmates. In doing so, you may be surprised by the variety of ways you and your peers resolve practical ethical problems. Even when you agree with someone else about the moral status of a particular dilemma, it is likely that you each will have somewhat different plans for implementing your solution to the problem. There is nothing wrong with that—it simply reflects the fact we are autonomous individuals who have the ability to ethically justify our actions.

Conclusion

The model we have presented provides a systematic, logical approach for resolving ethical issues. It is intended to help you structure your thoughts so that you can rationally resolve moral problems and clearly explain your reasons to other people. The model is *not* intended to eliminate emotions from your ethical deliberations. On the contrary, you need to employ your emotions in all three parts of the model. For example, recognizing an ethical dilemma begins when you feel awkward and uncomfortable about a situation; analyzing an ethical dilemma is incomplete unless you have asked yourself if you can respect yourself for the decision you are making; and implementing your moral action plan requires courage to carry out the corrective actions. Thus, your moral feelings play an essential role as you apply the model.

In some ways learning and using this ethical problem-solving model is similar to learning how to drive a car, play cards, or do math. It doesn't happen automatically. Employing this model the first few times may be somewhat slow and cumbersome, but before long it will be much less difficult, and after a longer period of time, it can become almost automatic. You may be concerned that you won't have time to employ this model. You may think that ethical dilemmas have to be dealt with as quickly as possible. While some situations may need to be resolved immediately, most require a period of time to be sorted out. One of the benefits of a systematic approach like this model is that it is a carefully reasoned approach that acts as a safety mechanism against rash decisions that will come back to haunt us at a later date. Whenever possible, we should proceed cautiously in matters dealing with ethics.

QUESTIONS FOR DISCUSSION

1. Think of a time when you were caught in an ethical dilemma. Maybe it was at work, at school, or during your leisure time with friends. How satisfied were you with your solution to the dilemma? Do you think your solution was fair?

2. Did the other people involved in the situation approve of your solution, or were they angry with you?

3. If you could jump into a time machine and go back to when you first encountered the dilemma, would you resolve it in a different way?

Ethical Dilemma Worksheet

Identifying the Ethical Dilemma

Get the facts:

- Is it a technical or an ethical problem?
- How significant is the problem?
- Who is affected by the problem?
- What is my role in resolving the problem?
- What are the two ethically conflicting actions?

State the dilemma:

_____

_____

_____

_____

_____

_____

_____

_____

_____

_____

_____

_____

_____

From *Issues in Recreation and Leisure: Ethical Decision Making* by Donald J. McLean and Daniel G. Yoder, 2005, Champaign, IL: Human Kinetics.

Ethical Dilemma Worksheet

Analyzing the Ethical Dilemma

Judge the dilemma:

- Apply each ethical theory to analyze the dilemma.
- Determine who or what is morally praiseworthy and blameworthy.

Come to a verdict:

_____

_____

_____

_____

_____

_____

_____

_____

_____

_____

_____

_____

_____

_____

_____

_____

_____

From *Issues in Recreation and Leisure: Ethical Decision Making* by Donald J. McLean and Daniel G. Yoder, 2005, Champaign, IL: Human Kinetics.

Ethical Dilemma Worksheet

Resolving the Ethical Dilemma

Create a moral action plan:

- "Sentence" those whose actions are blameworthy.
- Praise those whose actions are praiseworthy.
- Balance ethical analysis against the practicality of implementing corrective actions.
- State explicitly what corrective action you will take and your reasons for it.

_____

_____

_____

_____

_____

_____

_____

_____

_____

_____

_____

_____

From *Issues in Recreation and Leisure: Ethical Decision Making* by Donald J. McLean and Daniel G. Yoder, 2005, Champaign, IL: Human Kinetics.

PART II

Current Issues in Leisure Services

Community Recreation

FIVE

GOALS

1. To learn about the role of public recreation in the community
2. To become informed about naive legalism as a pitfall to ethical decision making and acting
3. To consider the issue of sexual harassment in community recreation
4. To consider the issue of safety in community recreation
5. To consider the issue of conflicts of interest in community recreation
6. To consider the issue of whistle-blowing in community recreation

Ethical dilemmas in leisure services occur in a variety of settings under a variety of circumstances. The travel agent, the manager of the local Boys and Girls Club, and the supervisor of a public outdoor recreation area all face a wide range of administrative issues that require ethical decision making. Some of these dilemmas are more likely to occur in some branches of leisure services than others. For example, environmental issues are common in park management, while problems with confidentiality are common in therapeutic recreation. Likewise, the exploitation of indigenous cultures has plagued international tourism for the past few decades. Later chapters discuss ethical issues that are relevant to specific branches of leisure services. The focus of this chapter is administrative ethical dilemmas common to all branches, such as sexual harassment, conflicts of interest, safety, and whistle-blowing. These general administrative ethical dilemmas are likely to occur in any branch of leisure services, whether it be public recreation, tourism, outdoor recreation, or therapeutic recreation.

In this chapter we will move from the general to the specific and address particular issues in the field of leisure services. First, however, recall that we mentioned in the first chapter that many people have the mistaken notion that studying ethics is difficult and ethical decision making is incredibly difficult. We have tried to counter some of those misperceptions in the first few chapters and we will continue to do so. Nevertheless, partially because of that undeserved negative perspective and a fear of ethics, some have tried to sidestep ethical decision making. While many of these alternatives are ingenious and seductive, they are weak substitutes for solid ethical thinking. One of the most prevalent tactics is to entirely rely upon the law for making decisions (see "A Warning About Naive Legalism").

We have established that appeals to the legal system are insufficient for resolving ethical dilemmas in the workplace. Now let us examine some common ethical dilemmas that leisure service providers may encounter at some point in their careers. We will begin this endeavor with the ethical dilemmas relating to sexual harassment, and then we will examine safety, conflict of interest, and whistle-blowing. As you consider the issues, focus on the ethical evaluation of these common dilemmas and avoid the temptation to resort to purely legal remedies. Ask yourself how you think these dilemmas should be resolved.

Sexual Harassment

Sexual harassment is nothing new. As far back as the Old Testament, chapter 39 in the book of Genesis describes a case of sexual harassment

A Warning About Naive Legalism

It may seem appealing at first to defer moral responsibility for ethical behavior to the legal system. Such action is termed **naive legalism** by ethicists. On the surface it seems a perfectly logical course of action. Today's administrators in general and certainly in community recreation have enough to do without devoting time and effort to resolving problems that have already been researched and discussed. Why not use the tools, or laws, that are already available? And there are a lot of those tools, too. Here are just a few:

- Occupational Safety and Health Administration Act (U.S.)
- Occupational Health and Safety Act (Canada)
- Environmental laws including the Clean Air and Water Acts (Canada and U.S.)
- Consumer Product Safety Act (Canada and U.S.)
- Americans With Disabilities Act (U.S.)
- Employment Equity Act (Canada)
- Equal Employment Opportunity Commission (U.S.)
- Canadian Privacy Act (Canada)

If laws and regulations are representations of collective moral sentiment, it seems we can't go wrong by simply following them. Not only will such a course keep us out of jail, but it should keep us on the straight and narrow moral pathway.

Unfortunately, this legalistic approach has serious shortcomings. Stevens (1979) points out that resorting to the law would be too expensive and cumbersome for dealing with most workplace ethical issues. Our law enforcement agencies and courts are overwhelmed as it is. For example, unless they result in tremendously large financial loss, cases involving conflicts of interest are too insignificant for the time it would take to deal with them in the courts. That is not to say that they are unimportant; however, dealing with them in this manner is not usually the best option. Moreover, as Stevens contends, the legal system is much more effective at dealing with antisocial behavior in the traditional criminal arena than in the workplace. It is simply not practical to shift the burden for solving most of our ethical dilemmas in the workplace onto the legal system.

Another problem with depending entirely on the legal system to solve ethical dilemmas is that we inadvertently undermine the moral justification for our laws. While a community's laws are obviously important,

(continued)

(continued)

they are only the tangible, practical signification of the more important fundamental collective moral sentiment. An exclusive focus on the law ignores the reason for the law in the first place. Wrongs occur first and are followed by laws and regulations. New situations create new ethical issues, and legislation is introduced to deal with them only when they become sufficiently commonplace. The law is forever playing catch-up with our moral sensibilities. Occasionally, the gap between dilemmas and legislation may be the result of new technology. Consider some of the issues related to copyrighted material made available for free on the Web, much to the dismay of the copyright holders. Only since 2000 have we begun to make, interpret, and apply legal guidelines for that situation (Field 2004). Before the expansion of copyright laws we had to deal with the ethics of copying and using certain electronic materials on a case-by-case basis.

Finally, naive legalism assumes that all laws are moral, or that right is what the law says is right. However, this is not always the case. For example, Jim Crow laws in the latter half of the 19th century and the first half of the 20th century segregated black Americans from white Americans, forming a rigid caste system that denied basic rights to African Americans. D'Angelo (2001) notes, "Segregationist legislation made for segregated telephone booths, water fountains, transportation, parks, restaurants and schools; most of those for blacks were poorly funded and inferior to those for whites" (3). Such laws are testimony to the potential for unethical legislation. Only when brave people questioned such laws and refused to follow them did the rules change.

Thus we should not assume that legal behavior and ethical behavior are the same. If laws are to provide justice, then the legal system needs to be founded on our moral reasoning. We cannot shift the burden of moral decision making to the courts. Our ethical responsibilities extend well beyond what laws forbid us to do. We should expect more of ourselves and others and go beyond simply obeying the law. Recall Kohlberg's (1976) argument that unquestioning allegiance to laws is but a preliminary stage in the process of becoming truly ethical actors.

This is not to say that laws and regulations are of no value. They certainly provide us with important direction. However, by themselves they are insufficient for ensuring ethical behavior. Let's consider a situation that could take place in any rural community in Canada or the United States. Such communities in general tend to be conservative, particularly the older citizens. The activities director of a long-term care facility for aging adults needs to hire two persons in the therapeutic recreation department. Two of the five equally qualified applicants are obviously of

Middle Eastern descent. A significant part of the job is to interact with the clients and their families. The folks in this community have not forgotten the terrorist attack of September 11, 2001, and they are careful whom they associate with. To them, all outsiders are suspect to some degree. Only after strangers have proven that they are not a threat does the community accept them, and this may take many years. Recent talk about the possibility of sleeper cells, or individuals who infiltrate communities and at some later time wreak havoc, has been common in this little town.

If the facility hires one or both of these Middle Eastern men, it will most likely lose business. This is no small matter, given that the financial condition of most nursing homes is extremely precarious. Moreover, for the clients and their families, the local facility is the only option if the family and friends are to stay reasonably close and be able to visit on a regular basis. The next closest nursing home is almost 50 miles away. Employment law states that employers cannot discriminate on the basis of national origin even though there seem to be extenuating circumstances in this case. The activities director must make a complex ethical decision that may be complicated by the law. Should she hire two applicants who are not of Middle Eastern descent and are as qualified, thereby maintaining the peace and prosperity of the small town? Or should she disregard her own feelings and the likely consternation of the community and families and abide by the law? To whom does she have the greatest responsibility? As you can see, it is not as simple as sticking to the law.

with an interesting twist. (A young man named Joseph worked in the home of a wealthy Egyptian named Potiphor. Several times, Potiphor's wife tried to seduce Joseph, but each time he refused to yield to the pressure. Smarting from rejection, Potiphor's wife concocted a story that led to Joseph's imprisonment.) But the legal concept, with its attendant definition, prevention guidelines, and penalties, is fairly new. The first mention of sexual discrimination and sexual harassment in the workplace is found in the United States Civil Rights Act of 1964. The United States Equal Employment Opportunity Commission (EEOC) increased awareness of the issue in the early 1980s by providing definitional guidelines. However, it was not until the 1991 hearings to confirm Clarence Thomas for the U.S. Supreme Court, which brought up claims by law professor Anita Hill of sexual harassment by Thomas, that the issue triggered a national debate. This case and the ensuing awareness was at least partly responsible for an increase in workplace sexual harassment cases, which rose from 6,127 in 1991 to 15,342 just 5 years later (http://chnm.gmu.edu/courses/122/hill/hillframe.htm).

Anita Hill's accusations of sexual harassment by Judge Clarence Thomas in 1991 brought sexual harassment to the attention of most Americans.

Sexual Harassment Defined

EEOC guidelines state that sexual harassment includes unwelcome sexual advances, requests for sexual favors, and other verbal or physical conduct of a sexual nature. Within this broad definition there are two types of sexual harassment. Quid pro quo harassment is when a person offers some type of employment benefit in exchange for a subordinate's submission to a sexual request. The other, more difficult to prove, type of sexual harassment is a hostile work environment in which unwelcome sexual conduct unreasonably interferes with an individual's working environment or creates an intimidating, hostile, or offensive work environment. The line between the two types of harassment is not always clear, and they often occur concurrently.

Sexual harassment is a significant workplace problem. Estimates of the number of incidences range considerably. An analysis of sexual harassment studies in the United States reported that research on the low end indicates 24% of women have experienced harassment and on the high end 58% of women have experienced harassment. Most of the variance can be attributed to two causes—lack of a consistent definition of sexual harassment and faulty study designs (Ilies et al. 2003). However, all studies agree that the effects of these behaviors are devastating to the agency and the individuals involved. Organizations stand to lose millions of dollars in lost productivity and expensive lawsuits and victims are often severely damaged both physically and emotionally.

Sexual Harassment in Recreation and Leisure

The field of leisure services may very well suffer from the devastating consequences of sexual harassment. Companies offering recreation opportunities may be less profitable than they could be. Nonprofit organizations that use recreation to enhance the lives of individuals are likely to at least partially miss the mark. And public agencies cannot serve their constituents effectively and efficiently if they must contend with the direct and indirect consequences of sexual harassment.

Because it is such a diverse field, no numbers are available indicating the frequency of sexual harassment in leisure services. However, there is no reason to believe that the rates are lower than in any other field. Some characteristics of the field may even create situations conducive to sexual harassment. For example, men and women work in a variety of situations that require creative work schedules, and behavioral expectations may be unclear in these novel settings. Furthermore, while progress is being made to increase the ratio of female to male managers in leisure and recreation, a significant gap remains, and because male supervisors are the most common perpetrators of sexual harassment, there may be more opportunities for sexual harassment. What's more, most leisure service personnel deal face to face with their customers, clients, and constituents. This is a factor because sexual harassment not only involves employees but can also involve those whom the employees serve.

Learning Activity: Is This Sexual Harassment?

Think about these situations, then indicate if you think it is or is not sexual harassment. Also, indicate why you think that way.

- An employee tells a coworker that a particular dress or suit makes her look "hot."
- An employee tells a coworker that his clothing makes him look "very nice" on a regular basis even after the recipient has told her he does not appreciate such comments.
- A female supervisor hugs a male subordinate in elation over the news of a promotion.
- A male supervisor hugs a female subordinate in elation over the news of a promotion.
- Pictures of partially clad women are posted in the break room of an aquatics facility.
- Men and women in revealing swimsuits are frolicking in the pool and sunning on the decks. These swimsuits may reveal more than some pictures that constitute a hostile environment.

Given the widespread condemnation of sexual harassment and unanimous agreement that its consequences can be devastating, it should seem fairly easy for leisure services personnel to make the ethical decision when it comes to sexual harassment. The law prohibits the sexual harassment of subordinates, peers, supervisors, or customers. Unfortunately, the law remains murky in several areas, especially in defining what constitutes a hostile workplace or offensive work environment. For example, consider whether the situations in the Learning Activity create a hostile environment.

Neville (2000) sums up the current work environment as it relates to sexual harassment: "What we have is a workplace that is stuffed to overflow with ambiguous rules of conduct, diverse corporate cultures, opposing personal beliefs, sharply differing attitudes, and a general blanket of uncertainty regarding this business of sexual behavior" (18).

Due to the limitations of sexual harassment laws and regulations, the burden of making the correct ethical choice falls on the individual. Using the following ethical approaches, we can evaluate alleged sexual behavior in the workplace.

- From a consequence-based (utilitarian) perspective, we could judge the appropriateness of an action based on the criteria of the greatest good for the greatest number of people. How does an action that is sexual in nature affect the employees, the company's owners, and clients over a period of time?

- From a rule-based (deontological) perspective, we could consider whether the person initiating the action would want to be the recipient of such action.

- From a virtue-based perspective, we must determine if an interaction or display is appropriate given the role expectations of the initiator and recipient of the action. For example, is it appropriate for a supervisor to make advances toward another supervisor or to a direct subordinate?

Given the unavoidable sexual nature of human beings, you will certainly face dilemmas related to sexual harassment. You must be familiar with the law, but you will also be required to make many ethical decisions beyond the law.

Safety

Is the world a safer place today than it was yesterday? That question has no simple answer. At the global level we are less safe because of humankind's increased ability to annihilate itself. New weapons of mass destruction are being designed as more traditional ones are being refined. Today not only do a few so-called superpowers have such weapons, but they are the route of choice for governments that want to become superpowers. In addition, our capacity to inflict devastating environmental damage grows each year. However, on a local level we are probably safer. Consider the evolution of automobile safety over the past half century, for instance. We have come from no seat belts and steel dashboards to lap and shoulder harnesses, front and side airbags, safety seats, and collision warning systems.

Safety Defined

The first step in an honest, comprehensive discussion of safety is to expose the myth of the completely risk-free workplace. Even the Occupational Safety and Health Administration (OSHA), the primary protector of working men and women in the United States, has recognized that fact. In response to several court rulings in the late 1970s, OSHA changed its primary mission of attempting to enforce a no-risk workplace policy to encouraging a "sufficiently risk-free workplace." All human activity carries some risk, and absolute safety must be sacrificed in the effort to accomplish even the most modest company goals.

Of course, safety can be increased, sometimes with relatively minor effort and expenditure, and at other times only with much expense, effort, and sacrifice. The analogy of wringing water from a wool stocking may help us understand risk-control efforts. With only a few twists, the water pours from the sock, but with each drop that is lost, subsequent drops become more and more difficult to squeeze out. The owner of the stocking has to twist extremely forcefully to get the final drops out. Even then, some moisture remains. Such is the case with risk reduction—it is easy at first but becomes more time-consuming and expensive as progress is made, and it is virtually impossible to remove all risk.

Because risk is inevitable, managers must decide how much risk their organization can accept and how safe they want the workplace to be. Make no mistake, these are ethical decisions. Recognition of the statutes mandating workplace safety is an aid but by itself is insufficient. Guidelines are available, such as those offered by OSHA and insurance carriers, but they are often unenforceable under law. Accidents occur and typically it is only then that rules are created to reduce the chance of additional injuries. It is up to the decision makers in the workplace to decide how much risk their employees and patrons should face.

Safety in Recreation and Leisure

While most fields strive to eliminate as much risk as possible for those they serve, the leisure services field accepts it. Some recreation organizations and companies even augment risk in an effort to provide exciting opportunities for their clients (Kelly 1987). For example, the distance between Buena Vista, Colorado, and Salida, Colorado, is about 30 miles. A perfectly good two-lane highway runs between the towns. Nevertheless, thousands of people pay $50 to rafting companies that provide them with helmets, life vests, and river guides for an exhilarating white-water ride down the Arkansas River from Buena Vista to Salida. Moreover, most airplanes take off, fly, and land safely; there is rarely a genuine need for anyone to bail out. Yet thousands of people strap on parachutes and jump out of planes that will be landing in just a few minutes. It's the thrill that drives millions of North Americans to do these and thousands of other risky recreation activities.

Leisure and recreation providers make profound ethical decisions about safety at every turn. This is even more obvious when we consider that participants and employees risk not only physical loss but also loss of emotional security and material goods. Such ethical decisions are even more significant because in many cases we make safety decisions based on information that participants and employees don't have access to. Moreover, managers often have expertise unavailable to those they serve.

Let's use the example of a youth tackle football program to illustrate the ethical nature of safety decisions. First, you must decide if your agency should even offer such a program. On one hand, you know that such

Starting and maintaining a youth tackle football program involves many ethical decisions about safety.

programs offer many benefits to participants, but you also know—probably more accurately than participants—the risk in playing. You are faced with a serious ethical decision. If you decide to offer the program, you must make additional ethical decisions as to how the program's level of risk should be handled. These are certainly administrative decisions but they are ethical decisions as well.

Very Safe Football Program

- New, regularly inspected equipment
- Trained coaches/officials
- Emergency medical technicians
- Limited number of games
- Rules limiting blocking and tackling
- Insurance for all involved

Very Unsafe Football Program

- Old, used equipment
- Pick-up coaches
- No medical personnel at games
- Long seasons with many games
- Very competitive league
- College football rules
- No insurance

As the administrator of the program, you decide where the program will be on the continuum of safety. If money is not a limitation, you may opt for a program that has the best equipment money can buy and extensively trained coaches and officials. A minimum of two emergency medical technicians would be at every practice and game. In an effort to have an extremely safe program, you would reduce competition and emphasize a philosophy of learning the game. You might also limit the number of games, institute rules about contact such as no hitting below the waist, and eliminate returns for kickoffs and punts. Finally, not only would you consult with your insurance carrier, you would agree to run the program on the terms stipulated by the carrier.

Of course, you're not likely to have unlimited resources, and you might experience pressure from others to offer a more traditional youth tackle football program. In that case, your options fall on the riskier end of the spectrum. You could ignore safety altogether and pray that no serious accidents occur, which probably isn't a good idea but is surprisingly common. Or you could

Learning Activity: Can You Be Too Safe?

Think about a sport that you are familiar with. Maybe you participated in it or know someone who did. This sport, like almost all sports, has elements of risk that need to be addressed by the program supervisor. Using 3-by-5 cards, label one card UNSAFE, one card RELATIVELY SAFE, and one card ULTRA SAFE. For each category or card, list five safety-related characteristics. (For example, if you chose gymnastics, one of the characteristics of an ULTRA SAFE program might be that a person with EMT certification be present at every practice.) Also, determine which type of program (UNSAFE, RELATIVELY SAFE, or ULTRA SAFE) is most expensive and which type of program is least expensive. Finally, consider which level of program safety is most ethical. What factors are part of your decision in determining how safe a program should be?

compromise some of the safety-related practices you would ideally like to have for the sake of the program. Regardless, you will make an important ethical decision after considering

- the potential consequences of the level of risk;
- the obligations you owe to the players, their parents, the recreation advisory board, and the community; and
- what you know in your heart is the right thing to do.

Conflict of Interest

During the course of a lifetime we assume many roles. We may find ourselves in the positions of spouse, parent, friend, supervisor, employee, board member, activist, and citizen all at the same time. Because each role has its own set of values and obligations, life is fraught with potential conflicts of interest.

Most of the time role obligations are compatible and we negotiate them with little difficulty. For example, parents are usually able to reschedule work for a day or two to fulfill their duties as primary caregivers when their children get sick. But on those occasions when the values and expectations for one role clash with those of another role, a serious conflict of interest ensues.

Conflict of Interest Defined

Conflicts often involve at least one role that is related to work or volunteer activities for an organization. Because of this, local, state, and federal laws have been adopted to curtail the often costly results of conflicts of inter-est. While these laws may be useful as guidelines, they are insufficient by themselves to control human action. State and federal laws almost exclusively relate to **self-dealing,** in which individuals place their own pecuniary, or financial, interests over those of the organization in such a way that the organization is harmed. Such a narrow definition fails to recognize that individuals have personal interests other than those related to money. We may also act in a manner that is harmful to our company, agency, or organization in our pursuit of personal relationships, status, and professional goals. Further complicating the issue, many of the cur-rent laws contain unspecified terms like *fairness* and *substantial harm.* Williams (1985) expands upon this common problem with conflict of interest laws: "The ambiguities which attach to the concept increase when the focus moves from the abstract definition to real events in public life" (7). Given this, dealing with conflicts of interest is a thoroughly ethical undertaking.

Conflict of Interest in Recreation and Leisure

While conflicts of interest often take place in the commercial sector, the most visible and damaging incidents occur in nonprofit organizations and public agencies. Because nonprofit agencies are largely dependent on financial donations and volunteers from the general public, any scandal that harms an agency's image can severely limit its ability to function. In addition, public scrutiny has become more intense for nonprofit organiza-tions and recreation-related agencies at the local, state, and federal levels since the mid-1970s. This increased transparency and accountability will continue to expose scandals resulting from conflicts of interest.

As noted, the basis for conflicts of interest is divergent values and obligations, and because of this, the leisure services field is particularly fertile ground for producing conflicts. Moreover, the recent full-scale com-mitment to developing partnerships with diverse groups and individuals in recreation and leisure portends the possibility of even more conflicts in the future. Kraus and Curtis (2000) note, "The trend of the 1980s and 1990s that seems certain to continue into the 21st century involves the full-fledged partnership among different sectors of the recreation, parks and leisure service field" (260). The authors go on to provide several examples of partnerships that involve diverse partners in projects ranging from joint use of facilities to subcontracting services. With greater diver-sity in partners there is greater potential for conflicts of interest because the different entities involved will have different missions, philosophies, and practices.

A few examples illustrate the range of possible conflicts of interest in leisure services:

- Board members may make decisions regarding the purchase of goods and services that personally benefit themselves at the expense of the agencies they represent.

- Workers in leisure services are encouraged to become members of their respective professional organizations that strive to establish and maintain the social position of the industry. Conflicts of interest may arise when employees neglect the responsibilities of their salaried position while devoting time and energy to these organizations.

- Park and recreation departments have been accused of being a home for individuals with "an edifice complex." These conflicts of interest involve the construction of sport and recreation areas and buildings that enhance the image of the decision makers while disregarding the genuine needs and capabilities of their constituents. The resulting structural legacies may quickly become financial burdens and maintenance nightmares for those who are stuck with their ongoing operation.

Conflicts of interest in the leisure services are not insurmountable obstacles, but they do require careful analysis of consequences, each role's duties, and diverse values and behaviors (including our own).

Whistle-Blowing

Employees have been blowing the whistle or disclosing information about their companies' illegal or unethical activities for a long time, but the practice has only become common knowledge for North Americans fairly recently.

As further testimony to the public's interest in whistle-blowing, *Time* magazine's 2002 Persons of the Year were three whistle-blowers: Sherron Watkins of the Enron accounting fiasco, Coleen Rowley of the scandal involving the FBI's failure to act on information about potential terrorist attacks, and Cynthia Cooper, who brought to light WorldCom's bookkeeping errors.

Whistle-Blowing Defined

Jubb (1999) identifies whistle-blowing as

> a deliberate nonobligatory act of disclosure, which gets onto public record and is made by a person who has or had privileged access to data or information of an organization, about

nontrivial illegality or other wrongdoing whether actual, suspected or anticipated which implicates and is under the control of that organization, to an external entity having potential to rectify the wrongdoing. (78)

Even without a formal definition such as this, we know whistle-blowing when we see it. Remember the kid who told the teacher on you for something you did on the playground? Back then we referred to such kids as tattletales, snitches, or rats. The concept is the same in whistle-blowing; the only difference is that the issues and the stakes are usually higher for adults.

Underlying this and other definitions is the principle that whistle-blowing is a morally uncertain action that involves a degree of disloyalty to the organization and to at least some individuals within the organization (Dandekar 1991). Typically, only a few individuals in an organization purposely commit serious wrongs. However, many others are at risk of being exposed by their compliance with the illegal or unethical deeds. In addition to contending with the vexing issue of disloyalty, the whistle-blower wages an uphill ethical battle because the accused individual or organization is presumed to be innocent.

© Associated Press

The risks can be very high for those who decide to disclose wrongdoing in their companies or organizations.

Related Films: Whistle-Blowing

Whistle-blowing is a common and emotion-laden human phenomenon. Consequently, it is the stuff of great (and not-so-great) movies. The following films and TV shows are representative of the many stories featuring an inside informant as a central character.

- *Serpico* (1972). This movie is based on a real-life undercover policeman who exposed widespread corruption in the New York police department.
- *All the President's Men* (1976). The still-unknown insider who provided vital information to the *Washington Post* about the 1960s Watergate break-in was known as Deep Throat.
- *Silkwood* (1976). Karen Silkwood was investigating shoddy practices at the nuclear power plant where she worked when she died in a suspicious car accident.
- *Brubaker* (1980). The new warden of a southern prison comes in as a prisoner to get a firsthand view of the facility. His discovery of corruption and his subsequent whistle-blowing put him at great personal risk.
- *City Hall* (1996). An idealistic deputy mayor uncovers corruption in New York's city hall.
- *Roswell* (1994). There are a lot of inside players in this TV series' complicated plot to expose what really happened when an unidentified flying object crashed in Roswell, New Mexico, in 1947.
- *Eraser* (1996). A woman with inside information on a crime becomes part of the federal witness program, but word inevitably leaks out and she must escape from those involved with the crime.
- *The X-Files* (1993-2002; 1998) In this TV series and movie, a lot of skulduggery takes place at the highest levels of government and business. Whistle-blowers try to enlighten the FBI heroes, but the informants keep getting killed.
- *The Insider* (1999). Jeffrey Wigand is fired from his high-level job in the tobacco industry. He blows the whistle about the industry's corrupt practices and gets a lot of people in hot water.
- *Exit Wounds* (2001). An unorthodox Detroit policeman exposes corrupt cops and their scheme to sell drugs.

Have you seen any of these films or TV shows? Who were the "good guys" and who were the "bad guys"? Have you seen other films or shows in this genre?

Because of these circumstances, going public with inside information is a courageous step with significant risk for the person initiating the charge. Those who bring wrongdoing to light may be in danger of extreme retaliation. Glazer and Glazer's (1989) documentation of the consequences of whistle-blowing include firing, demotion, transfer to a different position or location, character assassination, and social shunning.

Whistle-Blowing in Recreation and Leisure

While the vast majority of businesses, organizations, and agencies in the leisure services field act appropriately, some fall below society's expectations of how they should behave. A small percentage of people misuse their resources, mistreat their employees and constituents, and mislead the public. In many cases these wrongdoings are exposed only when a person who has privileged access to information comes forward. For example, the *Washington Post* interviewed National Park Police Chief Teresa Chambers in late 2003. In an article that ran on December 2, 2003, Chambers was sharply critical of the lack of staff and misuse of resources at U.S. national parks. Three days later Chambers was ordered to surrender her badge and gun and she was placed on administrative leave and prohibited from speaking with the media.

Potential whistle-blowers should answer several difficult ethical questions before making the final consequential act of public disclosure:

- How significant is the wrongdoing?
- Is the wrongdoing within the organization's ability to control?
- Has an attempt been made to inform the organization's decision makers of the wrongdoing?
- Are there ulterior motives for disclosing information?
- Who will suffer if the wrongdoing is disclosed?
- Who will suffer if the wrongdoing is *not* disclosed?
- What are the personal costs for the whistle-blower and the whistle-blower's friends and family?
- To whom is loyalty owed?

Because society usually benefits from whistle-blowing, state and federal statutes have been enacted in an effort to encourage the disclosure of illegal or unethical behaviors and to protect whistle-blowers from retaliation. Unfortunately, these regulations have been only partially effective. For example, New Brunswick is the only Canadian jurisdiction that specifically provides protection for whistle-blowers. In other Canadian provinces whistle-blowers risk their jobs and reputations when they disclose inside information (www.canadianlawsite.com/whistle-blower.htm#b). In the United States, a judge has ruled that many employees of the National Institutes of Health (NIH) are not covered by the Whistleblowers Protection Act (National Whistleblower Center 2005). This is particularly noteworthy given the fact that NIH makes numerous decisions that affect the safety of millions of Americans. Once again, we cannot escape the need for ethical decision making beyond the limits of the law.

Conclusion

Almost on a daily basis, individuals in leisure and recreation are required to make ethical judgments, regardless of their position in the company or organization. While we must be aware of employment policies and regulations, we cannot escape our responsibilities by simply abdicating decision making to a remote and sometimes ineffective legal system.

As we have demonstrated, making a moral call is particularly critical in personnel management.

- Far too many cases attest to the suffering of individuals and organizations from sexual harassment. But at the same time, a sterile work environment is not natural, enjoyable, or productive.

- Accidents in leisure settings, whether in offices, fitness facilities, or outdoor recreation areas, take a tremendous toll, but all human activity involves a compromise between human growth and complete safety.

- Promoting one's own interests at the expense of the organization limits the potential for achieving organization goals and objectives, but people must negotiate different roles and expectations in a society that exalts the individual over the collective.

- While whistle-blowing ultimately benefits society, the process may be costly for the whistle-blower. The Web site *Recognizing Retaliation: The Risks and Costs of Whistleblowing* (www.whistleblower.org/article.php?did =34&scid=72) lists several methods that companies or government agencies might use to dissuade employees from going public with damaging information. Methods include moving the focus away from the problem and onto whistle-blowers by manufacturing poor work records, threatening them into silence, humiliating them, setting them up for failure, prosecuting them, eliminating their jobs, and paralyzing their careers. Many informants confess, "I would never go through that hell again."

As you can see, not only are ethical decisions crucial, they are difficult. But then, we never said this would be easy.

QUESTIONS FOR DISCUSSION

1. It is often said that we cannot legislate morality. What does that mean to you?

2. Do you agree or disagree that we cannot legislate morality? Why?

3. Have we overreacted to the possibility of sexual harassment in the workplace?

4. Is it possible for an agency to be so safety conscious that it cannot accomplish its mission?

5. Are conflicts of interest more or less common than they were previously? Explain.

6. Are there some positions that are so sensitive for national security reasons that they should not be protected by whistle-blower laws? What might they be?

Commercial Recreation

six

GOALS

1. To understand that commercial recreation faces specific issues inherent to the field

2. To become familiar with the role of leisure and recreation in the local, national, and global economy

3. To learn about the issue of reciprocity in business

4. To consider both sides of the argument for gambling

5. To see that free markets offer controversial as well as mainstream recreation goods and services

6. To examine the practice of marketing to children

7. To develop an understanding of ethical egoism, the philosophy that individuals should always act purely in their own best interest

Commercial recreation is a major component of the leisure services industry in the United States and Canada. Edgington et al. (1995) indicate "that over 90 percent of all expenditures for leisure goods and services occur in the commercial leisure service sector" (292). Commercial recreation is defined by Crossley and Jamieson (1993) as "The provision of recreation-related products or services by private enterprise for a fee, with the long-term intent of being profitable" (6). Such a short and simple definition is misleading, as commercial recreation is anything but concise and well defined. Commercial recreation consists of such diverse goods, services, and venues that almost anything could fall under this general rubric. A brief list includes the following:

Fitness clubs	Night clubs
Golf courses	Restaurants
Bowling lanes	Resorts
Casinos	Cruise ships
Amusement parks	Camps
Manufacturers of toys, games, and sporting goods	

In addition, commercial recreation includes the providers of locales and equipment that make it possible for recreation activities to take place. Kelly (1996) refers to these indirect suppliers as one step removed from the recreation experience but essential contributors nevertheless. Marketers of recreation activities, programs and retail products, clothing outlets, motels, car rental establishments, "even the supermarket down the road from the public campground" (343) fit into this category. Commercial recreation providers include multinational corporations such as the Walt Disney Company and Carnival Cruise Lines as well as the thousands of small businesses that provide recreation goods and services at the local level.

The defining quality that sets commercial recreation apart is its ultimate purpose—the long-term intent of generating a profit. While this feature may help us define commercial recreation, it is also the basis for many of the ethical dilemmas to which we now turn our attention. Again, our intent is not to offer an exhaustive list of all ethical dilemmas but to provide examples of common ethical issues. The following dilemmas are not unique to commercial recreation or even to recreation in general, but they are common, and individuals working in this subfield will have to deal with these matters at some point in their careers.

Before we discuss some of the major ethical controversies of commercial recreation, however, let's digress for a moment to address an ethical pitfall that is particularly relevant to this subfield.

A Warning About Ethical Egoism

Ethical egoism is the theory that individuals ought to behave in their own best interest. It should not be confused with **psychological egoism,** the theory that individuals *can only* behave in their own best interest (Rosenstand 1997). According to psychological egoism, human beings are hardwired to act in ways that will benefit themselves. Doing otherwise, or **altruism,** is impossible; what looks like a purely selfless act is cloaked self-interest. For example, if devotees of psychological egoism observed a person making a large financial donation to the local Girl Scouts chapter, they would say the motivation was not really the desire to help girls fulfill their potential, but the desire for recognition, or a tax break, or a warm feeling from giving money to a worthy cause, or even a big payoff in an afterlife. Regardless of the situation, according to psychological egoism the ultimate motivation behind any act is that it benefits the actor in some recognized way. This is neither good nor bad; it just is. Ethical egoism, on the other hand, contends that we have a choice to either act in our own self-interest or act in the interest of others, and given these two options, it is always best that we act in our own self-interest.

As we consider moral issues in leisure and recreation in the free market, we must not fall victim to ethical egoism. Elements of ethical egoism can be found in early capitalist or free market theory. In 1776 Adam Smith, the father of modern economics, wrote:

> It is not from the benevolence of the butcher, the brewer, or the baker, that we expect our dinner, but from their regard to their own interest. We address ourselves, not to their humanity but to their self-love, and never talk to them of our necessities but of their advantages. (119)

This may be the most recognized excerpt from Smith's influential writings, and it is especially popular with those in North America who advocate for less government (Meyer 1998). Smith also suggested that in the free market an "invisible hand" lifts everyone when individuals strive for their own good. These ideas seem to be carte blanche for acting selfishly, that is, for ethical egoism. Careful reading of Smith's writings, however, reveals that Smith was by no means advocating unrestrained greed. Smith actually wrote more about the need for compassion and institutions that channel self-interest than about ethical egoism. Furthermore, Smith was the first person to offer any form of economic theory. Current economic theorists agree that his ideas are simplistic

(continued)

(continued)

by today's standards and contemporary marketplaces actually display more cooperation than individualism (Muller 1993).

Ethical egoism is contradictory because individual interests will inevitably conflict, at which point we will be forced to judge the good of one person as greater than the good of another. For example, if Sue and Tom are competing for the same promotion in their outdoor adventure company, the theory of ethical egoism argues that they should each do what is in their own best interest. Both believe that the promotion is best for them and they are willing to do whatever it takes to get the promotion. Sue would be forced to say (and act accordingly) that her interests are more important than Tom's, and Tom would have to say (and act accordingly) that his interests are more important than Sue's. The situation is logically irreconcilable, and any kind of unifying theory must be able to resolve such dilemmas.

Ethical egoism is irrational. Blackburn (2001) notes that a person who argues for ethical egoism may "kidnap the word 'self-interest'" (36). Let's say a person devoted to saving the white rhinoceros donates all her money to the cause and then goes to Africa to help out. In the process she comes down with malaria and never fully recovers. An opponent of ethical egoism would say, "She unselfishly sacrificed for a cause other than herself." The egoist would counter by saying that self-interest cannot be limited to a few tangibles such as wealth and health, but that "self-interest can be anything from accumulating money and being healthy to just having a pleasant feeling about what one has done." Such an argument is a **tautology** that does not explain anything, merely leading us around in a mental circle.

Finally, the theory of ethical egoism simply does not hold up in practice. People certainly act selfishly at times, but there are too many instances otherwise that refute the theory. From the beginning of time, people have seen human suffering and acted without regard to self. Social reformer Jane Addams is one such example. She forsook a life of affluence and worked tirelessly to establish Chicago's Hull House in 1889, the first settlement house for the poor and oppressed. In an effort to correct some of the social ills of the time and alleviate individual suffering, Addams used diverse forms of recreation such as art, dance, music, and sport (McBride 1989). Undoubtedly, some of our coworkers, friends, and family members have shown genuine concern for the welfare of others while disregarding their own interests. If the theory of ethical egoism is true, then it would always be reflected in real life. This does not seem to be the case.

Learning Activity: Egoism or Altruism?

The movie *Hero* (1992) presents more questions than answers if we watch it carefully and ponder its subtle messages. Sure, it has humor, romance, and excitement. But it also encourages us to think about the human condition. Dustin Hoffman plays Bernard LaPlante, a cynical small-time thief who rescues several people from an airplane crash. His deed triggers different responses from those around him.

Watch the movie and consider Bernie's motivations. Why does he act they way he does? What are the motivations of other key characters in the movie? Do his motives change over the course of the movie? If actions yield good results, does it really matter what the motivation for the action was?

Business Reciprocity

Reciprocity is the act of or the relationship between people involving the exchange of goods, services, favors, or obligations. Noonan (1984) writes, "Reciprocity is in any society a rule of life and in some societies at least, it is *the* rule of life" (3). In his influential book, *Bowling Alone: The Collapse and Revival of American Community* (1984), Putnam argues that reciprocity is the foundation of strong democratic societies. Gift giving, another term for reciprocity, can be good or bad. It can be so unambiguously unethical as to be illegal, including bribery and kickbacks, but it can also be, as Putnam argues, the glue that holds communities together and the oil that allows the machinery of society to function smoothly. The ethical challenge is to determine when reciprocity is wrong and when it is right.

We use three terms in this chapter and in other discussions involving reciprocity and business ethics. Although all three have some similarities, there are important differences that must be recognized.

- A **gift** is something given without an expectation of return.
- A **bribe** is something given to persuade or induce an action.
- A **kickback** is an illegal payback from a previous exchange.

Those who make bribes and kickbacks, which are generally frowned upon in business, often defend themselves by claiming they were simply making a gift and expected no return. The underlying motivation is a defining characteristic for these terms.

Business reciprocity is not exclusive to commercial recreation. Gifts, bribes, and kickbacks occur in the public and nonprofit sectors as well, including therapeutic recreation, community recreation, outdoor recreation, and the tourism and travel industry. However, reciprocity is more common and certainly more ethically challenging in commercial recreation than in other subfields. The public and nonprofit sectors have reduced but not eliminated the ethical dilemmas of business reciprocity by taking a rigid approach to gifts, bribes, and kickbacks. In most cases bribes and kickbacks are illegal. Gifts remain somewhat problematic, although the trend in public agencies is simply to ban all gifts regardless of the size of the gift and the motivation behind it.

The International Chamber of Commerce (ICC) has developed "Recommendations to Governments and International Organizations" to define and encourage appropriate behavior as it relates to extortion and bribery. This code can be viewed at the ICC Web site www.iccwbo.org/home/statements_rules/rules/1999/briberydoc99.asp. Also, an example of a private company that has addressed the topic of appropriate gifts and entertainment is the Sealed Air Company. Their code is available for perusal at www.sealedair.com/corp/conduct.html.

Learning Activity: Gifts or Kickbacks?

To illustrate the difficulty in determining what is acceptable and what is not, consider the four following scenarios. Which actions are ethical and unethical in each scenario? Is it clear which actions are unethical? What did you consider as you made your decision? Was there an overriding factor in your decision?

- **Scenario 1: Favors Between Friends.** John is the owner of a clothing store, and Valerie is the manager of a private fitness center. They've been good friends for years. As incentives for participation in fitness classes, Valerie often awards T-shirts and sweatshirts. Over the course of a year this amounts to a few thousand shirts, which she buys from John. Occasionally John gives Valerie and her husband a shirt or a cap, which adds up to a dozen shirts and a couple of caps each year. Valerie hasn't formally compared prices, but she is pretty sure John's price is competitive.

- **Scenario 2: Las Vegas Fling.** Each year a minor league baseball team in the western United States invites the sport writers from the area's major newspapers to spend a weekend in Las Vegas. The team covers all costs including airfare, lodging, food, drinks, and entertainment. For this year's gathering, the team is considering offering the writers $200 to try their luck in a casino and the services of a prostitute for those who choose to accept them. (Remember, prostitution is legal in Las Vegas.)

- **Scenario 3: Keys to the City.** A large town in western Canada is on the short list of locations for a theme park. The park would contribute greatly to the sagging economy of the region. When top executives

When is a gift just a gift, and when is it something more?

of the theme park company visit the community, each is presented with a key to the city. One of the perks of the key is the opportunity to purchase everything at half price for a week. Melinda buys a fur coat that she could never have afforded at full price, and Derrick buys the car of his dreams.

- **Scenario 4: The Toy Salesman's Puzzle.** A salesperson for a toy company travels to a foreign country to develop a market for the company's products. "Sure," the store manager says, "I'll sell your product. But space to display the toys is limited. For 10,000 American dollars I am sure I can find a very nice place, and for $20,000 I can put it right up in the front. Many people will see them and many people will buy them."

After a short pause the salesman replies, "That's a lot of money, but you've got yourself a deal. Should I make the check out to the company?"

"Just make the check out to me," he responds.

Gambling

Gambling means risking something of value, usually money, on an event that has an unknown outcome. It comes in different forms, including casino games, betting on sporting events, playing bingo, buying raffle tickets, and playing lotteries. In 2003, more than 25% of U.S. adults, or 53.4 million people, visited a casino, making a total of 310 million trips (American Gaming Association 2004, 1). Millions more purchased tickets for state-sponsored lottery games and visited horse and dog racing tracks. Furthermore, 88% of American males and 83% of American females have gambled (Fetto 2002). Gambling is popular not only in the United States but in Canada as well. The first sentence of the summary report in *Canadian Gambling Behavior and Attitudes* states, "Gambling is ubiquitous in Canada" (Canada West Foundation 2002). More money is spent on gambling than on tickets for sporting events, movies, theme parks, video games, and recorded music combined (Platz and Millar 2001). Kelly (1996) argues, "Along with popular culture, gambling may be the biggest leisure business of all" (352). In spite of its popularity, gambling, or gaming, a term preferred by the industry, is a controversial recreation activity. While economics has recently taken center stage in the debate, it is ultimately an ethical issue; even the economic arguments for and against gambling have an ethical basis.

Arguments for Gambling

Gambling is a fun leisure activity freely chosen by its participants. Platz and Millar (2001) researched college students' motivations for gambling and found that the top 10 reasons they gamble are the following:

1. Winning
2. Exploration
3. Excitement
4. Being with friends
5. Being with similar people
6. Risk
7. Observing other people
8. Autonomy
9. Escaping the daily routine
10. Meeting new people

It is hard to argue with any of these motivations, as they could easily apply to most other leisure pursuits. Even the first reason, winning, is not unusual. People participate in a variety of sports and games to compete and win. Moreover, a visit to virtually any locale where people are gambling will show that the participants have chosen to be there. No one has forced them to gamble against their will. The vast majority are adults who are capable of evaluating the risks and the benefits of the activity. A person under the age of 21 may occasionally be found on gambling premises, although gaming establishments and state governments go to considerable lengths to ensure that all players are adults.

Human beings may need a certain level of risk, and contemporary life in North America lacks some of the traditional means of experiencing risk (Iso-Ahola 1980). Some people tie elastic cords around their ankles and jump off bridges while others purposely swim with live sharks. Those with the resources and inclination may invest in the stock market as a way of getting their thrills. It is inevitable that some will pick numbers, roll dice, deal cards, or play the ponies as a relatively harmless way of meeting their personal needs. Whose business is it to determine how people get their thrill if no one is harmed?

Economics is one of the strongest and most popular arguments for legalized gambling. Gambling has pumped millions of dollars into struggling local economies, including East St. Louis, Illinois; Biloxi, Mississippi; Deadwood, South Dakota; Atlantic City, New Jersey; and the state of Nevada. New airports, community centers, roads, and schools are the tangible results of people placing their bets at a regulated, sanctioned casino or track. Furthermore, gambling has created thousands of steady, well-paid jobs. In 2002, the commercial casino industry alone was responsible for 350,000 jobs in the United States, the wages and benefits of which came to $11 billion. Another 400,000 jobs were supported by the casino industry's spending (American Gaming Association 1996). Because of these economic successes, communities, states, and territories are developing more and more opportunities for adults to enjoy themselves by gambling and help local and state economies in the process.

Arguments Against Gambling

Opponents of gambling argue that, sure, gambling is fun and exciting for some people. But robbing banks and vandalizing public property is fun and exciting for some people, too. The costs of gambling for individuals and society is simply too great when compared to the benefits. Besides, argue Leitner and Leitner (2004), there are many other wholesome leisure

What lies beneath the glitz and glamour—people being exploited or people just having a great time?

alternatives that don't have the serious downsides that gambling does. Participation in art, music, and writing as well as physical activities contributes much more to a person's self-esteem than gambling. If escape from reality is the goal, books and movies are better options. And if stimulation and thrills are sought, amusement rides, white-water rafting, and mountain climbing are available.

The economic benefits of gambling may be greatly exaggerated. The amounts and sources of gambling revenues must be carefully analyzed and then compared to the social costs of the activity. The gaming industry and other proponents have advertised that casinos draw millions of dollars into host communities. However, some studies suggest that gambling at best recirculates money that is already in the community, adding very few new dollars to the local economy. In Kansas City, Missouri, a survey found that 88% of gamblers in a casino lived within a 45-minute drive (Alm 1996). A study of Illinois riverboat casinos revealed that 85% of their patrons lived within a 50-mile radius of the boats where they did their gambling (Gazel, Thompson, and Brunner 1996). When the preponderance of spending in casinos comes from local residents, money does not flow into the local community, it flows out of the community.

The social consequences of gambling have been documented, although they have not been widely recognized. For one, higher crime rates are associated with gambling. Communities with legalized gambling have rates of crime that average 84% higher than the crime rates of nongambling communities (Shapiro 1996). Rates for personal bankruptcy are also significantly higher for gambling communities. Of course, no discussion of the social costs of gambling would be complete without addressing the growing phenomenon of compulsive gamblers. Abbott, Cramer, and

---

Related Films: Gambling

Gambling has been a favorite topic of Hollywood over the past 50 years. Classic gambling movies include the following:

- *The Hustler* (1961). Ruthless Bert Gordon takes Eddie Felson, a small-time pool hustler, on the road to learn the ropes. But Felson soon begins to realize that making it to the top could require a steep price.
- *Cincinnati Kid* (1965). An up-and-coming poker player tries to take down a master of the game.
- *5 Card Stud* (1968). After a card shark is caught cheating, he is lynched by the other players of the game except for one, Van Morgan. The players begin to die one by one, and Van Morgan has to find out what's going on before he ends up dead.
- *The Sting* (1973). A con man seeking revenge for his murdered partner teams up with a master of the big con to win a fortune from the man who killed his partner.
- *The Seduction of Gina* (1984). In this made-for-TV movie, newlywed Gina discovers blackjack and becomes obsessed with the game.
- *Rounders* (1998). A young man vows to his girlfriend he'll give up gambling, but to save his best friend who's in debt to a Russian mobster, he gets back in the game.
- *Casino* (1995). Two mobsters move to Las Vegas, and as they live and work in the city, the details of mob involvement in the casinos of the 1970s and 1980s are revealed.

Have you seen any of these movies? If so, do you think they accurately portray gambling? Do most of the movies focus on the positive or the negative elements of gambling? Do most have happy endings?

Sherrets (1995) estimate that 5 to 10 million Americans are compulsive gamblers. Further exacerbating the situation is evidence that over half of casinos' revenues come from the 4% of their patrons who are pathological gamblers (Grinols and Omorov 1995). Perhaps most disturbing is the growing number of young people suffering from gambling addictions.

Lorenz (1995) sums up gambling addiction at the turn of the century: Until the mid-1970s, the typical compulsive gambler was a white, middle-aged male. The profile of today's compulsive gambler is truly democratic, including all ages, races, religious persuasions, socioeconomic levels, and education. Whether sixteen or sixty, the desperation and devastation are the same.

The most insidious damage of gambling may be the erosion of the work ethic in North America. In 2000, a radio advertisement for the Massachusetts state lottery suggested two means to financial security. One option was to study diligently through high school and college, work hard for another 30 or 40 years, and live within one's financial means. The other option was to play the Massachusetts lottery. This advertisement is particularly appealing to those on the lowest rungs of the socioeconomic ladder as evidenced by the fact that the poor spend a larger percent of their income on gambling (Herring and Bledsoe 1994). Browne, Kaldenberg, and Browne (1992) note that gambling is one more way of exploiting the most vulnerable individuals in society and that state-sponsored lotteries in North America are examples of social conflict theory in which the affluent elite continue to take advantage of the less affluent.

Providing Controversial Leisure Services

The private commercial sector is the economic engine of all democracies in the 21st century, and a growing portion of economic activity in the United States and Canada is in leisure and recreation. We spend three times as much on recreational goods and services as we spend on cars, and we spent $81 million on online games (electronic games accessible via a computer or computer network) alone in 1998 (Bryce 2001). Leisure products are as diverse and dynamic as the 320 million people in North America. From cards to computer games, from Caribbean cruises to roller coasters, from youth soccer games to professional sport, the market has it or will have it soon. But giving people what they want may not always be the best thing to do. Some leisure activities might be harmful to participants and to society. For example, one-dollar beer nights may be fine once in a while, but these special events can lead to a variety of problems if they take place too often.

Arguments for Providing Controversial Leisure Services

Adults and young people are anxious to pay for an impressive array of leisure goods and services. Every time a person pays for a pair of running shoes, buys a glass of wine, rents a DVD, or starts a recreation business, jobs are created and taxes are generated to build schools, protect individuals from terrorist activities, and maintain parks and open spaces.

Market economies are based on meeting the needs and desires of consumers. There is no reason for producers of leisure goods and services to offer commodities for which there is no demand. For instance, new technology has largely eliminated the demand for VCRs, so fewer and fewer are produced. It is inevitable that consumers' needs and desires will change over time, and companies must keep abreast of those changes lest they become the dodo bird of free enterprise.

Many people desire to participate in activities that involve alcohol and interaction with people of the opposite sex. This type of recreation takes place in clubs, bars, and other venues. This has not changed over the past centuries, and it is unlikely to change any time soon. If recreation providers do not respond to these needs with structured and regulated leisure services, they will occur anyway, most likely in venues that are harmful to participants and society. These recreation activities won't produce tax revenues when they go underground, either. The United States' experiment with the prohibition of alcohol is a perfect example. From 1920 to 1933, alcoholic beverages could not be made, sold, or consumed in the United States. Thornton (1991) has noted that Prohibition increased crime, which in turn put an undue burden on the justice system, removed a source of tax revenue, and caused many people to switch from alcoholic beverages to opium, marijuana, cocaine, and other dangerous substances.

Arguments Against Providing Controversial Leisure Services

The leisure services field has an obligation to do more than offer what people want. Leisure and recreation have the potential to lift the human spirit and to create healthier and more productive individuals. Unfortunately, commercial recreation has flooded society with activities that appeal to our baser appetites. For example, bars outnumber art galleries in virtually any community. And how many of the most popular movies are little more than displays of violence, titillating sexual scenarios, and special effects, and how many seriously investigate the important issues that affect individuals and society?

When making money is the single most important criterion for providing recreation, society is in grave danger. Owners and operators know that they can consistently fill their bars by offering reduced rates on large quantities of alcohol and staging wet T-shirt contests. Giving people what they want may line the pockets of a few individuals for a short time, but it can contribute to alcoholism, and that results in broken lives, dysfunctional families, and deteriorating communities. We need only to look at examples from history to see the disastrous results. Ancient Rome did not meet its demise because of dwindling resources or plagues, but because its citizens grew fat, lazy, and immoral on a steady diet of violence, debauchery, and spectacle.

Learning Activity:
Debate on Recreational Marijuana Use

The class should be divided into two teams of equal numbers. The teams should have no more than 10 people each: If several class members remain after teams are constructed, the extras should serve as judges to determine which side makes the most convincing argument. Team one will argue in favor of recreational use of marijuana, and team two will argue against it. When determining teams, it is not necessary to have students who are pro-marijuana on the team that will argue for legalization and students who are opposed to marijuana on the other team. In fact, it is valuable to place students in the position of arguing a position they do not necessarily support. This has the potential to give them a thorough understanding of the issue. It is always helpful to see both sides of an issue.

- Teams are given 10 minutes to plan their opening statements. Each team will then have 3 minutes to make their initial case.
- Following the opening statements, teams will regroup to prepare their rebuttals. The time allowed for this should not be more than 8 minutes.
- Each team will have the opportunity for a 3-minute rebuttal.
- Following rebuttals, 5 minutes will be allowed for teams to prepare a final statement.
- Each team will present a 3-minute final statement.
- To add a little pizzazz, secret ballots should be cast by those who were not on a debate team to determine who won the debate.

The total time for this learning activity should be around 50 minutes. This may work best for classes that are longer than 1 hour. For classes that are shorter in duration, it is possible to select teams and give instructions in one class, let the teams do some research on the topic outside of class, and then have them debate the next time the class meets.

Marketing Goods and Services

Marketing plays a prominent role in the distribution of recreation goods and services. Because of the ever-increasing array of things available in North American markets, products cannot reach consumers without careful marketing. Marketing is much more than promotion, and even first-semester students of marketing know the four Ps—product, price, place, and promotion (O'Sullivan 1991). Underlying these four components is a vast amount of research into the needs and wants of consumers of both genders and all races and ages. Anything as powerful as marketing can be controversial. While there is disagreement about many marketing activities, in this chapter we'll focus on only one—the practice of targeting children in the marketing plan.

Arguments for Marketing to Children

How many children would have missed the vacation of a lifetime without the marketing of Disneyland? Again, marketing is not merely promotion of a product or service, it is based on determining people's needs and then responding to those needs. For example, Walt Disney recognized that parents wanted and needed safe environments where they could take their children and have fun with them. After considerable market research on activities, locations, and prices, Disneyland was established, followed by Disney World and other Disney theme parks (Jackson 1993).

Similarly, how many kids would never have experienced the joy and health benefits of skateboarding if marketers had not informed them of all the equipment available? How many adults would never have precious memories from their childhood of hanging out with friends, drinking sodas, and eating junk food without the marketing industry? Simply put, lives are enriched by marketing.

The classic definition of marketing is the process of supplying a product that meets a need. Marketers do not create needs, they merely respond to needs that already exist. This is true for children as well as adults. Marketers never force anyone to buy a particular product; they simply present information.

Marketing to children is a phenomenon of the late 20th century. Before then, young people were largely ignored in the process of researching needs and designing products to meet those needs. Adults decided what foods children would eat, what toys they would play with, and what clothes they would wear. The child of 2005 is much different than the child of 1990 or 1950. Today's 15-year-olds are not defenseless children. They are more savvy consumers than their parents were at that age, and in some cases they are more knowledgeable than their parents. For example, some families rely on the advice from children in the purchase of many electronic items.

Today kids have more control over and responsibility for their lives. One in four children grows up in a household with only one parent (U.S. Census Bureau 2000). Many get up for school on time, pick out the clothes they'll wear, prepare their own meals, and go to stores on their own to buy things for themselves and their families. According to Guber and Barry (1993), "Forty-nine percent of kids buy food for their family or participate in grocery shopping" (16). Advertising helps children make informed decisions about the purchases they make every single day.

Government agencies, consumer advocacy groups, and businesses themselves regulate marketing, especially marketing that targets children. The Federal Trade Commission is one of the key government agencies that regulate marketing at the national level. One of its main responsibilities is to stop false or deceptive advertising. The U.S. Consumer Product Safety Commission acts as a catchall agency covering areas of marketing not addressed by any other agency. Furthermore, all states have agencies that regulate marketing practices. State agencies along with federal agencies tightly control the marketing of items like tobacco and alcohol. Finally, the National Advertising Review Board, a self-regulatory board created by the advertising industry and the Council of Better Business Bureaus, screens all national advertisements for honesty and refers questionable advertisements to the Federal Trade Commission. In short, the interests of consumers and producers are served when marketing is done in an ethical manner.

Arguments Against Marketing to Children

Children are our most valuable asset. The marketing industry certainly believes that, but their perspective is quite different from ours. They value children simply because they hold more than $120 billion of spending power (Guber and Barry 1993). McNeil (1992) breaks the children's market into three components. As a **primary market,** children in the U.S. and Canada have well over $8 billion dollars of their own money to spend on toys, food, clothing, and many other items. As an **influence market,** they instigate over $130 billion in family purchases. As a **future market,** children will be massive consumers of all products at some time in their lives. McNeil ominously notes, "Of the three dimensions of the children's market, this has by far the greatest potential" (15). Why is this so ominous? Many scientists predict dire environmental consequences if the current rate of consumption continues. If marketers are successful

© Getty Images

Are these young people sophisticated consumers or easy targets for marketers?

in convincing our young people that the good life consists of consuming as many goods as they can, the earth may face a very serious crisis within our lifetime.

Marketing may be the most powerful economic force in contemporary societies. Although the marketing industry at times downplays its influence, the fact that virtually all successful products employ advertising suggests otherwise. Skinner provides further evidence of the role of marketing in society (1990): "It is estimated that nearly half of every dollar spent on goods and services is used to pay for the cost of marketing activities" (11). Marketers use the term *targeting* to describe their efforts in getting a particular message to a particular group of people. In this process, children are definitely sitting ducks.

While kids are especially vulnerable to marketing ploys for several reasons, one in particular stands out—peer pressure. Anyone who has spent any amount of time with children knows that friends are important, and for most preteens and teenagers, acceptance by peers is the most significant part of their lives. Market research has increasingly turned to focus groups to exploit this fact. The first question researchers ask a group of young people is typically, "What is cool?" The second question is, "What is not cool?" Children want what is popular with their peers, and the worst thing in the world is having clothes or toys that are uncool.

Unfortunately, children have few allies when facing the marketplace. Parents and other adults are of little value when it comes to helping children become wise consumers. Even if parents have the time to do so, they are a part of a materialist system themselves, and any message about the dangers of buying more and more things stands in stark contrast to their own consumer practices. McNeil (1992) notes that consumer education for children in school is "often done much like parental instruction—on a hit or miss basis." He continues, "Their learning is more incidental than intentional, even though becoming a consumer is basic to our way of life" (9).

The devastating consequences of unfettered marketing to children are nowhere more obvious than in North America's epidemic of childhood obesity. In 1995 the American Academy of Pediatrics (AAP) argued that TV ads are at least partially responsible for childhood obesity. When children are bombarded daily by hundreds of advertisements for high-fat foods made to look as popular and delicious as possible, the result—childhood obesity—should come as no surprise. To compound the situation, television and its ubiquitous ads for unhealthy snack foods are increasingly watched by children in the absence of knowledgeable and caring adults. Our children are easy targets.

Learning Activity: Analysis of Children's Advertising

Students will analyze advertisements in magazines that are popular with children. Each person is to bring to the following class an advertisement that is directed at children. Each is asked to answer questions about the ad. (It is ideal if a visual presentation device is available to project the advertisement image so that all can see the ad while the student answers the following questions.)

1. At what group is this advertisement targeted? Age? Gender?
2. What makes this advertisement attractive to the targeted population?
3. What are the benefits (positive) of this advertisement?
4. Are there negative elements of this advertisement? Are there negative messages embedded in this advertisement?

It is encouraging to note that the practice of marketing to children can be stopped or dramatically altered. In 1996 the U.S. Food and Drug Administration (FDA) banned the advertisement of tobacco aimed at children when an avalanche of indisputable research showed that children are particularly susceptible to advertising and that smoking has many negative health consequences. If it can be done for tobacco, it can be done for other unhealthy products.

Conclusion

At this time, the free market is the most powerful force in the world, and a growing part of the market is leisure and recreation. The defining characteristic of this economic system is that it produces profit for owners and those who work for them. The profit motive, while being central to capitalism, is a mixed blessing, resulting in several compelling issues for those in leisure and recreation. The use of gifts and bribes, popularity of gambling, provision of controversial recreation goods and services, and marketing to children are only a few of the issues that confront us.

We must not be duped into adopting a philosophy based on our own interests all the time. The theory of ethical egoism is linked to and often supported by a superficial understanding of the free market system. Like unfettered capitalism, ethical egoism leads to exploitation and suffering for many. No invisible hand will miraculously transform selfishness into altruism. As leisure service producers and consumers, we must carefully consider our own behavior, remaining fully aware that we are part of local, national, and global societies.

QUESTIONS FOR DISCUSSION

1. Why are economies in developed countries relying more and more on the production, distribution, and consumption of leisure-related goods and services? (Although this issue was not addressed in this chapter, it is relevant to our field. You will need to think hard to respond to this question.)

2. Is profit the only motivation in the commercial sector?

3. How should North Americans do business in countries that are rife with corruption?

4. Should the field of leisure services embrace or rebuff gambling?

5. Should producers of leisure service and goods give people what they want, even if that means going against their own personal values?

6. Should the providers of leisure goods and services target their marketing efforts at children?

7. Is ethical egoism a viable philosophical theory? Is ethical egoism a moral theory?

SEVEN

Therapeutic Recreation

GOALS

1. To recognize that therapeutic recreation faces specific issues inherent to the field
2. To learn about the role of codes of ethics in resolving ethical dilemmas
3. To understand the issues of paternalism and autonomy
4. To consider the issue of the right to appropriate treatment
5. To become aware of the issue of confidentiality
6. To understand the issue of provider–client relationships

Therapeutic recreation is a relatively new field. Edgington et al. (1995) indicate that in the United States the Red Cross provided a few services in military hospitals in the 1950s, but it was the later passage of legislation, most notably the Americans With Disabilities Act in 1990, that established the field. Therapeutic recreation has suffered through the challenges common to all new social endeavors. In particular, agreement on a definition of therapeutic recreation has remained elusive, which comes as no surprise since defining any concept that includes the terms *leisure* or *recreation* is automatically challenging. After examining several old and contemporary definitions, Sylvester, Voelkle, and Ellis (2001, p. 17) offer the following description:

> Therapeutic recreation is defined as a service that uses the modalities of activity therapy, education and recreation to promote the health and well-being of persons who require specialized care because of illness, disability or social condition. Furthermore, recognizing the potential of leisure contributing to the quality of life of all people, therapeutic recreation facilitates leisure opportunities as an integral component of comprehensive care.

In this chapter we'll consider some of the dilemmas that face those who work in this branch of recreation. By incorporating several scenarios we'll address key problems, including paternalism and autonomy, the right to appropriate treatment, confidentiality, and provider–client relationships. These issues are not unique to therapeutic recreation, but anyone associated with this subfield will have to deal with them at some point. In fact, the position that individuals and agencies take on these controversial topics will be evident every single day. But first, let's consider one of the most common barriers to ethical decision making in general and in this subfield in particular (see "A Warning About Codes of Ethics").

In this chapter we will consider four key topics: paternalism and autonomy, the right to appropriate treatment, confidentiality, and provider–client relationships. While these are separate issues, they nevertheless share many similarities. Consequently, we will find no hard and sharp line dividing them. We will address paternalism and autonomy first because they set the stage for discussion of the other three topics.

Paternalism and Autonomy

Paternalism may be defined as doing something to or for another person without that person's consent (McNamee, Sheridan, and Buswell 2000). Examples of such behavior include the lifeguard who stops children

A Warning About Codes of Ethics

In this chapter, *codes of ethics, codes of practice, codes of conduct,* and *ethics policies* will be used synonymously. Often they are lumped together under the rubric of **soft law** (Campbell and Glass 2001). Such codes are promoted as providing guidance for facing difficult ethical issues, and they are considered one of the hallmarks of a profession. Codes of ethics have proliferated as the drive to secure professional status has increased, not only in leisure services but also in every field that desires to be seen as a profession. The discussion of codes of ethics is included in this chapter because the subfield of therapeutic recreation has been particularly active in this area.

Purpose and Potential for Codes of Ethics

When problems arise, it is tempting to simply refer to an ethics code for a proven solution. After all, codes of conduct should inform us about appropriate responses to a wide variety of ethical dilemmas. But we must be careful. Some codes might be helpful, of course, but because of certain limitations, they are poor substitutes for moral contemplation and ethical decision making.

Although recent times have witnessed a proliferation of ethical codes, many organizations still do not have them, especially smaller operations. A study of 472 Canadian companies indicated that only 50% had codes in place. The George S. May International Company's recent survey found that about 20% of U.S. businesses have a written code of ethics. Their full report is available at http://ethics.georgesmay.com/6.htm (Business Ethics Takes on More Importance As Business Scandals Make Headlines). While these studies focused on the private sector, other studies indicate that the incidence of conduct codes is similar in the public and nonprofit sectors (Deck 1997). Furthermore, codes are beneficial only when they are collectively designed, consistently supported, and constantly monitored. These efforts require significant amounts of time and money, resources that are unlikely to be available in many organizations. Half-hearted attempts at establishing codes of ethics have little value and in some cases are even counterproductive.

Limitations of Codes of Ethics

Codes may be the product of questionable motivations. Some are merely moral wallpaper designed to protect professionals at the expense of those they serve. Newton (1978) has suggested that codes are nothing more than a convenient method of limiting advertising, suppressing

(continued)

(continued)

competition, and forbidding contradictions of professional judgment. In some cases, adopting a code of conduct may be a preemptive tactic to prevent the imposition of more restrictive sanctions by government.

One of the most damning critiques of codes of ethics is their generality and subsequent ambiguity in application. Consider the following statement that is often found in conduct codes: *Professionals should at all times display the utmost respect for persons.* This seems fine on the surface, but what happens when the interests of several groups of persons are at issue? Does respect for persons mean that mentally handicapped individuals should determine their own treatment plans? Does respect for persons mean that we should tell clients everything, even when sharing information will likely cause them needless suffering?

On the other hand, some codes are too specific to be helpful. Perhaps in the effort to correct the weakness of being too vague, they attempt to address concrete situations. While this may be an admirable effort, it presents just as many problems as it seeks to correct. A code that addresses every eventuality would be impossible because human activity is so diverse and unpredictable. In addition, new dilemmas occur every day as a result of improved technology, shifting demographics, and changing values. Keeping such a code current would be impossible.

Finally, considerable evidence from different sources suggests that codes of ethics simply do not have much effect. For example, Schwartz (2001) interviewed employees from four major Canadian firms that had codes of ethics. The workers indicated that the codes were of little value to them because they believed they knew right and wrong without a code of ethics, they generally did not face ethical dilemmas at work, and even if issues did come up, they felt that common sense was enough to help them work through such issues.

Cleek and Leonard (1998) designed an interesting experiment involving graduate and undergraduate students at a large public university. They asked students what alternative they would choose in a hypothetical ethical situation. One group of subjects was simply told that their company had a code of ethics while the other group was given a relevant ethical statement from the code. The study found no statistical difference in the choices of the two groups, meaning the ethical statement itself did not appear to have any effect on the subjects' decisions.

There is no substitute for the hard work of ethics, and we should be aware of overreliance on codes of ethics. Of course, one of the first steps in dealing with ethical issues in our professional lives should be a careful consideration of the appropriate codes. After that, we must use our own abilities and experiences to systematically determine the best course of action.

from running at the swimming pool and the public recreation director who decides not to share information with citizens about a local theatrical group that wants to perform a controversial play. The restriction of **autonomy,** or self-governance, is inherent in paternalism.

Related Films: Movie Portrayals of Persons With Disabilities

The Web site called *Films Involving Disabilities* (www.disabilityfilms.co.uk/categories.htm) lists hundreds of movies that focus on disabilities or feature persons with disabilities. It is easy to navigate the site because the films are categorized according to type of disability. Movies that are particularly good include the following:

- *One Flew Over the Cuckoo's Nest* (1975). Based on Ken Kesey's book of the same name, in this movie a prisoner fakes mental disability to be transferred to a mental hospital.

- *My Left Foot* (1989). In this true story, Christy Brown, who suffers from cerebral palsy, learns to use his only functional limb, his left foot, to become a painter, poet, and author.

- *Lorenzo's Oil* (1992). A child is diagnosed as suffering from adrenoleukodystrophy (ALD), an extremely rare, incurable degenerative brain disorder. Frustrated at the failings of doctors and medicine, his parents educate themselves in the hope of discovering something that can halt the progress of the disease.

- *What's Eating Gilbert Grape* (1993). Gilbert Grape cares for his autistic brother Arnie while trying to find a life of his own.

- *Tuesdays With Morrie* (1999). A man meets with his mentor, who is dying of Lou Gehrig's disease (ALS), every Tuesday in the last months of the older man's life.

- *Girl, Interrupted* (1999). A young woman who is depressed and directionless after finishing high school in the late 1960s ends up in a mental institution, where she befriends several of the young women in her ward.

- *A Beautiful Mind* (2001). This film is based on the life of John Nash, a brilliant mathematician who was also schizophrenic.

Have you seen any of these movies? Do they portray people with disabilities accurately? Are they respectful of people with disabilities? Are they disrespectful? Explain your answer to the previous question.

Learning Activity: Comparing Codes of Ethics

In the therapeutic recreation field, the American Therapeutic Recreation Association (ATRA) has developed a code of ethics (www.atra-tr.org/ ethics.html), as has the National Therapeutic Recreation Society (NTRS) (www.recreationtherapy.com/history/ntrs.htm). Obtain copies of these two codes and then answer the following questions.

- What are the primary similarities between the two codes?
- What are the primary differences?
- Which code do you believe is best? Why?
- What problems can you see in having two different codes in one relatively small branch of leisure services?

As these examples illustrate, paternalism can be contentious. Few would argue that a lifeguard should not act in the best interest of young swimmers by blowing a whistle to stop them from running, but the actions of the recreation director are open to debate. Part of the dilemma involves the competence of the recipient. In most situations young children are not able to think and act in their best interests. Nor can an unconscious victim of a boating accident decide what type of medical attention she needs, so someone has to act for her. Other cases are not so clear, however, and that is where ethical decision making is necessary.

Helen and Ivan: An Example

Helen and Ivan were in love, and they wanted to get married. While both were adults, they functioned at a lower intellectual and emotional level due to developmental disabilities. Ivan and Helen lived with their families and worked at the Green Valley Learning Center. The agency was an important component of their lives. Not only did the center provide work experiences for them, it also provided education and recreation opportunities. In fact, it was at one of the dances sponsored by the center's recreation department that Ivan and Helen first met. At each social event sponsored by the center thereafter, the staff observed the budding romance. The relationship certainly had its ups and downs. It was not unusual for Helen and Ivan to be madly in love on Monday and Tuesday, sick of each other on Wednesday, and back in love on Thursday, ready for another wild weekend of love and war.

Their marriage was opposed from the beginning. Both sets of parents were against it and unsuccessfully attempted to undermine the relationship. Most of the center's recreational staff had grave misgivings and counseled against the marriage. They believed it was in the best interest

Learning Activity: Paternalism, Recreation, and You

The instructor asks one or two students to share a time when someone acted paternally with them. This example can be in any setting. In fact it most likely will not be in a recreation setting. The students should be asked to describe the situation and to share their feelings about the actions. Then the instructor will ask students to think about a time when they were treated paternally in a recreation setting. This may be more difficult, but if the instructor allows time for students to recall experiences, they will come up with good examples. (The instructor may want to think of an example in his or her own life to share in an effort to get students thinking about their own experiences.)

© Human Kinetics

People who work in recreation must at times act paternally. These swimmers must be controlled for the sake of their own (and others') safety.

of Ivan and Helen to remain part-time lovers and adversaries rather than full-time spouses. But while agency staff and parents argued against the marriage, they knew they could not actually forbid it. Legally the only thing they could do was to try to convince the young lovers that this was a bad idea.

But Helen and Ivan were not persuaded, and efforts to stop the marriage only made the couple's resolve stronger. The couple married, and parents and staff waited for the fights and inevitable divorce. But Helen and Ivan remained married. They had their struggles but the union lasted, while some of the marriages of the recreation staff who were against the marriage ended in divorce.

This is an example of paternalism—or, more accurately, it is a fairly rare example of thwarted paternalism. In most cases the party who is subjected to the paternalistic act succumbs to the efforts of those who usually have their best interests at heart.

Codes of Ethics and Paternalism and Autonomy

On the topic of paternalism and autonomy, the ATRA code of ethics provides only limited guidance. It states, "Therapeutic Recreation personnel have a duty to preserve and protect the right of each individual to make his or her own choices. Each individual is to be given the opportunity to determine their own course of action in accordance with a plan freely chosen" (principle 2). Does this mean that mentally disabled individuals should be allowed to make their own choices? This may be problematic when some severely disabled persons have difficulty understanding or communicating. So we are left to deal with these issues largely on our own.

Competence is particularly relevant to therapeutic recreation because clients display different levels of competence. Furthermore, therapeutic recreation providers often have a high degree of authority over those they serve. As VanDeVeer (1986) argues, competence is an imprecise concept. Individuals may exhibit periods of competence or incompetence, as in the case of early Alzheimer's disease patients. One moment they may be capable of acting in their own best interest and the next moment they may be utterly incapable. Also, in some instances people are average or even gifted in specialized intellectual realms while lacking much of the common sense required for everyday living. The middle ground between full competence in every aspect of life and complete incompetence is a capacious and uneven landscape that requires not only technical discernment but ethical judgment as well. Such is particularly the case with the next topic we will tackle: justice.

Opportunity and Leisure

Justice concerns what is good, fair, and equal. **Distributive justice** is when social goods are made available to those who deserve to receive them. The constitution of the United States grants all people the social goods of life, liberty, and the pursuit of happiness. Certainly, the opportunity to recreate falls within the broad category of the right to pursue happiness. John Kelly, one of leisure studies' leading writers, has argued that leisure and recreation are not privileges earned but rights granted. They are the domains of freedom, and recreation is one of the primary means by which we reach our full potential as human beings (1987). Dustin, McAvoy, and Schultz (2002) go one step further, arguing that it is the duty of park and recreation workers, including specialists, to create settings where each person can grow and develop to his or her potential.

Limitless recreation opportunity for all seems like a good idea, and at the conceptual level it is hard to argue against. Unfortunately, practical concerns require leisure service providers and especially recreation therapists to consider the moral and ethical dimensions of the concept. For example, what is meant by *all?* Does it include visitors? Does it include legal aliens who have the right to work? Does it include illegal aliens who work but do not possess green cards (lawful permanent residency)?

We must also consider forms of recreation. Does the pursuit of happiness mean that everyone should be able to jet to Aruba or walk to the local basketball courts? Should citizens of a country have the right to visit their national parks, their state parks, or just their neighborhood parks? Should they receive financial aid to help them go to parks?

Moreover, some leisure activities are socially unacceptable or even illegal. Should they be available? How about gambling, pornography, or extremely dangerous recreation activities like rock climbing without protection?

The Right to Appropriate Treatment

Most of us would agree that competent health services are a part of the guaranteed right to life, liberty, and the pursuit of happiness. Politicians of every ilk have argued for years not about whether health care should be available for every citizen, but about how such services should be delivered. We have already made the case for recreation opportunities, so it seems reasonable that therapeutic recreation is entitled to anyone who needs it as well.

Many people are in favor of this position, including ATRA. The ATRA code states, "Therapeutic Recreation personnel are responsible for ensuring that individuals are served fairly and that there is equity in the distribution of services. Individuals receive service without regard to race, color, creed, gender, sexual orientation, age, disability or disease, social and financial status" (principle 3). Here again, we are faced with difficult questions. Does that statement include individuals who function at a low mental ability? And what about those who bring the debilitating conditions upon themselves, like drug and alcohol abusers? What about the unemployed or the homeless?

Some have argued that the resources for providing therapeutic recreation are not infinite, so we need to be realistic and determine how to ration precious leisure resources. Considerations for receiving recreation therapy might include

- the ability to pay for services,
- the ability to qualify for third-party reimbursement for services,
- the expense of delivering services,
- the ability to communicate needs and desires for particular services, and
- the likelihood of exhibiting measurable positive results from services.

Of course, under this system not everyone would qualify for the therapy that would improve the quality of their lives and the lives of those around them. For example, consider David, a 32-year-old mentally ill man who lives on the streets of a large city. He certainly cannot pay for services himself, nor does he qualify for Medicare benefits. His illness discourages him from coming in for services and it is too expensive to go out and find him. Because communication with David is difficult, evaluating the effectiveness of a therapeutic recreation plan is virtually impossible. Will David receive the therapeutic recreation services that could benefit him? Not likely.

Using Leisure As a Reward or Punishment

Clearly, recreation provides many significant personal and social benefits. Therapeutic recreation professionals analyze the needs of individuals and prescribe specific recreation programs that include activities with anticipated results. These activities lay a foundation for the personal growth of clients. In the process of providing services they often employ the principles of behavior modification, which raises the thorny question of whether or not it is ethical to use recreation opportunities as a reward or punishment to change behavior.

Consider Sam, a 14-year-old juvenile delinquent who lives at the Triple J Ranch for Troubled Youth. In many ways Sam is a typical teenager. He likes to play video games and watch television. But above all, Sam likes to fish. It is one of the few activities that Sam and his father used to do together, and for this reason it is very important to him. But Sam's father is incarcerated and won't be going on any fishing trips with Sam or anyone else for the next 40 years.

The Triple J uses several therapeutic interventions, one of which is the opportunity for or denial of recreation activities. But the past month has been a rough one for Sam. Early in the month, he was caught lying to a counselor. His punishment was to have his video-game playing priveleges suspended for a month. Later that week, Sam and another boy were fighting in the cafeteria, and he lost TV privileges for a month. Shortly thereafter, things went from bad to worse. Staff checked Sam's room and found another boy's wallet. After being confronted, Sam admitted to stealing the other boy's property. That action resulted in the loss of the fishing trip that Sam had been eagerly anticipating for the past few months.

What are the moral implications of denying Sam the recreation opportunities that he enjoys so much? Playing video games, watching television, and fishing are not hurting Sam or anyone else. In Sam's case, as in the

© Photodisc

Are recreation activities like this a right that should not be denied, or a privilege that can be denied by those in positions of authority?

case of many young persons who get into trouble, their behavior is largely the result of a troubled childhood. Sam was neglected and abused for the first 12 years of his life. Other than a handful of fishing trips his dad took him on, there was little joy in his life. These activities may serve as a relief valve to let off the stress and anger that Sam has amassed over his short lifetime. Is it really in his best interest to deny him his beloved activities?

On the other hand, few things mean enough to Sam to be tools for changing his behavior. Without significant change, Sam's life will be even more difficult than it is now. If he cannot stop lying, stealing, and fighting, he will have to move to a more restrictive setting where there is no chance of doing the recreation activities he enjoys. While it is unfortunate to deny him these recreation activities, it is perhaps in his best interest to do so.

As this example illustrates, recreation therapists must be careful not to violate individuals' rights to recreation opportunities and appropriate treatment. While it may not be simple or inexpensive to provide therapeutic services, it may still be the right thing to do. Similarly, those of us in the leisure services cannot disregard the rights of clients to speak in confidence or to enjoy a level of personal privacy, our next topic.

Confidentiality

The issues of confidentiality and privacy are not unique to therapeutic recreation or leisure services. In fact, the most conspicuous examples are found in counseling settings, religious confessionals, the legal arena, and health care services. However, therapeutic recreation often takes place in settings that are conducive, even purposely designed, for the transmission of sensitive personal information.

Confidentiality Crisis: An Example

Imagine a recreation leader sitting around a campfire with a small group of female campers after a long day of hiking. The campers and the leader are feeling good about themselves and are comfortable with the group. After all, each person had to trust and depend on others while crossing streams, setting up camp, and preparing food. The conversation is not a formal debriefing or group counseling session, just casual banter sprinkled with jokes and good-natured ribbing. As might be expected with young adults, the conversation gets around to romantic relationships. As the talk becomes more personal, a camper named Heidi shocks the group when she states that her lover from a year ago tested positive for the HIV virus. She goes on to say that she is scared to death to get tested. The group leader, while trying to hide her dismay, knows that Heidi is friendly with several young men in school and has talked about recent dates she has gone on.

The next day during a water break on the trail, the leader and Heidi find themselves sitting together several yards from the rest of the group. The leader initiates the discussion by mentioning that she appreciates Heidi's participation in the camping trip and her willingness to open up to others. With some trepidation, she encourages Heidi to get tested for HIV.

Heidi explains that she knows she should but it's too risky. She is afraid that Fred, her current boyfriend, will find out and leave her. Realizing that refusing to get tested puts Fred and possibly others in grave danger, the leader again advises Heidi to get tested, telling her that if she does not the leader will be forced to alert the public health authorities. Heidi becomes defensive and angrily tells the recreation leader that she is not her mother, a probation officer, or a nurse. She also reminds her of the context of the campfire confession, a group of people sitting around a campfire sharing some of their most personal feelings in the process of developing caring and trusting relationships.

© Nancy R. Cohen/Getty Images

Confidentiality and privacy issues frequently come up in therapeutic recreation.

Considerations in Confidentiality and Privacy

We'll return to this scenario, but for now let's consider some additional information about confidentiality. Confidentiality and privacy have been controversial issues for several decades; however, in Canada and the United States the dilemma has become even more contentious in the last few years. First, advancements in technology have led to more effective collecting, analyzing, storing, and disseminating of data, including personal information. That harmless survey you filled out last month was probably the result of a great deal of technology. Your name was probably randomly selected by computer. A statistical program likely entered your responses into a data set that could be manipulated and analyzed with a few keyboard strokes. With one or two more buttons, the information could have been printed out or sold to other parties with unknown, perhaps unscrupulous, motives.

Second, personal information is incredibly valuable. Marketing is based on consumer information and market researchers are constantly designing ways to gather it. Marketers are willing to pay for personal data, and the more personal the data, the more they are willing to pay. Today, North Americans are less willing to give away what they know they can sell.

Learning Activity: Google Up Confidentiality Agreements

Students are given the assignment to go to the search engine Google (www.google.com) and enter the phrase *confidentiality agreements.* This will yield a large number of examples of different agreements. Students should be cautioned not to go to the first two or three Web sites with confidentiality agreements as this will provide a smaller number of different documents. Students will make a copy of an agreement and bring it with them to the next class.

In class, one student will go to the board and serve as recorder. The purpose of this learning activity is to look for commonalities in all confidentiality agreements. The instructor will select a student to share one key element of his or her agreement. Perhaps the student says that the agreement he brought with him has a definition of confidentiality. The recorder writes *definition* on the chalkboard. The instructor then asks how many students found a definition of confidentiality in their agreements. They indicate by raising their hands. The recorder puts down the number of people who found that element in their agreements. This process is repeated until all elements (with corresponding numbers to indicate prevalence) are on the board. The instructor can then sum up what a good confidentiality agreement should contain.

Finally, concurrent with the recognition that personal data is a valuable commodity is the awareness that individuals have the right to control information about themselves and their families. When privacy is violated and confidentiality is broken, people are inclined to seek compensation in the courts for their loss of this basic right.

As a consequence of these trends, confidentiality is legally protected. However, protection is not unlimited. If, for example, a person shares information that contains a threat of serious harm to others or to themselves, those in authority are not only exempt from confidentiality but are legally mandated to report the statements. The courts also have the authority to force doctors, journalists, legal personnel, and counselors to divulge information from confidential conversations.

The other side of the coin is that the ability of the human services fields to help individuals and society rests upon a trusting relationship between client and provider. Logical arguments for breaking confidentiality may resonate with therapists and other professionals, but for many clients such arguments fall on deaf ears. Once the recipients of services perceive that their or others' private statements were disclosed, they might refuse to speak freely. When trust is damaged, meaningful therapy comes to a halt. The individuals lose the potential benefits of working with trained therapists, and counselors and society at large suffer for it.

Returning to a Confidentiality Crisis

Let's return to the scenario of the young woman who disclosed that she could be infected with HIV. The group leader is also an assistant professor in the therapeutic recreation department at the local university and, being aware of codes of ethics, she could turn to one for the answer to her ethical dilemma. As expected, the NTRS code states: "Professionals respect the privacy of individuals. Communications are kept confidential except with the explicit consent of the individual or where the welfare of the individual or others is clearly imperiled. Individuals are informed of the nature and the scope of confidentiality" (II.2). That statement is some help, but this is an ethical decision that rests solely with the leader, and she must sort out for herself the validity of the campfire statements; her relationship to the camper, the university, and her profession; and the short- and long-term effects of her disclosure. Again, codes are at best an aid in the ethical decision-making process—they are not the final answer to a dilemma.

We'll turn our attention now to a problem that is common not only in nearly all professional situations but in many personal situations as well.

Multiple-Role Relationships

Few issues have the potential to be so helpful and harmful at the same time as the phenomenon of playing several different roles in a relationship. It is impossible to limit the discussion of this problem to the professional setting because a common source of the trouble is mixing our private and public lives.

Norman and Jill: An Example

It was like a small sliver in his hand. It didn't bother Norman most of the time but on occasion when he moved his fingers just so . . . ouch! It was like that when he had spoken to his fiancé, Jill, a few minutes ago. There had been something just under the surface that he couldn't quite put his finger on but that made him very uncomfortable.

Norman met Jill 18 months ago when she participated in a horseback-riding therapy program. Norman was a certified recreation therapist who was convinced of the therapeutic potential of riding and working with large animals. Jill had been one of six adult participants in his first group. She'd been struggling with a number of emotional issues and the combination of the strength and peacefulness of the horses and Norman's thoughtful counseling had helped her sort through most of her problems.

About halfway through the 5-week program, Jill volunteered to care for Norman's horses when he had to leave for a few days. By the end of the program Jill was caring for the animals on a regular basis. Through this process Norman and Jill became friends and a romantic relationship blossomed a couple of months after the program ended. Now they were making plans for a summer wedding. Norman had the nagging feeling that at times Jill saw him as much as a therapist as a life partner. Maybe that was okay; after all, they did love each other.

Results of Multiple-Role Relationships

Multiple-role relationships can be troublesome in all branches of human services in which there are providers and recipients of social services. A classic case, and the basis for several Hollywood movies, is the psychotherapist who becomes sexually involved with a client currently in therapy.

It is fairly easy to see the harm of such an unbalanced and exploitative relationship. The American Psychological Association (APA) and all major mental health organizations absolutely condemn such behavior. The NTRS code of ethics specifically states, "Professionals promote independence

Related Films: Movies That Show Consequences of Complex Relationships

The following movies illustrate the dangers of multiple-role relationships. Several, although not all of them, focus on romantic relationships between therapists and clients.

- *Spellbound* (1945). A psychiatrist who is treating another psychiatrist falls in love in this Alfred Hitchcock classic.
- *Betrayal* (1978). A psychiatrist convinces his female patient that having sex with him is therapeutic.
- *Lovesick* (1983). A psychiatrist who falls in love with a patient is advised by the spirit of Sigmund Freud.
- *Chattahoochee* (1989). A man with post-combat syndrome enters into a strange relationship with his counselor.
- *Prince of Tides* (1991). A man talks to his sister's psychiatrist about their family problems and falls in love with her in the process.
- *Final Analysis* (1992). A psychiatrist falls in love with his patient's sister, who is married to a Greek mobster.
- *The Color of Night* (1994). A psychologist falls in love with a murdered colleague's patient as he tries to find the murderer.

Have you seen any of these movies? Have you seen other movies of the same genre? Is there a power differential between the therapist and the client? What are the stages of moving from an appropriate therapist–client relationship to one that is not appropriate? Once a therapist–client relationship becomes inappropriate, is it possible for it to be restored to a healthy professional relationship?

and avoid fostering dependence. In particular, sexual relations and other manipulative behaviors intended to control individuals for the personal needs of the professional are expressly unethical" (II.1). Unfortunately, as we shall see, many multiple-role relationships are not so well defined and unquestionably prohibited.

While service providers may be fully aware of the possible negative consequences of multiple-role relationships, sometimes such relationships may be unavoidable. This problem may be exacerbated in smaller communities where relatively few providers of such services exist. In some cases the refusal to take on multiple-role relationships may mean denying critical services. Many potential clients simply may not have the resources to travel long distances to access other providers.

One of the most complex multiple-role relationships is that which includes the roles of therapist and friend. We may be tempted to believe that therapist and friend are two nearly indiscernible elements of a single role, but they are not. One can be a friend without acting as a therapist, and it is possible to be an individual's therapist without any type of emotional involvement or friendship. This issue is further compounded by general recognition of the value of a therapeutic bond based on trust, compassion, and empathy—three hallmarks of friendship.

Then there is the thorny issue of sequential multiple-relation roles. Few of us can fail to see the danger of concurrent roles such as therapist and employer or therapist and best friend. But what if the roles are sequential, one following the other? The initial therapeutic relationship may be the origin for another relationship. Perhaps a recreation therapist has recognized the technical and interpersonal skills of a participant during an expedition. When the trip is over and the client has worked through his issues, the therapist may be inclined to hire the former client as a camp counselor. This progression of relationships is the direct result of the initial therapist–client relationship and the employment relationship would never have happened otherwise. Let's keep in mind the slippery slope of multiple-role relationships as we revisit the previous scenario with Norman and Jill.

Returning to Norman and Jill

Did Norman act unethically? Did Jill act unethically? As a client, does Jill even have any responsibility to act one way or another? Jill, the client, initiated the additional relationship. She volunteered to watch the horses for Norman. Jill certainly did like horses and it was therapeutic for her to be around them. Does that let Norman off the hook? While they became close friends by the end of the therapeutic program, it wasn't until a few weeks later that they actually fell in love. Could Norman be expected to ignore the age-old progression of acquaintance to friend to lover? On the other hand, the original relationship was that of therapist and client. Norman was in a position of authority, and while he did not abuse that authority, Jill certainly recognized it. **Transference,** a phenomenon in which patients, clients, or even students view their therapists or professors in an excessively positive light, thereby increasing their own vulnerability, is very common.

Conclusion

Therapeutic recreation, like other sectors of leisure services, has its share of issues that may seem purely technical at first. However, a more thoughtful assessment reveals that many are predominantly ethical decisions. Because of the nature of some therapeutic recreation clients, paternalism and autonomy concerns will always require constant vigilance. A serious ethical burden is placed on the shoulders of recreation therapists and administrators who are called upon to make decisions for those who are unable to do so on their own. Issues involving justice and leisure are always controversial, but especially so in therapeutic recreation because of the potential for disregarding the rights of disabled persons. Regarding confidentiality and privacy, it is not uncommon for professionals to be forced to choose between the rights of individuals and groups in such dilemmas. Moreover, because multiple-role relationships are standard in this branch of recreation services, ethical judgments about the types and levels of relationships are often necessary. Finally, although codes of ethics address the issues we have previously discussed, they have limitations in determining responses to ethical dilemmas.

QUESTIONS FOR DISCUSSION

1. Will codes of ethics improve and become more helpful in the future?
2. Have you ever been the recipient of inappropriate paternalism? How did you respond?
3. If withholding therapeutic leisure activities in a residential setting is inappropriate, what alternative things or activities could be withheld to change behavior?
4. At what point does sharing information become an unethical and unnecessary spreading of information?
5. How can leisure service providers care deeply about those they serve but avoid entering into friendships or inappropriate relationships?

EIGHT

Outdoor Recreation

GOALS

1. To realize that outdoor recreation faces specific issues inherent to the field
2. To understand that holding uncontestable positions is an impediment to ethical decision making
3. To understand the concepts of anthropocentricism, biocentrism, ecocentrism, and theocentrism
4. To consider the issue of species reintroduction
5. To understand the issue of charging fees for using national parks
6. To consider the issue of no-rescue wilderness areas

North Americans may participate in more outdoor recreation than any other people. This recreation includes white-water rafting, sailing, climbing, and rappelling as well as less strenuous but equally fulfilling activities such as casual strolls and picnics in local parks. The popularity of outdoor recreation can be attributed in part to the incredible natural resources of this great continent. White-capped mountains, dense hardwood forests, wave-washed beaches, vast deserts, lush swamps, and crystal-clear lakes invite people to test their limits, learn new skills, or simply relax. With such wonderful resources that are valuable to so many, there are bound to be ethical dilemmas. We will address some of those dilemmas, but first, a caution is in order.

A Warning About Uncontestable Positions

When we think of courage, we most likely think of the brave deeds that take place on battlefields or in burning buildings. Maybe we think of a child standing up to a bully on the school playground, or maybe we envision ourselves in a noble confrontation with a coworker or supervisor about a serious problem at work. However, courage comes in other forms, too. While we might not recognize it, thinking and acting ethically takes a great deal of courage.

Human beings seek and require a certain degree of stability in thought and action without which we simply could not survive. Our cognitive abilities allow us to establish conditioned or learned responses to the situations we confront on a continual basis. We do not need to reinvent the wheel each time we act, so to speak. That is why when we approach a traffic light we do not have to think everything through as if it were the first one we ever saw. We know, or assume we know, that red means stop, green means go, and yellow means slow down and proceed cautiously. The templates in our minds also tell us that applying pressure to the gas pedal will make us go faster and applying pressure to the brake will slow us down. We also believe from the mental pictures we have previously developed that other drivers will behave in predictable manners as well.

But stability in our thought processes can be taken to an extreme. At some point, stable and beneficial thinking drifts into unproductive dogmatism. Consider that if everyone maintained complete loyalty to established beliefs, or their own cognitive schemas, we would still be living on a flat earth in the center of the universe. Eight-year-old children would be working 12 hours a day in dangerous coal mines, and those with even the slightest disability would be condemned to a life of pity and ridicule. Fortunately, brave souls mustered the courage to take action against the status quo. Such action would never have happened without individuals honestly reconsidering their personal belief systems.

Reconsidering a position does not automatically mean reversing it. It means making a genuine attempt to reevaluate the assumptions on which our actions are based. It is entirely possible that our beliefs and values will not change at all, and it is possible that what may have been an ethical stance at one time is no longer ethical because of changing circumstances and new information.

For example, nearly everyone in the United States in the early 1800s believed that women should not be allowed to vote. Given the social conditions and widespread attitudes about the roles of women, this was arguably an ethical position. For most women then, the world ended at the porches of their homes because of their unrelenting and unshared domestic duties, and they themselves believed they did not need the right to vote. Three events led to changing beliefs and women receiving the right to vote in the United States:

- African American men (another group considered unqualified to make such decisions) were given the right to vote.
- Women showed their ability to contribute beyond the home through events such as World War I.
- European cultures began to allow women full participation in the political process.

Finally, in 1920, nearly a century after the suffrage movement began, the 19th Amendment gave women suffrage. A new ethical standard was established, and today almost no one would suggest that women shouldn't be able to vote.

The point is this: We simply cannot allow **uncontestable positions** to be part of our cognitive and ethical constitutions. Regardless of how strongly we feel about certain issues, we must not allow dogmatic thinking to creep in and impede our ongoing moral development. Our positions on significant issues ought to be able to stand up under scrutiny. If they cannot, we have to discard them and replace them with positions that we can reasonably and logically defend.

Some issues are more vulnerable to dogmatic thinking than others. For example, once people determine their positions on abortion, euthanasia, social welfare, and political affiliation, they are extremely resistant to change regardless of new information or societal transformations. It seems that some issues in outdoor recreation are similarly vulnerable to dogmatism. Unswerving beliefs tend to be found on issues like hunting, animal rights, species reintroduction, and entrance fees for national parks.

Learning Activity: Hunting Debate

Beliefs about hunting are commonly uncontestable. First, everyone should indicate by raising their hand whether they believe hunting is ethical or unethical. Second, at least four but no more than seven students who believe hunting is ethical and an equal number of students who believe the opposite will debate the issue. The group of students in favor of hunting must argue that hunting is *unethical* and the students against hunting must argue that hunting is *ethical*. The pro group gives a 3-minute opening statement, followed by a 3-minute opening statement by the con group. Each group then has 5 minutes for a rebuttal.

The debate ends with each group presenting a 3-minute closing on their position. While this short activity will not likely change students' beliefs about the ethics of hunting, the temporary role reversal will give them a chance to see the issue from the other side. It will also provide an opportunity for them to think about their own uncontestable positions.

As we have seen thus far, personnel in outdoor recreation face a wide variety of ethical issues. To help us understand these complex concerns, we will group outdoor recreation ethical issues into three broad categories:

1. Those related to **anthropocentrism, biocentrism, ecocentrism, and theocentrism.** The underlying question is where we position human beings in relation to other natural objects.

2. Those related to preservation, conservation, and ecosystem management. The underlying question is what our responsibilities are to the environment.

3. Those related to outdoor education and leadership. For some, the underlying question is what our responsibilities are to others in the outdoors.

A number of specific dilemmas exist within each of these broad categories. After a brief discussion of the categories, we'll consider selected issues. Do not be misled into thinking that choices about the following issues are merely technical. While there is a great deal of technical information to consider, ultimately these are ethical decisions.

Anthropocentrism, Biocentrism, Ecocentrism, and Theocentrism

Traditionally, ethics concerned itself only with situations that affected individuals or groups of persons. Aristotle, Thomas Aquinas, and Immanuel Kant advocated such an anthropocentric position.

Great Thinkers

- Aristotle is considered one of the great thinkers in history, and his influence is evident in many societies around the world. An ancient Greek who studied under the great philosopher Plato, Aristotle wrote not only on ethics but on many other topics including mathematics, logic, physics, biology, philosophy, and politics (McKeon 2001). While most of Aristotle's ideas have been reworked and refined, they nevertheless laid the groundwork for much of what we know today.

- Thomas Aquinas was a 13th-century Italian philosopher who based many of his ideas on interpretations of Aristotle. His works on the nature of God and his exposition of natural law made him one of the major Roman Catholic theologians, and he has influenced many generations. A Dominican priest, Aquinas has been referred to as the Angelic Doctor and the Prince of Scholastics (Finnis 1998).

- Immanual Kant is regarded by many as the most influential thinker of modern times. A German philosopher of the 18th century, Kant laid a theoretical foundation that several of today's philosophers continue to build upon (Kuehn 2001).

- Albert Schweitzer was born in 1875. He spent the first 30 years of his life studying science, music, and theology and writing, and he devoted the rest of his life to serving humanity, primarily as a medical missionary in Africa. He has been called the greatest Christian who ever lived. Schweitzer was awarded the Nobel Peace prize in 1952 (Berman 1986).

According to anthropocentrism, all natural objects exist for the sake of human beings. While some attention is paid to the treatment of animals and natural objects, anthropocentrism clearly states that it is not for their sake but for their potential to make life better for human beings. From this perspective, **moral standing,** the term used to designate worthiness of ethical consideration, applies only to competent human beings.

A more recent philosophical position, biocentrism, gives moral standing to all living things. The most well-known advocate of this position was Albert Schweitzer, who aptly described his philosophy as "reverence for life."

Ecocentric ethics moves even further from anthropocentric ethics and gives moral standing to natural nonliving things, in particular ecological systems. Thus, forests, wetlands, lakes, grasslands, and deserts merit ethical consideration not only because they affect humans but also simply because they exist.

Finally, theocentrism may be seen as the ultimate movement away from the focus on humans and other life forms on earth. Everything, including life itself, is measured against God. Animals do not take second place to

Learning Activity: Moral Standing

To determine your beliefs in terms of applying moral standing to living and nonliving objects, draw a line from one side of a piece of paper to the other. On one end write *rock* and on the other end write *competent adult human*. (This exercise assumes that you believe rocks do not have moral standing and that competent adults do.)

On the continuum, decide where you would place such people and things as a human infant, a human fetus, a severely mentally handicapped adult, a brain-dead adult, a dictator, an individual ape, a family of apes, a dolphin, an insect, a tree, and a forest. What is your rationale for your choices? Are you generally anthropocentric, biocentric, ecocentric, or theocentric?

humans. Everything is tied for second place. Moral standing may be given to humans and other entities but only as they exist to reflect and praise God. In and of themselves, they have no value (Bouma-Prediger 2001).

Effects of Outdoor Recreation on Animals

Providers of outdoor recreation opportunities affect animals in many ways. For example, guides and outfitters for people who desire to hunt and fish are becoming more and more common. The fact that these individual service providers have an effect on animals is indisputable, but the actual effects are hotly debated. The effect of other outdoor recreation providers such as river guides, wilderness leaders, expedition directors, and park interpreters is less obvious, but they nevertheless have a significant effect on animals. Even resort owners who arrange for tourists to swim with dolphins and manatees affect the animals. Dolphins and manatees are wild animals that survive in oceans and estuaries by being cautious. When they interact with humans, they lose some of those protective behaviors and suffer because of it. Although recreation practitioners undoubtedly affect animals, their influence is relatively minor compared to the influence of natural resource managers and administrators. Through their decisions, these men and women have the potential to create or eliminate habitat, the defining element in wild animal populations. In this way, large numbers of animals are either aided or harmed.

Humankind's effect on animals has been discussed for centuries, often quite adamantly, by everyone from philosophers and lawyers to politicians and laypersons. As the following overview will demonstrate, the treatment of animals by humans is not a simple issue.

© Photodisc

In what way have people directly and indirectly impacted this species?

Arguments for Animal Liberation

Although several biocentric arguments for animal liberation exist, we'll focus on two of the more common. Singer (1990), professor of bioethics at Princeton University since 1999 and arguably the academic most closely associated with the animal liberation movement, has used the idea of **speciesism** as the basis for his argument in favor of better treatment of animals. Borrowing from the terms sexism and racism, he suggests that conventional treatment of animals is similar to the discriminatory treatment previously accorded to women and to people of color. Just like women and nonwhite persons, many animals have moral standing. This moral standing is not because animals possess souls or have the capacity to reason, but because they can suffer. Singer includes only some classes of animals as capable of suffering (dogs are certainly able to suffer—amoebas are not). He provides little explanation for the potential of suffering for the species that lie between these two extremes on the scale of complexity. Of course, humans can suffer also, but because of our advanced mental capabilities, we might suffer differently. Singer's position is generally utilitarian and particularly focuses on consequences. He argues that because our task as human beings is to minimize suffering, the way we treat animals must dramatically change. According to Singer, practices such as medical testing on animals, hunting, fishing, and the use of animals in circuses must be eliminated.

Animal liberation proponent Tom Regan (1983) argues from a different biocentric perspective. Although the suffering of animals is a consideration, he suggests that animals have rights because they have inherent value. They should be seen not as means to our ends but as ends in and of themselves. Even if animals do not suffer or suffer very little in the process of being used by humans, they should be liberated. The use of animals for any type of entertainment is wrong. Zoos, circuses, rodeos, and keeping pets are unacceptable from this perspective.

Arguments Against Animal Liberation

Within the anthropocentric paradigm, there are two lines of thinking. In the first perspective, the world consists of two and only two distinct classes of animals—human beings constitute the first category while all other animals constitute the second category. According to this hierarchy, men and women are qualitatively different from animals. Human beings have certain characteristics that set them above the rest of the earth's fauna. Perhaps it is that only human beings can reason or that only human beings have souls. In any case, along this line of reasoning, some suggest that with dominion over animals comes a responsibility to help keep species alive and to not inflict undue pain and suffering on individual animals. Others in this camp believe that human beings' only responsibility is to perpetuate our own species, and all other animals possess value only as they contribute to that end.

The second perspective on animal rights considers human beings and all other animals not as two distinct classes, but as classes along a continuum. Human beings anchor one end and bacteria anchor the other. Earthworms, cockroaches, birds, fish, rats, chimpanzees, and all other animals occupy various positions along the spectrum. Increased rights are permitted to animals according to the number of humanlike qualities they possess. Thus, mammals have more rights than insects, and bipeds such as apes have even greater rights. Only human beings, however, are granted full rights.

The different levels of animal treatment are the result of human beings' understanding of their place in the world, or their degree of anthropocentrism. Of course, that perspective will profoundly affect an individual's approach to the next category of outdoor recreation issues, preservation and conservation.

Preservation, Conservation, and Ecosystem Management

As noted, North America has a tremendous wealth of natural resources. However, these resources face greater demands from more users and more recreation activities. Consider the demands on a trail in 1903 and the demands on that same trail in 2003. A hundred years ago, hikers and a few horseback riders used the trail in the warmer months. After the snow began to fall, a rare soul on snowshoes might tread the path. Today, that trail must accommodate not only hordes of hikers and horses but also a variety of all-terrain vehicles (ATVs) and mountain bikes in the spring, summer, and fall. In the winter the trail is host to snowshoers, sledders, skiers, and snowmobilers.

Situations such as these have laid the groundwork for a field of study and practice devoted to preserving, conserving, and managing our natural resources. Managers are required to make ethical decisions about natural resources every day.

Species Reintroduction

Wild animals have always been part of the way people experience nature, and rare and elusive animals hold an especially powerful attraction. Ironically, the desire to experience nature and all of its elements, along with commercial and residential development and the resulting loss of habitat, has made viewing animals impossible in some areas. For example, Canada's blue pike is a fish that is gone forever, no one will ever again watch a passenger pigeon fly overhead, and the Florida cougar will never be seen again. The World Conservation Union (IUCN) Red List of Threatened Species lists over 10,000 endangered species worldwide and 242 extinct species for North America alone (www.iucnredlist.org).

Our influence over other species today is unprecedented. While the displacement and occasional disappearance of animal species is a natural phenomenon, it typically takes a century or more for it to happen. Not so when human beings are involved. For instance, in less than 40 years, gray wolf populations in the lower 48 states of the United States plummeted thanks to a concerted effort to eliminate what was considered a pest.

That same influence can also affect species in a positive way. Just as our cognitive capacity and technical abilities helped us virtually eliminate a species, they can be the foundation for bringing the species back. Guns, traps, and poisons can be replaced by reintroduction plans, high-tech tracking devices for individual animals, and education programs. It is merely a matter of deciding whether we want a species to remain, disappear, or reappear. While we cannot re-create a species that has become extinct, we can reintroduce a species to a particular area.

While the biology of species reintroduction is considerably complex, working through the political and philosophical issues poses the greatest challenge because people tend to hold such strong opinions on the subject. Sometimes people who will never be directly affected by a reintroduction program are passionate about it. Some reintroduction programs receive little attention and thus are not too controversial. Most people are not aware of the ongoing effort to reintroduce the river otter to many of the watersheds in the United States. Only a few more are aware of the peregrine falcon reintroduction program in some of the large cities in the United States. But just about anyone who is interested in outdoor recreation is familiar with the controversial effort to reestablish viable populations of gray wolves. These efforts are led by the United States Fish and Wildlife Service and assorted nonprofit agencies. We'll use this example to illustrate the many ethical dilemmas faced by outdoor recreation decision makers when dealing with species reintroduction.

© Tom Brakefield/Corbis

Species reintroduction can raise many ethical dilemmas.

In the 1800s the United States and Canada were home to large populations of gray wolves. While the number of wolves in Canada is still relatively high, such is not the case in the United States. The last half of the 19th century saw the near-eradication of many large wild mammals in the United States. Buffalo, elk, mountain lions, and grizzly bears were destroyed at an alarming rate, but nowhere was the eradication effort as intense or as successful as that for the gray wolf. Only a handful of the animals remained in the United States outside of Alaska by 1900. In the last couple of decades, however, an attempt has been made to reverse the extermination.

Yellowstone National Park in northwestern Wyoming has been the site of an intense battle over wolf reintroduction. Once a stronghold of the species in the 19th century, no wolves have lived within the park boundaries since 1923 because of hunting pressure and loss of habitat. When the question of wolf reintroduction was first raised, groups and individuals immediately aligned themselves on one side or the other of the issue—everyone had a vested interest in the project. The loudest voices against reintroduction were those of the livestock industry, and the loudest voices in favor were those of national conservation agencies. After extensive research, discussion, and lobbying in Washington, the wolf reintroduction project in Yellowstone National Park exists within a fragile truce. Let's look at some of the arguments for and against wolf reintroduction.

Arguments for Gray Wolf Reintroduction

Human beings are newcomers to North America, and Europeans are particularly new. Most of the animals that are here today, including the gray wolf, were here long before Europeans arrived. For thousands of years, the wolf held a privileged position at the top of the food chain, but in a relative blink of an eye, the human species displaced the wolf. Fortunately, human beings are uniquely capable of correcting the wrongs they have committed. Through gray wolf reintroduction we can right the wrongs of our parents and grandparents. If there were ever an opportunity to fix the damage of the past, this is surely it.

Public lands, including national and state parks, are owned by the citizens of the United States. Because of this, every American citizen has a voice in the operation of wild places like Yellowstone National Park. The management of the land and the animals that live there is controlled by federal agencies including the United States Fish and Wildlife Service and the National Park Service. These agencies carry out the policies that are jointly established by the aforementioned agencies and citizen advisory boards. Moreover, public land management is expensive and paid for entirely by federal taxes. Citizens who pay taxes should have a say in how their money is spent. Surveys of citizens indicate that the majority of people in the United States support efforts to reestablish most species. Whether they live in Wyoming, Texas, or New Hampshire, people favor the reintroduction of the gray wolf to Yellowstone National Park. In fact, less than 11% of Americans are opposed to wolf reintroduction in Yellowstone National Park (www.defenders.org/wildlife/wolf/yeswolf.html).

Positive economic effects are another argument in favor of wolf reintroduction. Many communities near outdoor recreation areas have limited revenue sources, and traditional sources of economic activity are dwindling. Such is the case with the communities that surround Yellowstone National Park. Mining, farming, and ranching have been in decline for the past two decades. One of the bright spots for the local economies in Wyoming, Montana, and Idaho has been tourism. Visitors to Yellowstone indicate that the mere possibility of seeing a gray wolf is part of the attraction. For many tourists the presence of the gray wolf adds an extra dimension to the outdoor experience that can be found in few other places in the world. The money from outside sources (tourists) is essential to maintaining viable communities by supporting private businesses and local services such as schools, hospitals, and public recreation programs. Moreover, wildlife attractions do not have the negative aspects of some other tourist attractions such as land-based casinos in Colorado and massive biker rallies such as those held in Sturgis, South Dakota.

Arguments Against Gray Wolf Reintroduction

The most vociferous argument against wolf reintroduction comes from the cattle and sheep ranchers in the areas that border Yellowstone National Park. While the debate rages as to the extent of the damage, no one would argue that gray wolves do not occasionally kill and eat livestock. Although most of the cattle and sheep are not actually within the park boundaries, the wolves do not recognize the park boundaries and occasionally stray out of the park to kill livestock. The profit margin in the livestock business is narrow and the loss of even a few animals significantly affects a rancher's ability to earn a living.

Men and women settled the western states with the support and encouragement of the federal government. In many cases they left lives of relative security to take on extreme risk and hardship. For those who made the sacrifices and survived, a way of life and mindset were established that included the taming of the wild land. This meant controlling, or killing, predators that were perceived as direct competition. The reintroduction of the wolf is a reversal of this hard work and a threat to the ranching lifestyle that many dream of passing on to future generations.

By reintroducing wolves and telling local ranchers to get along with their new four-legged neighbors, the United States government is imposing an unfair mandate. This is particularly ironic given the previous authorization from the federal government to go forth and tame the land for production and the ultimate good of the country. It is a classic case of manipulation and broken promises. Most of the people in Washington, D.C., who are making the decisions about wolf reintroduction, will likely never be on a ranch near Yellowstone and will certainly never have their livelihood threatened by the predator. Ranchers are left holding the bag not only by politicians and citizens groups, but by tourists as well. Tourists only visit for a short time and don't have to deal with the negative elements of wolf reintroduction.

Species reintroduction has been an issue only since the 1970s. The next ethical dilemma in outdoor recreation management that we will discuss, natural resource rationing, has been practiced and often hotly debated for a surprisingly long period of time.

Rationing Outdoor Recreation

Responding to the growing recreation demands on North America's natural resources, public sector managers have been forced to adopt new strategies for providing access while protecting resources. One approach is **rationing,** the planned allocation of resources, services, and opportunities for outdoor recreation. Although rarely disputed as a concept, when rationing is actually implemented, confrontations may occur. McLean and Johnson (1997) offer eight rationing techniques:

- Queuing—Providing access at a later date or placing users on a waiting list
- Lotteries—Randomly drawing names from a prefigured pool
- Need-based priority—Giving extra opportunities or special access to those with special circumstances
- Access to use rules—Requiring a particular level of skill to access a program or facility
- Time allotment—Limiting the amount of time persons can access services
- Demarketing—Attempting to decrease awareness and demand
- Vouchers—Providing a limited number of vouchers for access or participation
- Pricing—Charging fees for services and access

All of these rationing techniques can be controversial, but establishing fees for access to public land is the most controversial technique of all.

Fees for Admission to National Parks

Much research has been undertaken and a great deal has been written about the use of fees for public programs and resources, including national parks. Such a wealth of information may lead the manager to believe that deciding whether to charge fees is a technical decision. While we need to be aware of the information that is available, a decision about the use of fees for national parks is ultimately an ethical exercise.

Arguments for Fees at National Parks

Managers of North America's natural resources have the daunting task of conserving forests, lakes, deserts, grasslands, and other sites. At the same time they have to promote these areas for the use and enjoyment of the public. If they fail to protect the natural resources and the sites are degraded, public use becomes a moot point as precious little will remain to use and enjoy.

Charging entrance fees for national parks, while not the entire answer to the challenges these managers face, is one of the most efficient options available. Fees can reduce the effects of users on land and water resources by lowering the number of visitors. Each natural resource has a carrying capacity, a level of use beyond which the resource begins to deteriorate. The ability to institute and manipulate the price of fees gives the manager the chance to operate at an optimal capacity. At optimal carrying capacity the area can restore itself and retain its ability to provide enjoyment to users forever.

While other rationing techniques are valuable, fees provide additional benefits. Several studies indicate that the funding for maintaining national parks has been inadequate for several decades. Fees can greatly reduce the gap between the fiscal resources that are needed and the fiscal resources that are available. Where better to generate additional revenue for maintenance than from the people who visit the parks and contribute to the need for maintenance?

On-site surveys of park users show general agreement with park fees. Most individuals indicate they would not refrain from using the parks if an appropriate fee were initiated. Experimental fee programs over the past decade bear this out. In addition, differential pricing strategies and free days on certain weekdays allow equal opportunity for all regardless of economic status.

The public often takes for granted the quantity and quality of natural resources on this continent. This lack of appreciation is partially the result of unlimited access to national parks. Charging a modest fee will impress upon users the worth of the natural resources and establish an understanding of appropriate use. Most, but not all, national parks in the United States and Canada charge a fee. These fees range from a few dollars at some of the less visited parks to $7.00 at Banff National Park in Canada (www.pc.gc.ca/pn-np/ab/banff/visit/tarifs-fees_E.asp?park=1) to $20.00 at Yosemite National Park in California (www.us-parks.com/misc/National_Park_fees/park_fees.shtml). The only hope of fulfilling the mandate of conserving our resources and promoting use and enjoyment is to educate the public about the need to maintain the parks with revenue from sources other than taxes, and fees do just that.

Arguments Against Fees at National Parks

The introduction of fees at national parks is focused on efficiency at the expense of effectiveness. More (1999) has noted that, "Economics is above all a science of efficiency—efficiency in the allocation of scarce resources to produce the maximum possible benefit to society" (234). Fees are contrary to at least part of the mission of national parks, the use and enjoyment of all citizens. A policy cannot be effective if it is inconsistent with the organization's mission. User fees exclude low-income citizens from using national parks, which stands in stark contrast to the primary purpose of the national park concept. In addition, visitors, unless they are from another country, have already paid for the parks through federal taxes. Charging a fee is no less than a double tax.

A great deal of evidence suggests that the use of fees at a few parks will lead to a total reliance on fees to fund all parks. Already, some politicians propose that the parks should be completely self-sufficient. Some assume that if reasonable fees cover a small part of the costs, higher fees may cover more of the costs. As fees continue to increase there will come a point where the number of visitors levels off and then begins to decrease. Soon, the break-even point will be reached and the parks can indeed be self-sufficient. However, self-sufficient parks will not serve all citizens, as is their mandate. They will serve only those who are able to pay (Hayhurst 2001).

Finally, fees detract from the education of the public and the generation of even broader and deeper support for national parks. Over a century ago North America's national parks were established in the belief that some places were so special that they needed to be protected. Knudson (1984) has argued that visitors to national parks "do not always comprehend the purposes and behavior appropriate to these special places. To them, any public park is a place where the public can do whatever comes to mind" (231). Paying an entrance fee may augment the belief that the user has a right to misuse the national park. The quick and easy solution of charging an entry fee is only a short-term fix that may compound the problem in the long run.

Outdoor Education and Outdoor Leadership

Outdoor education is experiential learning that occurs primarily in the natural environment. Outdoor leadership is influencing and teaching people in and about the outdoors. These are not new concepts as much as they are newly recognized concepts. Outdoor education, while less common and certainly less formalized than it is today, occurred in North America as soon as Europeans arrived in the 16th century. The continent was a harsh wilderness, and it was only through understanding the land and working with it that people were able to survive. The same can be said about outdoor leadership. Both concepts contain in varying degrees an element of the other (Priest 1990). For example, we would immediately identify the educational role of natural resource interpreters, also known as naturalists, at a national park. On further investigation, we would also realize that the same person is leading and influencing visitors. Likewise, an adventure leader obviously guides and influences those in her care, but she is also educating them about themselves and the world around them.

Outdoor education and outdoor leadership are not without their controversies. One such controversy is the use of technology in outdoor adventures. As we have seen in several other situations, at first glance the issue seems to be a technical problem. We might think that with enough research, we can neatly solve the problem by answering the question, "Can we?" Of course, we must move beyond whether we *can* to whether we *should*. "Should we?" is the question of ethics.

No-Rescue Wilderness Areas

The past century has witnessed a major philosophical shift of North American attitudes about wilderness. For nearly 300 years wilderness was something to be conquered and eradicated, but over the last century, recognition of the inherent value of wilderness has grown and culminated in the passage of the Wilderness Act of 1964 in the United States. Today, wilderness is defined as a large block of land untrammeled by humans. From a slightly different perspective, it is also a unique opportunity to experience freedom, challenge, risk, and self-reliance.

© Spectrum Stock Inc.

No-rescue wilderness areas are a major controversy in outdoor recreation.

Ensuring that opportunity requires a management approach based on consistent policies and procedures. The debate about instituting a no-rescue policy has gone on for decades. Some argue that managers should designate a small portion of wilderness lands where users would be entirely on their own if they encountered serious difficulties. No government rescue teams would be dispatched for them. Strict enforcement of policies that limit the number of backcountry users and prohibit the use of motorized vehicles would make rescue by friends and volunteers extremely difficult. Others argue against such a policy for a number of reasons, as we will see.

Arguments for No-Rescue Wilderness Areas

Citizens of Canada and the United States possess natural and government-protected rights of self-determination. They have the opportunity to realize their potential in many ways. Most grow through the social venues of school, work, and human relationships. A few develop, however, by looking inward and challenging themselves, often purposely putting themselves in situations where they must call upon hidden reserves of mental and physical strength. Such a challenge is possible only when the risks are genuine and the stakes are high. Fabricated challenges and perceived risks just don't measure up.

Venturing into wilderness areas alone or with a few friends—fully aware that no one will come to the rescue when challenges present themselves—is the last venue for this type of personal development. Facing life-threatening physical, mental, and emotional ordeals in the wilderness is not for everyone. But it should not be denied to the minority who desire to grow by overcoming personal tests of this nature.

Individuals who go to the wilderness to experience the dangerous edge of life return as new beings. They understand their true limits, not the artificial limits imposed by a society that has become obsessed with safety. Society benefits from their private victories in the wilderness because they become the self-reliant few who rise above mediocrity and lead in times of crisis. Their stories of survival in no-rescue wilderness areas demonstrate to the rest of society that challenges can indeed be overcome and that we can call upon untapped resources when we really need them. A few individuals will inevitably be lost in no-rescue wilderness areas, but the benefits far outweigh the costs.

In addition, rescues are potentially damaging to the environment. Consider that vehicles driven over sensitive tundra areas in the summer leave signs that remain for as long as 18 years (http://arctic.fws.gov/seismic.htm). Similarly, formations in caves can be extremely fragile. Because rescues in such places are particularly complex, irreversible damage can be done. It would require extraordinary discipline for rescuers to avoid harming the environment while rescuing an injured adventurer.

Furthermore, rescues can be costly. According to *USA Today* (2004), in 2003 alone the U.S. National Park Service spent $3 million on rescue operations to save climbers, rafters, spelunkers, snowmobilers, and other adventurers. Local law enforcement agencies usually pay for rescue operations that do not take place in national parks, and these costs have risen over the past 10 years. For example, the Grand County Sheriff's Department in Utah now averages 80 rescue operations a year, up from the 9 missions they undertook just a decade ago. The typical cost for a rescuer to even walk out of the office is $245.

Arguments Against No-Rescue Wilderness Areas

Human beings by nature want to help others. We have survived only because we are able to work together against threats to individuals. One person facing a 600-pound grizzly bear is not much of a fight, but a grizzly bear against five hunters—well, that is a different story.

Allowing hikers and climbers to suffer and die in no-rescue wilderness areas is to deny that we are human beings. It has even been suggested that human beings are most complete when they are rescuing and helping others.

Much has been written about the high cost of rescues undertaken by national park personnel, but most rescues are carried out by friends and complete strangers who volunteer their time and money and risk their own lives to get individuals out of harm's way. Such actions strengthen society more than anything else. Those who are saved experience in a profound way the love of their fellow human beings. Those who do the saving are rewarded with the deep knowledge that they contributed in a tangible way to the welfare of injured and suffering individuals and to society. Communities large and small take pride and come together when rescues are undertaken.

National Park Service policy prescribes that efforts be made to rescue hikers, campers, and climbers regardless of whether they are near a busy campground or in a remote wilderness area. (This policy pertains only to national parks and not necessarily to other public lands, and it does not apply to private land.) Policies do not materialize out of thin air; they are the collective will of society expressed through local, state, and federal boards and advisory committees. The majority of people are opposed to allowing suffering if they can help it.

Consider for a moment an unthinking and unprepared father who leads his children into a no-rescue wilderness area just before a terrible storm blows in. It is one thing to allow the father to perish because of his actions, but what about his children? There is simply no way a just and caring society could sit idly by and allow that to happen.

Even if a handful of individuals benefit from no-rescue wilderness areas, the cost to society is far too great. While a no-rescue wilderness area may be a romantic notion, it is in reality a dreadful, immoral concept.

Conclusion

The outdoor recreation issues discussed in this chapter are only a sample of the challenges that this sector will face in the years to come. Careful analysis of data collected over the past two decades clearly indicates that the demands placed on our natural resources and the men and women who work with those resources will increase. Certainly sound information will be necessary for technical decision making and acting. But by itself, qualitative and quantitative data are insufficient for the task. They need to be coupled with ethical decision making and acting. Only then will managers, leaders, and educators be able to properly use and care for our natural resources.

Learning Activity: Survey of Attitudes Toward No-Rescue Wilderness Areas

This survey is not statistically valid, but it does serve to get us thinking about the issue of no-rescue wilderness areas. Each student is given a 3-by-5 card. Students are not to write their names on the cards. There are only two items of information that are required. First, students should answer the following question with a simple yes or no: Are you in favor of some no-rescue wilderness areas in North America? The second piece of information is whether the student is male or female. While students are doing this, the instructor should draw a box like this on the blackboard:

	Yes	No
Male		
Female		

The instructor shall collect the 3-by-5 cards and record the number of responses in the proper category or box. This will lead to an interesting discussion if there is a difference in attitude according to gender, and even if there is no difference according to gender.

QUESTIONS FOR DISCUSSION

1. Are there any ethical issues unique to the field of outdoor recreation?

2. What is the difference between holding uncontestable ethical positions and "sticking to your guns"?

3. Do human cultures naturally progress through the stages of anthropo-centrism, biocentrism, ecocentrism, and theocentrism?

4. Is the reintroduction of species simply messing with nature, ultimately resulting in negative consequences?

5. Are fees for national parks setting a precedent? Will we soon have to pay fees if we want to go to our neighborhood parks and playgrounds?

6. Would you backpack in a no-rescue wilderness area? Why or why not?

NINE

Tourism

GOALS

1. To realize that tourism faces specific issues inherent to the field
2. To realize that ethical relativism must be recognized in ethical decision making and acting
3. To consider that tourism affects and is affected by culture
4. To understand the sex tourism industry and its effect on travelers and hosts
5. To learn about the relationship between tourism and the natural environment
6. To understand the issue of virtual reality and its relationship with tourism

No comprehensive discussion of leisure would be complete without addressing tourism. It is one of the fastest growing social and economic phenomena since 1950 and there is little reason to believe that the growth will decrease. Tourism includes the trip to visit the grandparents as well as the once-in-a-lifetime adventure in an exotic locale. It includes an afternoon's ride through the countryside as well as that one-day extension at the end of a business or educational conference. Responding to the needs and wants of travelers, the tourism industry requires committed, knowledgeable personnel to make technical and ethical decisions on a daily basis.

In the 1980s there was little discussion about the ethics of tourism, but since then things have changed. Several factors have contributed to the rise of ethical issues related to tourism. First, tourism on such a massive scale is a recent phenomenon. Sure, people traveled in the past, not just for business but for pleasure as well. But travel would not have been an option for most people; it was limited to the highest socioeconomic classes

A Warning About Ethical Relativism

Before we discuss several ethical controversies related to tourism, we should briefly deal with the thorny problem of **ethical relativism.** If we place **absolutism,** the belief that there is always one indisputably right perspective, on one end of a spectrum, we would place relativism, the belief that local values and rules always prevail, on the other end. Neither of these extremes is particularly useful in making ethical decisions, and we have to incorporate the strengths of both perspectives into a reasonable decision-making model.

Let's consider Ron and Cathy and their 7-year-old son, Logan. They are adventurous travelers to say the least, and they are currently on a tiny, remote island in the South Pacific. As Ron and his son rest in a small hut they've rented from one of the local fishermen, young Logan begins to climb a nearby fish-drying rack. Ron tells his son to come down from the shaky wooden structure, but Logan ignores his father's request. After Ron tells Logan a second time to stop climbing and gets the same response, he grabs the little boy, ties him to the side of the hut, and flogs him with a broom. When Cathy returns to the hut and finds the bruised and bleeding Logan still tied to the side of the hut, she is aghast. When she asks Ron about the situation, he calmly explains that Logan disobeyed him and is being punished. "You know," he says, "folks around here discipline their children a little differently than we do back home. But when in Rome, do as the Romans do."

Ron is justifying his disciplinary actions through ethical relativism. While this concept is particularly salient to our discussion of tourism because conflicts among different cultural values and behaviors are unavoidable, it can be a threat to making sound ethical decisions. Philosophers have struggled with the proper balance between relativism and absolutism for at least 2,000 years. The Greek historian Herodotus (500 b.c.e.) offered a classic example of the danger of absolutism when he asked a group of Greek men how much money it would take for them to eat the corpses of their fathers. They gasped. Next Herodotus asked a group of Indian tribesmen how much money it would take for them to cremate their fathers' corpses. They were horrified by the question. Of course, it was custom for Greeks to cremate their deceased and for the Indians to pulverize the bones of their ancestors and eat them for spiritual strength. Herodotus' point was that customs must be considered when determining right from wrong (Blackburn 2001). We must not err in thinking of Ancient Greece as Ancient Athens. Ancient Greece was a conglomerate of very different cultures, the most notable of which were Athens, Sparta, and Carthage. Herodotus, considered the first historian, lived on the edge of Greece and Turkey. It was a crossroads for travel, and thus a place where one could be exposed to a large number of different cultures. Moreover, "he traveled extensively throughout the ancient world: to Greece, Babylon, Egypt, Italy, Sicily and elsewhere" (Blanco, 1992, p. xi).

But ethical relativism must be limited—surely there are standards that hold true for all cultures. The challenge is to determine what is merely different and strange from a cultural perspective and what is wrong regardless of the setting. Blackburn (2001) suggests that most human behavior consists of local implementation of a few universal standards:

> Every society that is recognizably human will need some institution of property (some distinction between mine and yours), some norm governing truth telling, some conception of promise-giving, some standards restraining violence and killing. It will need some devices for regulating sexual expression, some sense of what is appropriate by way of treating strangers or minorities or children or the aged or the handicapped. It will need some sense of how to distribute resources, and how to treat those who have none. (22-23)

With that in mind, let's think about local practices and right and wrong as they relate to the most common of human activities, eating and drinking.

Learning Activity: Eating and Drinking

Given that eating and drinking are essential to human life, it takes a bit of thinking to realize that these endeavors are 5% physiological and 95% social and psychological. The basic purpose of eating and drinking is getting food and drink into the body, but there are thousands of variations on these activities. Because they are primarily socially constructed, their wrongness or rightness most often depends on the particular social setting.

Write each of the following eating or drinking activities on 3-by-5-inch index cards. Then put them in a hat, draw one at a time, and discuss whether they seem wrong to North Americans because of cultural considerations or whether they are wrong regardless of cultural differences. Are there any absolutes in this list?

- Eating horsemeat. There is even a word for eating horsemeat—hippophagy. Horses are eaten in France, Germany, Japan, and Kazakhstan (White 2003).

- Eating dog meat. Eating dog is common in parts of east and southeast Asia. The South Korean industry involves about 1 million dogs, 6,000 restaurants, and 10% of the population (Saletan 2002).

- Drinking blood (nonhuman). Many cultures in Africa, especially those in particularly arid regions, drink animal blood.

- Serving food that is known to be dangerous. While some foods can be harmful if not properly prepared, the most dangerous foods are certain mushroom species and several puffer fish species (Fish and Wildlife Research Institute 2000).

- Denying nutritious food to children. In some cases children are denied nutritious food because of war, drought, or other extenuating circumstances. However, in some situations children do not get nutritious food because their parents and other caregivers choose not to provide them with the appropriate food due to lack of knowledge or effort. A steady diet of fast food may be the classic case of this phenomenon.

- Cannibalism. Human cannibalism has existed in prehistoric and primitive societies on all continents. It may still be practiced in remote areas of New Guinea, and it existed until recently in parts of west and central Africa, Sumatra, Melanesia, and Polynesia; among various Indian tribes of North and South America; and among the aborigines of Australia and the Maoris of New Zealand (Occultopedia 2004).

(GreenPACK 2004). When our parents and grandparents were young, a major trip probably amounted to going to another state or province for a few days or a couple of weeks. By today's standards, that's hardly even considered travel. McLaren (2003) notes, "Before WWII, travel for pleasure was the province of the very rich" (2). As usual, more people and activity means more dilemmas. Another factor is the diversity that is now a universal element of the tourism industry. Given the vast differences in the motivations of both tourists and travel providers and the variety of available destinations and experiences, it should be no surprise that problems might arise. Finally, tourism is problematic because the economic stakes are high for individuals, organizations, and nations. Tourism is often touted as the world's largest industry. "With annual revenues of almost $3 trillion, its economic impact is second only to that of the weapons industry" (McLaren 2003, 5).

Suffice it to say, some of the kinks, including ethical and moral questions, are still being worked out in this new and potent global industry. Tourism faces many dilemmas, but we will address only four of the more prominent concerns: tourism and culture, sex tourism, tourism and the environment, and virtual tourism.

Tourism and Culture

Culture is all the information of and about a society including art, music, language, values, stories, as well as tangible items from cars to salt and pepper shakers. Culture is the inertia and the structure that keeps society intact. Ironically, the first research to consider the effects of visitors on other cultures was undertaken by anthropologists who were investigating unknown (to them) lands and peoples in the first half of the 20th century. Anthropologists sought to offer the world a picture of other cultures. However, they came under criticism from fellow academics when some studies were exposed as questionable interpretations of cultures by overzealous researchers (Punch 1986). Questions arose concerning the possibility of observing a culture without inevitably changing it, even minutely. Today, sociologists and anthropologists agree that all in-depth studies of a culture have the potential for disturbance, and the more invasive and numerous the interactions, the more potential they have for causing cultural change. It is a small leap from the intrusion of researchers to the intrusion of tourists.

In the United States, the Pennsylvania Amish are an example of the complex relationship between tourism and culture and the ethical concerns that the tourism industry must address. Amish communities are scattered over much of Canada and the United States, but those who live

Related Films: Culture Clashes

Many movies are based on the theme of cultures that come into conflict; following are some of the better ones.

- *Fiddler on the Roof* (1971). This musical tells the story of a Jewish peasant and his family in prerevolutionary Russia.

- *Deliverance* (1972). A weekend trip in backwoods America turns threatening as four urban men battle unfriendly terrain and locals.

- *Witness* (1985). A policeman goes undercover in an Amish community to protect an Amish boy who witnessed a murder.

- *The Emerald Forest* (1985). An American dam engineer in Brazil searches the Amazon rainforest for the Indian tribe that kidnapped his son. In doing so he begins to understand the damage the dam project is inflicting on the rainforest and its people.

- *Gorillas in the Mist* (1987). Movie based on the true story of Dian Fossey, a researcher who went to Africa to study the vanishing mountain gorillas.

- *Black Robe* (1991). Huron Indians lead a Jesuit priest through the wilderness of Quebec in the middle of winter to find a distant mission.

- *Mississippi Masala* (1992). To the dismay of their families, an Indian woman and a black man fall in love in Mississippi.

- *Thunderheart* (1992). An FBI agent who is part Sioux but has little knowledge of his heritage is sent to a Sioux Indian reservation to investigate a murder.

- *Krippendorf's Tribe* (1998). When an anthropologist is paid to find a lost New Guinea tribe but fails, he creates a fictitious tribe instead.

- *Catfish in Black Bean Sauce* (2000). A Vietnamese brother and sister who were adopted and raised by an African American couple are reunited with their birth mother.

Have you seen any of these movies? If so, were you able to pick out the cultures that were in conflict? Did both cultures survive intact or did one become dominant? Can you think of a particular moment or incident in the movie that captured the essence of cultures in conflict? As you think about one or more of these movies, do you think it is inevitable that some cultures will overcome other cultures? A related question: Is it possible that any culture will last for a long time?

in and around Lancaster County, Pennsylvania, are the most well-known. They strive earnestly to separate themselves from worldly ways, so they do not own or drive automobiles, they farm exclusively with horses, they wear simple clothes of blue or black, and they have little exposure to mass media. Amish homes do not have televisions, Internet connections, or radios. Few Amish attend school beyond the 8th grade, and they are pacifists. Their agricultural lifestyle that eschews many modern conveniences appeals to visitors who desire a peek into what they believe to be the idyllic lifestyle of days long past. Over 5 million people visit Lancaster County each year. This amounts to nearly 350 tourists for each Amish person. Moreover, tourists generate $400 million in economic activity, or about $29,000 for each individual Amish man, woman, or child in the county (Hostetler 1993).

Positive Effects of Lancaster County Tourism

North America loses thousands of acres of prime farmland each year to commercial and residential development, and the agricultural land that remains is increasingly owned and operated by large corporations. With

Amish communities hold great appeal for many tourists.

the resulting demise of the small family farm, farming is simply not an option for more and more Amish men and women each year. While the Amish are known for their austere and self-reliant lifestyle, they still need some income to survive. Fortunately, tourism has created opportunities for many Amish to work in or close to their community. For example, Amish food, natural and wholesome, is extremely popular with tourists. Amish restaurants provide diverse employment opportunities from ownership to cooking to serving. Genuine Amish goods such as furniture and quilts enjoy an almost fanatical following and demand a premium price. An additional benefit of these economic opportunities is that every member of the family can contribute to the production and sale of such goods and services.

Tourism dollars contribute to the growth and maintenance of communities regardless of their cultural makeup. Tourism money goes toward building roads and filling potholes, providing fire and police protection, and operating hospitals. The Amish make a great effort to not be of the world, but they still must live in the world, which means they use the county's roads, benefit from fire and police services, and go to the hospital when necessary.

Exposure to cultures such as the Amish provides many benefits for non-Amish visitors. Honesty, simplicity, and lack of stress are plainly visible in Amish communities, and many visitors are rejuvenated and ready to return to their fast-paced lives after only a few days in an Amish community. Moreover, it is human nature to fear and disrespect that which we do not understand. Amish culture is beguiling but can be misunderstood, and firsthand observations can alleviate such misunderstanding.

While we tend to think of the arrow of influence going only from the Amish to the visitors, greater interaction with mainstream culture has positive consequences for the Amish as well. Hostetler (1993) writes that, "Among the young, change is evident in the wearing of store-bought suspenders, sweaters with zippers and buttons, and (among the young boys in winter) warm caps rather than brimmed hats" (391). Some Amish communities allow use of gas-powered tractors in farming. This contributes to greater efficiency in agricultural practices. The use of more modern farm machinery also allows more opportunity and diversity in agriculture. In the area of health, the mainstream culture has contributed to improvements for the Amish people on a number of different fronts. In Michigan, Amish families have been encouraged by the state to install septic systems to more effectively handle waste water (U.S. Water News Online 2002). Also, scientific research from the dominant culture has proven that continued marriage exclusively within local Amish communities has contributed to a higher rate of babies born with disabilities.

Amish leaders have recognized this fact and have taken measures to limit this phenomenon. Overall the Amish have been more inclined than ever before to seek medical care when persons in their communities are seriously ill or injured.

Negative Effects of Lancaster County Tourism

While the potential benefits of Amish tourism cannot be denied, neither can the potential harm. As mentioned, culture is the structure on which all societies reside. Consequently, anything that significantly disrupts culture has the potential to devastate the society. Respect and obedience to parents and elders are important in Amish culture. Easily influenced like all children, Amish children may observe and imitate the authority-challenging behaviors of the children of tourists. Outward displays of materialism are also unacceptable to the Amish but are fairly evident in visitors. Over time the contrary values and behaviors of a dominant culture can erode the values of a smaller culture. Hostetler (1993) begins his book on Amish life with the following introduction:

> Small communities, with their distinctive character—where life is stable and intensely human—are disappearing. Some have vanished from the face of the earth, others are dying slowly, but all have undergone change as they have come into contact with an expanding machine civilization. The merging of diverse peoples into a common mass has produced tension among members of the minorities and the majority alike. (3)

Another criticism of tourism is the commodification of culture. Wyllie (2000) writes that, "When culture is commodified it loses its authenticity and much of its meaning for people" (65). Products, whether they are tangible goods or services, become commodified when they are produced for the primary purpose of being sold, in this case to tourists. An Amish quilt constructed of plain but durable materials is very different from the brightly colored but less functional counterpart that is sold in the visitor center. Likewise, a demonstration of plowing a field with horses lacks the spiritual significance that the Amish ascribe to farming. Unless cultures like the Amish are careful, commodification can create a serious cultural void that may lead to societal collapse.

Finally, not everyone benefits to the same degree from tourism. It appears that non-Amish entrepreneurs profit much more than the Amish whom visitors flock to see. Kraybill (1989) notes that tourism is an annoyance for many Amish. Visitors clog the narrow country roads and peer into homes and schools to get a glimpse of the simple life. Perhaps the most outrageous tourist act is to photograph the Amish. Almost all Amish object on religious grounds to having their picture taken. Nevertheless, some tourists refuse to be denied their pictures. An Amish man spoke for many when he said of tourists, "They invade your privacy. They are a nuisance when I go to town for I can't go to any public place without being confronted by tourists who ask dumb questions and take pictures" (Hostetler 1993, 319).

The Pennsylvania Amish are a classic example of the complex, controversial relationship between tourism and culture, and as we have seen, the difficult questions are ethical rather than technical. Let's consider some other ethical tourism issues. To do that we'll have to make a huge leap from the Amish of Lancaster County to the ever-growing sex tourism industry.

Sex Tourism

It is no secret that tourism in general faces several ethical quandaries. If we add an additional component, sex, to the mixture, we have the makings for some volatile moral issues. Although human sexuality is a common,

© Digital Vision/Getty

The sex tourism industry results in particularly thorny ethical dilemmas.

even universal experience, its cultural expression is as varied as one can possibly imagine. But before we address particular issues, we need to turn our attention to the difficulty of defining sex tourism.

Defining Sex Tourism

For most people, sex and tourism seem like two words that have little reason to even exist in the same sentence. They may think that sex and tourism don't make sense together or aren't compatible in the least. Others might think of sex tourism as middle-aged European or North American men traveling to developing countries and purchasing the services of a prostitute. While this is certainly an instance of sex tourism, the phenomenon is much more diverse and considerably more ethically challenging.

For example, it is possible that spring break, as practiced by a large number of college students each year, can be considered sex tourism. Mewhinney, Herold, and Maticka-Tyndale (1995) used focus groups and interviewed Canadian college students who traveled to Florida for spring break. They determined that there are five key elements of a spring break vacation, including "a group holiday with friends traveling and rooming together, a perpetual party atmosphere, high alcohol consumption, sexually suggestive contests and displays, and the perception that casual sex is common" (254). In a study 3 years later, the same researchers (Maticka-Tyndale, Herold, and Mewhinney 1998) found that 55% of men in their sample intended to engage in coital activity while on spring break. Certainly, most of us would condemn affluent North American men who purchase sex from a prostitute in a developing country. On the other hand, considerably fewer of us would rebuke a coed who goes to the South Padre Islands over spring break, falls madly in love with the man of her dreams, and engages in sexual relations with him. The expansive area between those two extreme examples of sex tourism requires considerable ethical deliberation.

Qualities of Sex Tourism

Oppermann (1999) suggests several characteristics of sex tourism that will broaden our understanding and may prove helpful in determining what activities might be unacceptable (immoral) and acceptable.

- Intention and opportunity—It would seem to make a difference if tourists travel for the single purpose of indulging in sexual activity. Research suggests that relatively few travelers who are involved in sexual activity make that activity their sole purpose for traveling. In many cases, they simply have sexual encounters because the opportunity presents itself (Harrison 1994).

• Monetary exchange—An exchange of money for sexual favors may help define the ethics of sexual encounters while traveling, but unfortunately this is not always cut and dried. What about female travelers to the Caribbean Islands who are courted by young men who never specifically ask for money for their companionship? While they never ask for monetary compensation, the young men do expect to be offered gifts in return for their time, perhaps even an airline ticket to Canada or the United States.

• Relationship between seeker and provider—Conventional prostitution may be ethically unacceptable, but in some developing countries, men may see themselves as rescuers of damsels in distress, even marrying native women they meet in bars. Is this exploitation? If so, who is exploited and who is exploiting? For many sex workers, prostitution may be an avenue to a better life for them and their dependents.

• Sexual encounter—While the definition of a sexual encounter may seem obvious at first, it is not. Sex is not limited to vaginal intercourse. Oppermann (1999) questions the criteria for a sexual experience: "Would oral sex, hand jobs or watching be enough to qualify? There are many places that offer peep shows where customers commonly masturbate. Some tourists may simply use such facilities for that purpose" (259).

Gray areas that become evident as we consider these qualities call into question the knee-jerk reaction to condemn all sex tourism. If condemnation were justified, it would likely be necessary to denounce over half of the sexual activities of human beings on the planet. We'll now shift gears and address the specific issue of using sex to market tourism.

Sex As a Marketing Tool for Tourism

Sex has been used to market everything from automobiles to zucchini. The trend in the last few decades has been to use even more sex-related pictures and text to sell a wide range of products because sex is entwined with powerful human emotions. Tourism, especially international tourism, is no exception to this trend. Oppermann, McKinley, and Chon (1998) note that eroticizing the South Pacific has been a major promotional strategy in the international tourism industry. Furthermore, they point out that the four Ss of sun, sea, sand, and sex dominate promotions of Caribbean destinations. They assert that "the use of sexual imagery and sexual innuendo is widespread in tourism marketing" (20).

Categories of Sex in Tourism Marketing

We'll first consider the ways sex is used in marketing tourism, and then we'll consider whether it is ethical to use sex to market tourism given some of the potential problems in the sex tourism industry. In their 1998 analysis of sex in promotional materials of Pacific tourism destinations, Oppermann, McKinley, and Chon found that sex was a common theme. They found three basic methods for using sex in the promotional materials.

- Body shots—These images comprise the most obvious category. Most body shots were of locals, which "most commonly—and in many cases most blatantly—portrayed these people in a sexual manner" (26). While body shots of visitors were not as common, they were plentiful and typically showed tourists in skimpy swimwear around a pool or at the beach. As might be expected, the majority of body shots were of women.

- Suggestive postures—The second category of sex in advertising for these destinations was suggestive postures of both singles and couples. The authors argue that such images convey availability of females or display the presence of intimate relationships between visitors and locals and visitors and visitors.

- Sexual messages of language—The third category consists of sexual messages of language, and the authors suggest that this category includes text that runs the gamut from fairly blatant references to sexual encounters to more subtle innuendos of romantic destinations and activities. An example of this might be an advertisement for a nudist resort that included sexual messages such as, "Shed your inhibitions at our resort. No need to get dressed to swim or play games, or even for drinks or dinner!"

Ethical Predicaments in Tourism Marketing

The potential ethical issues in the use of sex to promote tourism fall into three categories, the first of which has to do with the inaccuracy of tourism representations. For example, advertisements only show the smiling faces and healthy bodies of native people. They do not portray the harsh reality of destinations that suffer endemic social and political problems. Visitors are distracted from these important issues by the titillating images and are subsequently unaware of the real living conditions for most people in these areas. Visitors are therefore unlikely to advocate for improvements and increased human rights in such localities. Second, the marketing of sex tourism may lead to unfulfilled expectations and the exploitation of individuals and communities. When people, especially women, are seen merely as sex providers, they are perceived as objects without emotional, intellectual, and physical needs. Finally, there are practical issues to be considered such as the spread of sexually transmitted diseases and the increased use of hard drugs by sex workers and those purchasing sexual services.

Learning Activity: Subliminal Sex in Advertising

This learning activity will take some preparation but it is worth it. The instructor must first secure a video titled *Ad and the Id: Sex, Death and Subliminal Advertising*. The video is a 30-minute documentary that was produced in 1992 by the University of California. Most university libraries have the film or can get it.

Students will undoubtedly view this film differently. Some will like it and some will think the producers were crazy. This provocative movie analyzes from a psychoanalytic perspective the images of sex and death in advertising. It does not, however, deal with the sexuality in advertising that is obvious; rather it considers the subtle but powerful messages about sex that are camouflaged within ordinary advertisements. After showing this film, the instructor should lead a discussion of the video's contents. Questions to get the conversation started might include:

1. Who agrees with the video? Who disagrees with the video? Who agrees with some of the content of the video?
2. Why do you agree or disagree with the video?
3. The film was produced in 1992. Have things changed since then?
4. How is sexuality used in advertising?
5. Is there too much sexuality in advertising?
6. Why is sex such a powerful component in marketing?

Note: The instructor should realize that while this is a thoughtful video, it does offer some unconventional ideas about advertising.

Marketing is notorious for challenging our perceptions of what is acceptable and what is unacceptable in advertising. While sex is not the only controversial area in marketing, it is the most prominent. Tourism workers will be called upon to make ethical decisions about the use of sex as a marketing tool for decades to come.

Tourism and the Natural Environment

Tourism as we know it depends on the physical environment. While we cannot overlook its intellectual, emotional, and social elements, tourism must take place somewhere for travelers to realize its much-heralded benefits. The interdependence of tourism and the environment has resulted in several environmental issues.

Some of the controversies regarding tourism and its effect on the physical environment are well known, albeit superficially. Wyllie (2000) notes that, "It is probably fair to say that of all the criticisms leveled against tourism, those citing its harmful environmental effects are the most telling and serious" (108). However, while people tend to recognize the problem on a general level, they fail to understand the full complexity of the environmental injuries caused by tourism and travel, which include the following (Mathieson and Wall 1982):

- Destruction of vegetation
- Air pollution
- Water pollution
- Disturbance of wildlife
- Extraction of unique rock formations by souvenir hunters
- Soil erosion
- Ribbon development (building complexes in a continuous row along a road)
- Traffic congestion
- Architectural pollution

Lobeke National Park

Lying close to the equator and bordering the Congo, the southeast corner of Cameroon contains one of the most dense, lush, and vibrant jungles in the world. This area of several hundred square miles is ideal habitat for a large and unusually concentrated number of endangered forest elephants, western lowland gorillas, and countless other exotic plant and animal species. After several discussions with the World Wildlife Fund and negotiations with officials of neighboring governments, the prime minister of Cameroon finally signed a decree officially designating the area as Lobeke National Park in 2001. The dream of preserving this pristine habitat with its incredible flora and fauna seemed to be coming true.

A decade later, Lobeke National Park is an excellent backdrop against which to study the relationship between tourism and the environment. In the 1970s and 1980s, the most ominous threat to the area was unsustainable logging that was scarring the land and destroying the wildlife. While national park designation abated the lumber menace, it created an equally serious but more complicated threat—tourism.

Lobeke National Park in Cameroon is an illustration of the complex relationship between tourism and the environment.

Currently, access to the park is extremely difficult. Efforts are underway to construct roads and bridges, to develop sites for fueling vehicles, and to build lodging facilities. Of course, this will mean an enormous increase in human activity in the jungle. Unfortunately, the wildlife that is the main attraction of this jungle is extremely elusive. Unlike species such as the white-tailed deer of North America that have become accustomed to humans and have even flourished near developing areas, elephants and large primates show no signs of adapting to human interference. They choose to retreat further into the jungle. Because they are the main attraction, tourists pursue them and thereby exacerbate the problem. Ultimately, these animals will leave the area permanently or, if no retreat is possible, slowly die out. This is but one example of the ethical environmental dilemmas that tourism faces.

Types of Tourism

While all forms of tourism have the potential to damage the environment, Lawton and Weaver (2000) suggest that three particular types of tourism pose the greatest threat. Within the broad category of nature-based tourism, they offer the subcategories of **3S tourism, consumptive and captive tourism,** and **adventure tourism.**

3S (sun, sand, and sea) tourism is one of the most controversial forms of tourism and may be the most potentially harmful to the environment. Primary destinations include the Mediterranean and Caribbean basins, the South Pacific, and parts of the Indian Ocean. Several factors make this form of tourism especially threatening. For one, it is the fastest-growing sector of tourism. Additionally, some have argued that 3S tourism is particularly hedonistic, thereby elevating the quest for pleasure above all other considerations, including the environment. Finally, popular recreation activities such as golf and scuba diving may be extremely detrimental to the natural resources of these areas.

Consumptive and captive tourism is dependent on the environment and includes recreation activities such as hunting and fishing (consumptive) and places such as zoological parks (captive). Opponents of such activities argue that killing, capturing, and incarcerating animals is obviously harmful to the environment, while proponents argue that techniques such as catch-and-release fishing, habitat restoration, and park development more than offset the negative consequences to the environment.

Adventure tourism includes activities such as white-water rafting, skydiving, wilderness hiking, sea kayaking, mountain climbing, caving, and orienteering. New adventure-based recreation opportunities are created every day. It is argued that in the process, beaches, rivers, mountains, and deserts suffer irreversible harm. An example is the use of expandable bolts, or pitons, on mountains. It is impossible for human beings to scale sheer rock walls, so expandable bolts are sometimes placed in the rock to give climbers something to grasp. Bolt placement requires drilling holes in the rock. This allows climbers to climb mountains that were previously insurmountable, but because some of the most famous walls in the world are now permanently scarred, the U.S. National Park Service has banned the use of pitons in many areas (Grappling with rock climbing 1993).

Ecotourism to the Rescue?

Although the term has been used and abused so often that it has actually mystified the concept, **ecotourism** refers to "tourism in which the natural environment and its flora and fauna are the main attraction and their preservation and enhancement are primary concerns for promoters and tourists" (Wyllie 2000, 106). As this definition suggests, one of the core elements of ecotourism is sustainability. The mission of ecotourism is to blend the needs of tourists and the needs of the environment in such a way that is advantageous for both.

Unfortunately, ecotourism has had mixed results. Costa Rica is the best example of the positive side of ecotourism. The designation of 25 national parks, buffer zones, and restricted areas has been instrumental in preserving the country's natural resources and in some cases has reversed damage from previous travel-related activity.

In some cases, however, unethical providers have merely used the concept as a guise for continued exploitation of the land and native people. Duffy (2000) reported a situation in Belize where tourists and the commercial tourism provider seriously damaged coral reefs without any sanctions at all. Although the proposal and subsequent development of ecotourism has a strong environmental component, this concern may be undermined by commercial and political interests. A further limitation is that ecotourism appeals to a small fraction of all travelers. For those who are interested in the environmental condition of their destination, most are concerned only with their particular vacation site for a specific time period (usually a week or 10 days, the length of the trip) and are less concerned about the general environmental health of the area. Finally, Wyllie (2000) leaves us with a sobering statement that should challenge us all:

> Perhaps we should pray that ecotourism does not become anything larger than a niche market. If most of us become "born again" ecotourists and forsake our favorite haunts, such as Waikiki, Miami Beach, Las Vegas and the like, the pressures on the world's most fragile ecosystems would quickly become unbearable. (108-109)

Learning Activity: Webbing Carrying Capacity

Carrying capacity is one of the key concepts as we discuss environmental damage by visitors. The instructor will write the term *carrying capacity* in the middle of the blackboard. Students provide words or very short phrases that are related to this topic. The instructor writes each on the board around the key concept of carrying capacity and draws a line to other concepts that have some type of relationship to it. Before long, it becomes obvious that the term is related to many concepts, each of which is related to one another or at least to most of the other phrases and concepts. The instructor will then provide a concise definition of the term. The instructor should look up the precise definition prior to the learning activity.

Virtual Reality and Tourism

Virtual worlds and experiences will be widely available in the future. Determining when that will finally happen is the basis of many books and articles. But for us, the question is not when, it's what. Will we be able to visit an encampment of American Indians in the 1600s? Will we be able to travel to the most beautiful place on earth or beyond and savor a romantic interlude with the person of our dreams? Will we be able to watch and even interact with the rarest animals on the planet without disturbing them at all? Will the disabled experience everything—seeing, hearing, running—that the nondisabled experience?

The potential of such a future is tantalizing, but we must also consider the possible negative effects of virtual reality (VR). We ask you to put your skepticism about virtual reality on hold and consider the ethical conundrums posed by this mind-boggling phenomenon.

Defining Virtual Reality

The VR we will discuss is not the VR of the current generation of amusement arcades and home video systems. Although these technologies are marketed as VR, the commercial sector is overstating its products. They are relatively simple prototypes of what is to come. VR is a developing technology that allows participants to create simulated experiences of both real and unreal, but at the same time believable, situations. Cruz-Neira et al. (1992) have defined three essential elements of virtual reality: visualization, interactivity, and immersion.

Visualization is the most basic component and includes stereoscopic vision, look-around capability, and the ability to see other VR participants. Considerable progress has been made in this area but much remains to be done.

Interactivity refers to the degree of control the participant has over the experience. Participants must be able to affect their environment. For example, if a participant in a virtual tourism environment calls out to a virtual vendor, the vendor must respond in some way. He may look at the caller and shrug his shoulders, he may speak in his foreign language, or he may respond in the participant's language. Such responsiveness contributes to the essential sense of control.

Immersion is the final, and heretofore elusive, quality. Players must be able to believe they are in a real world. This will be accomplished through the manipulations of all the senses—sight, hearing, taste, smell, and feeling.

© Brand X Pictures

Along with the potential of virtual reality to change tourism as we know it, there will come new ethical dilemmas.

VR Tourism

Can you imagine the ability to move not only geographically but temporally as well? And to do so without the dangers and inconveniences of modern travel? You and I would be able to watch the ancient Egyptians as they built the pyramids. We wouldn't have to settle for looking at the deteriorating artifacts of the glorious past—we could actually be in that past. We could see the Egyptians working on the pyramids, hear the solid thud of the massive blocks as they drop into place, feel the sand slipping under our feet, and smell the gentle morning breeze from the Nile. Is this science fiction? Perhaps, but remember that the science fiction of yesterday has often become the reality of today. Let's now consider the potential effects of virtual technology on some of the tourism-related issues we addressed earlier in the chapter.

The Effects of VR on Cultures

For many tourists, the chance to experience the culture of another society is the driving force behind their travel. This is problematic for two reasons. First, culture can be as secretive and elusive as any rare animal. At times, much of a culture is so subtle as to be detectable only by a trained anthropologist. At other times, something entirely different masquerades as culture, often the pseudoculture that native people believe the tourists desire to see. Second, the discovery of a different culture can have disastrous effects for its people. Fifty years of exposing the Sherpas to western values has seriously affected this sensitive culture. Sir Edmund Hillary's conquest of Mt. Everest in 1953 would not have been possible without his Sherpa guide, Tenzing Norgay. Since that time, more and more mountain climbers have employed Sherpas in climbs of virtually all Himalayan peaks. Because guiding or carrying for a climbing party is extremely lucrative compared to traditional labor, it is the work of choice for most young men. To be seen and subsequently hired requires Sherpa men to pack up their families, leave their small mountain villages, and live in the city of Kathmandu. This has contributed to the dilution of traditional Sherpa culture. The following quote is but one example of the effect of tourism on such a culture: "When someone in the family dies, the Sherpa way is to keep the body at home for two or three days to mourn. But if you live in Kathmandu and rent a house belonging to a Hindu, he wants to get a dead body out of his house immediately. So it is really not a Sherpa home anymore" (Reid 2003, 45).

It is also possible that as virtual cultural experiences are developed, we will see a decline in the recognition of the value of cultural diversity. Why go to the trouble of protecting a culture if you can conveniently visit and revisit it for a small fee? Some would argue that employing virtual tourism to see, feel, taste, smell, and hear other cultures is the final step in the commodification of all culture. When items become commodified, their inherent use value is reduced while their value as things that can be exchanged on the free market increases. Culture could be produced, reproduced, and sold like a computer or a car tune-up. We wouldn't have to worry about the comparisons between the real culture and the virtual culture because the original would have disappeared, leaving nothing to compare.

The Effects of VR on Sexual Expression

Sexual activity comes with consequences, some of which are wonderful and some of which are devastating to individuals and society. In sex tourism today, most of the consequences appear to be of the latter type. But in a virtual world we could eliminate broken hearts, unwanted pregnancies, exploitation, and sexually transmitted diseases. Impotence? Forget it. Viagra? Who needs it? In virtual reality, men and women could be the kind of lovers they only dreamed of being. And sexual partners could come in an incredible variety. Participants could even change gender without surgery and hormone therapy, perhaps in the process developing a greater tolerance and appreciation for the opposite sex.

Although there are potential benefits of virtual sex and sex tourism, there are also potential dangers. Some people have difficulty differentiating between real and unreal. An array of drugs and counseling techniques are marketed and prescribed to help persons with mental disorders such as schizophrenia sort out the real from the imaginary (Edelman 1996). In an area as emotionally charged as human sexuality, it is possible that the confusion between virtual sex and real sex might become more pronounced and more devastating. It is possible that some could retreat into a virtual world where they do not have to worry about rejection or negative consequences of their actions.

Already the effects of cybersex, a feeble example of the sex trips that may lie ahead in the future, are causing alarm. Sex addiction, much of it related to pornographic material and cybersex experiences currently available on the Internet, is on the rise. Although not yet recognized by many professionals, sex addiction has been linked to sexual crimes, damaged relationships, and broken families. Opponents of virtual sex cite the statistics for harm linked to use of the Internet for sexual gratification, and they worry about the next generation of technology (Schneider and Weiss 2001). The *Attorney General's Commission on Pornography Report* (1986) notes that three out of four U.S. citizens believe that pornography leads some people to lose respect for women.

Most religions have expressed concern about sexual expression outside marriage. A trip into the realm of virtual sex would be taboo for Christians, Muslims, Hindus, Buddhists, and many others. The prohibitions against using computers to generate a virtual sexual experience are based not on possible consequences but on strongly held beliefs about what sex should and should not include. These beliefs are not likely to change in the near future and promise to be the basis for at least one side of the debate on VR sex.

The Effects of VR on the Environment

More people are traveling than at any other time in history. According to McLaren (2003), international tourist arrivals increased from 25 million in 1950 to 698 million in 2000, and are predicted to grow to 1.56 billion by 2020. In addition, people are traveling to environmentally sensitive places in numbers that will inevitably lead to environmental destruction. But virtual reality has the potential to sidestep that issue altogether: In the future VR may make it possible to believe that we are someplace else.

Above the timberline in the Colorado Rocky Mountains during the spring and summer it is stunningly beautiful. Thick mats of small, brilliant flowers stretch amid piles of jagged boulders. The growing season is quite short, usually about 3 months. Consequently, damage to the grasses and flowers takes several years to disappear. The grooves of roads and trails remain even after 50 years in some places. It is easy to imagine the harm that could be done if swarms of backpackers walked through these fragile areas. But with VR, tourists could see and smell timberline flowers and feel gentle mountain breezes without causing environmental damage and without worrying about being stranded in a dangerous late-season snowstorm.

Virtual adventure tourists could hammer pitons into rock walls to their heart's content. After a day of virtual climbing, they could return to the real world for a good night's rest. The next morning they could gaze at the same route or new ones without ever seeing the ugly cracks and holes left by their virtual pitons, because in a virtual world, pitons do not leave marks. That sheer rock wall could be as clean and unspoiled as the day it was first discovered.

But again, a note of caution is in order. Perhaps VR might not be able to protect the environment after all. VR might actually mean the end of the pristine areas and rare species that are so popular today. If a person could experience such areas and animals virtually, would there be a need to pump millions of dollars into preservation? Consider zoos and aquariums. For the average tourist they may actually be better than the real thing. SeaWorld in Orlando, Florida, offers an experience called *Shark Deep-Dive Sea World* that cannot be matched in the real environment of any ocean in the world (www.floridatravelusa.com/articlesnew/seaworldmay04p036.html). Participants put on a wet suit, climb into a shark cage, and travel on a submerged track in a huge salt-water tank complete with floating vegetation, coral reefs, and white sand. In the

Learning Activity: What Makes Something Real?

It may seem easy to answer this question, but most of us find ourselves resorting to saying, "I really don't know what makes something real, but trust me, I know real when I see it." But in the future, we may be able to create visuals, smells, and anything else to stimulate the senses just as naturally occurring sights and odors would. It may even be possible to create negative consequences, if that is what people want. For example, if people want to experience what it would be like to catch the winning pass in the Super Bowl and get tackled really, really hard in the end zone, it might be possible to do that with a tactile suit. Of course that is off in the future, but it may one day be possible.

Students pair up and discuss the question, "What makes something real?" After 10 minutes, have the class come together and have each person share what they decided. If students will put effort into this learning activity, they will see that the line between real and virtual is thin indeed.

process they are able to see and almost touch more than 50 types of sharks. Actually swimming in the ocean with the possibility of catching a glimpse of a shark pales in comparison. Which of these two experiences is most attractive to the average North American, and which will receive the most attention and financial support?

Conclusion

In this chapter we have looked at some of the ethical issues that the tourism sector faces. Leaders in this sector will need to make difficult ethical decisions about these and other quandaries. We've also peered into the future in the last few pages—a future that is exciting and a little frightening at the same time. Obviously, we cannot know the future with any certainty. However, tourism, just like all other leisure sectors, must attempt to anticipate what will happen rather than simply respond to what has already occurred.

Tourism is rife with complex ethical issues that sometimes masquerade as technical problems. As we have seen, however, moral questions underlie most of the issues. If we fail to recognize this, our actions will be unproductive. As promoters, providers, and consumers of tourism, we must ponder the rightness or wrongness of our actions. And as with most other issues, we do not have the luxury of putting these tough ethical decisions off for a few years, because the clock is ticking.

QUESTIONS FOR DISCUSSION

1. What trends or events do you think will have the greatest impact on tourism in the future?

2. How do you respond to the following statement? Cultures change. It doesn't matter whether the change is caused by tourism or technology or war.

3. Since sexuality is a natural human function, shouldn't international sex tourism be accepted but carefully regulated?

4. How do you respond to the following statement? We must accept that humans affect their physical environment. There can be no human activity without some environmental degradation.

5. Have you had any type of virtual experience? How was it? How far away from a "real virtual experience" are we?

PART III

Applications and a Look Ahead

TEN

Professionalism and Recreation and Leisure

GOALS

1. To understand the concept of professionalism
2. To learn about the historical development of professionalism
3. To understand two different perspectives on professionalism
4. To evaluate leisure services as a profession
5. To learn about the obstacles to the professionalization of leisure services

Professionalism

Professionalism is a critical element of the 21st century, profoundly affecting individuals and societies. Sociologist Eliot Freidson (1994) states:

> There seems to be rather remarkable unanimity about professions—agreement first, that they represent a distinct kind of occupation which is of special importance to the effective and humane functioning of modern society, second, that they have been growing in number and importance throughout this century, and, third, that they will increase in number and importance in the future, into the next century. (106-107)

We need to understand the implications that the presence or absence of professional status might have on the roles and ethical obligations of leisure service providers. For example, do professionals have ethical responsibilities that go beyond those of nonprofessionals? To be able to answer this question, we first need to investigate how the idea of professionalism evolved and then consider the arguments for and against defining leisure services as a profession. While it is up to you to decide whether you think leisure services is a profession, by thoroughly examining the concept of professionalism and its ethical implications you will better understand the ethical responsibilities required of service delivery that is based on a professionalism model.

In this chapter we will consider professionalism as a general concept, briefly investigating its historical development and ethical implications. Then we'll consider whether leisure services qualifies as a profession by examining its traits and roles. Finally, we'll look at some of the problems that help prevent leisure services from being recognized as a profession.

Trait-Based Definition of Professionalism

Let's begin by briefly examining the history of professionalism. Sociologists and historians generally agree that the emergence of modern professions can be traced back to Victorian England (Kimball 1992; Polanyi 1944). However, two different schools of thought about the development of professions in that era have come to the forefront. The more traditional interpretation suggests that professions are the offspring of the guilds of 17th-century England. Polanyi argues that the largely unregulated free markets of the time posed a serious threat to the intellectual class (bourgeoisie), so workers created associations of like-minded persons (guilds) to protect themselves from the power of the owners who were controlling the lives of their workers. Eventually, guilds evolved even further into close-knit groups of craftsmen who developed their own standards for the products that they offered to the public. Over time, other traits, most of which were initiated to consolidate control of the production and distribution process, were initiated. Today, it is alleged that certain traits are common to professions. While sociologists and researchers disagree on the number of traits there are, most agree on at least the following shared characteristics of professions.

- A unique body of knowledge
- Professional preparation, including accreditation and certification
- Professional organizations and a concern for ethics

A Unique Body of Knowledge

In an effort to gain control of their labors, guilds, the predecessors of professions, sought to draw sharp boundaries around their particular areas of expertise (Polanyi 1944). This involved the institution and distribution of information and principles distinctive to their particular fields. Supporting the idea of special skills and knowledge, but using the term *systematic body of theory,* Pavalko (1972) argued that "the skills that characterize a profession flow from and are supported by a fund of knowledge that has been organized into an internally consistent system, called a body of theory" (5). However, knowledge and theory are not simple notions.

Abbott (1988) argues that knowledge comes in at least two forms, abstraction (theory) and concreteness (application). He claims that for an occupation to meet the criteria of a profession, it must strike a balance between these two forms: "At either extreme, the profession tends to lose credibility; too great abstraction appears to be mere formalism, too great concreteness is judged to be no more than a craft" (165).

Professional Preparation

Ultimately, other institutions and the general public confer professional status on any occupation. A basis for this confirmation is strong societal influence of a field, which can be enhanced by the professional preparation of its members. Formal preparation usually takes the form of higher education; however, an important component of preparation, the development of a particular **ethos,** may be transferred in practical settings. The diversity of tasks and settings within leisure services challenges the preparation process of the field.

Accreditation and Certification

Related to professional preparation is the process of accreditation and certification. The park and recreation field has successfully instituted accreditation; the National Recreation and Park Association (NRPA) and American Association for Leisure and Recreation (AALR) list 85 colleges and universities in the United States and Canada that meet their accreditation standards (Houghton 2002). Certification for those who provide recreation and leisure services has grown over the past decades. This is not to say that certification in different disciplines and in the United States and Canada is the same, though. For example, formal certification for recreation therapists in Canada has not progressed as quickly as it has in the United States (Thomas and Ostiguy 1998). Nor has certification been adopted as readily in the travel and tourism industry as it has in community and outdoor recreation. Examples of certification include Certified Recreation and Park Professional (CRPR),

© John A Rizzo/Getty Images

Accreditation is designed to ensure quality in higher education programs; certification is designed to ensure quality for practitioners.

Certified Therapeutic Recreation Specialist (CTRS), and Certified Outdoor Leader (COL).

However, certification is controversial. The strongest argument in favor of certification is that the public will be better served. Over a period of time, certification programs establish standards of practice to prevent untrained and unprepared individuals from working in the field. Opponents of certification argue that many capable workers, some of whom have been in the field for decades, will not be certified because they may be intimidated or choose not to pursue certification for other reasons. Opponents also dispute the idea that certification promotes better service. It is relatively easy to find certified workers who lack the essential skills, knowledge, and judgment for their position. Moreover, there are concerns about the validity of the tests. Assessing the ability to put up a tent is fairly easy, but measuring judgment and attitude is far more difficult and arguably more important. A recreation administrator may be able to provide the legal definition of sexual harassment on a test, but sorting out the subtle nuances of such behavior in the workplace may only be gained through years of experience.

Professional Organizations and Ethics

The plethora of national organizations reflects the diversity of missions and applications in leisure services. In addition to the international and national organizations in the following list, nearly every state and territory in the United States and Canada has at least one organization.

- American Association for Leisure and Recreation (AALR)—Serves recreation practitioners, educators, and students who advance the profession and enhance the quality of life of all Americans through creative, meaningful leisure and recreation experiences.
- American Camping Association (ACA)—Dedicated to enriching the lives of children and adults through camp experiences.
- American Therapeutic Recreation Association (ATRA)—Represents the interests and needs of recreational therapists.
- Association for Experiential Education (AEE)—Develops and promotes experiential education.
- Canadian Camping Association (CCA)—Dedicated to the growth, development, and promotion of organized camping for all populations in Canada.
- Canadian Parks and Recreation Association (CPRA)—National voice for a vibrant grassroots network with partnerships that connect people who build healthy, active communities and affect the everyday lives of Canadians.

- International Ecotourism Society (IES)—Unites travel and conservation worldwide through research, publications, consultations, and advocacy.
- International Festival and Events Association (IFEA)—Advances festivals and events throughout the world.
- National Intramural-Recreation Sports Association (NIRSA)—Resource for professional and student development, education, and research in collegiate recreational sport.
- National Recreation and Park Association (NRPA)—Advances parks, recreation, and environmental conservation efforts that enhance the quality of life for all.
- North American Association of Environmental Education (NAAEE)—Network of professionals, students, and volunteers working in environmental education throughout North America and in over 55 countries around the world.
- Resort and Commercial Recreation Association (RCRA)—Nonprofit organization established to further the resort and commercial recreation industries through services to professionals, educators, and students, as well as to increase the profitability of commercial recreation enterprises.
- World Leisure and Recreation Association (WLRA)—Worldwide association of persons and organizations for discovering and fostering conditions that permit leisure to serve as a force for human development and well-being.

In addition to advocating for the profession and offering educational and networking opportunities, associations typically provide ethical advice and decision-making assistance. Most national and state organizations have developed codes of ethics and accompanying policies, though, as we saw in chapter 7, codes of ethics must be employed very carefully.

Role-Based Definition of Professionalism

The other approach to defining a profession focuses on the nature of the relationship between those who serve and those who are served. Central to this approach is the idea that professions provide services and make social welfare their paramount concern (Clarke and Stewart 1986; Coalter 1990; Vielba 1986). From this perspective, much less attention is paid to individual consumer choice (the bedrock of marketing) than to meeting collective societal needs. Of course, the needs of groups are often expressed

Learning Activity: Specialized Knowledge?

Opinions differ about the unique body of knowledge or systematic body of theory possessed by the park and recreation field. What do you think?

Students gather into groups according to the subfields in which they are interested. For example, there may be a group for natural resources management, one for therapeutic recreation, and one for public leisure services. If there are more than four people who are in a particular subfield, then two or more groups of three or four students should be made. These groups go to separate areas in the classroom to answer the following questions:

1. Is there a unique body of knowledge or systematic body of theory for your subfield?
2. If so, what are three or four examples of this unique body of knowledge or systematic body of theory?
3. If not, why is there no unique body of knowledge or systematic body of theory in your subfield?
4. Is there really any profession that has a unique body of knowledge or systematic body of theory?
5. Does not all knowledge come from some place else? For example, isn't the body of knowledge in medicine, one of the classic professions, simply a compilation of information from the fields of chemistry, biology, and even physics?

After discussing these questions in the small groups for 15 minutes, students return to their original seats and report their answers to the rest of the class.

through individuals, but the desires of individuals are always weighed against the social good.

Such an approach to defining professionalism casts doubt on leisure service organizations that adopt a pure marketing philosophy treating the individual consumer of goods as the ultimate judge of a product's value. The relationship or role-based approach to defining professions privileges public and nonprofit leisure and recreation providers over their commercial counterparts that must generate profit, although this is not to say that some public sector providers do not treat clients merely as customers and that some commercial providers do not strive to contribute to the social good.

McLean and Johnson (1993) argue that professionalism is defined primarily by the role professionals assume rather than a list of traits or characteristics evident in certain occupational groupings. The key feature that distinguishes professionals from nonprofessionals is that clients expect professionals to protect their interests whereas they do not necessarily expect nonprofessionals to act on their behalf.

Compare our relationship with our doctor to that of the local car salesperson. We expect our doctor to give us an honest opinion on our medical condition, and likewise our doctor expects us to report our health symptoms and lifestyle activities accurately. Our relationship with our doctor is therefore founded on a high level of trust. However, when purchasing a used car, we and the salesperson expect each other to be less than completely forthcoming as we both attempt to negotiate a deal. The salesman may indicate that we should buy quickly because, "Another person is *very* interested in the car and will be back later this afternoon." Likewise, even if it's true we probably won't say, "I've been shopping all day and I'm desperate. I really need to get a car." The social relationship between the car salesperson and ourselves is based not on trust but on deception. The deceptive behavior is not immoral in this situation, as it is understood by both parties that a certain amount of misrepresentation is required to play the bargaining game. But the fact that the interactions between the seller and buyer are founded on deception rather than trust indicates that it is a nonprofessional relationship.

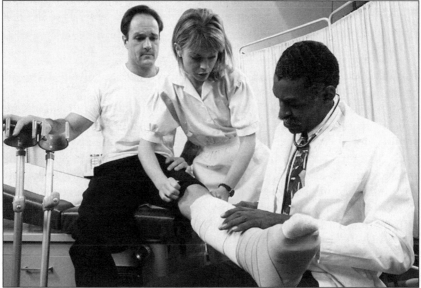

© Photodisc

A trusting relationship between provider and client is essential to professionalism.

We find ourselves entering into trust relationships when we are unable to adequately assess and look after our own interests. Professionalism is therefore founded on benevolent paternalism of the professional toward the client. Occupations in which the clients are aided by paternalistic treatment are thus candidates for professionalism.

Several writers in leisure studies strongly question whether recreation qualifies as an occupation in which clients are better served by paternalism in leisure services. For example, Coalter (1990) believes that professions are based on the relationship between provider and those whom the provider serves. He states, "Professional status is not an inherent property

Learning Activity: Making Theory Real

In the previous pages, we have discussed the relationship between recreation providers and recreation clients or consumers. Some have made the argument that everyone benefits from a professional relationship, while others argue that the power differential between the professional and client is unproductive at best. All of this has been at the theoretic level, and it is time that we considered real-life examples of this positive or negative professional–client relationship in leisure services. If there is a solid basis for either side of this issue, there will certainly be examples to support it.

Each student is given a 3-by-5 card. They are not to write their names on the card unless they want to. The instructor asks students to give two brief examples from their own experience. One will be a concrete, real-life instance in which the relationship between provider and recipient of leisure services may have met the professional ideal. There might have been a high degree of trust and all parties benefited.

The other example will show how a leisure service professional may have discouraged play and spontaneity and made the consumer more dependent on someone to provide their leisure.

The student will put a star by the example that reflects her or his own position.

The cards are then collected by the instructor. The instructor will read some of the examples to the class. The authors may comment on their own examples for clarification purposes only. After reading an equal number of examples on both sides, perhaps 10 each, the class will vote on where they stand on the issue. The instructor will say, "Hold up your hand if you think that the relationship between leisure service provider and client/consumer is basically productive." Then the instructor will say, "Hold up your hand if you think that the relationship between leisure service provider and client/consumer is basically unproductive, maybe even destructive."

Have two people with different opinions provide reasons for their perceptions on professionalism in leisure services. Allow for some discussion.

of an occupational group but refers to a particular set of relationships with others" (107). However, Coalter does not fully agree that this type of relationship between the professional and the client is desirable. He suggests that most fields employ an authoritative top-down model in which professionals determine the clients' needs and then go about meeting those predetermined needs. Such a model lacks the genuine partnership between facilitators and citizens that is essential for an informed and empowered citizenry and a properly functioning democracy.

Similarly, Lord, Hutchison, and VanDerbeck (1991) have taken the position that leisure and recreation providers tend to discourage play and spontaneity and instead encourage clients to depend on professional leadership for their recreation activities. Rather than facilitating leisure choices, they argue that professionalism is a political relationship in which the professional is cast in "the role of policy and decision-maker for the client" (277).

The Public Interest

One of the problems with the definitions of professionalism that we have examined so far is that they focus on only two stakeholders: the professional and the client. The debate over the merits of professionalism tends to overlook the public interest. Consider the example of national parks. National parks provide habitat for large vertebrates such as bears, moose, and reptiles. Tourists visit many of these parks in great numbers, and the parks satisfy the diverse needs of individual tourists who want to experience nature. The vast majority of these tourists have good intentions toward the animals that inhabit the park, and they don't intend to disturb the natural habitat. Yet the presence of millions of well-meaning visitors can cause dramatic declines in animal populations that do not adapt well to the presence of human beings. The visitors do not realize the negative effect they are having on the park because the disruption of wild animal behaviors and possible decrease in animal populations happens over a long period of time. Fortunately, professional staff members are in position to monitor these developments and take corrective action by limiting visitor access. The park staff has the professional responsibility to deny leisure services to individual consumers in order to protect the animals. This action, while it may be unpopular with some visitors, will maintain the essential wildness of the park for future generations.

The notion that professionals' primary duty is to serve the public interest rather than the interests of clients or the profession has increasingly been accepted as the main justification for granting professional status to an occupation. The rise of the ethics course in the curriculum of traditional professional schools such as law and engineering may have resulted partially from the public's increasing awareness that some members of these professions were not protecting the public's interests. It began to occur to many professional associations that if the public lost faith in the moral responsibility of these professions, eventually those same occupations would be regulated by government agencies and thus lose their professional autonomy.

The accounting profession is just such an example of a profession's moral accountability being called into question. The accounting industry's primary purpose is to objectively verify the accuracy of the fiscal reports and operations of businesses and agencies in the nonprofit and public sectors. The Arthur Andersen accounting firm, one of the largest in the nation, worked with the Enron Corporation, an energy company, for several years. Due to illegal business practices, Enron collapsed. The ensuing investigation found several discrepancies in the company's financial records—discrepancies that would have been discovered and reported by any reputable accountant. Arthur Andersen was convicted of obstructing justice when it shredded documents showing that it had helped falsify Enron's accounting records. Until the exposure of these financial deceptions, both the accountants at Arthur Andersen and the executives at Enron benefited tremendously from their business relationship. However, the cost of Enron's collapse was borne mainly by investors and rank-and-file Enron employees (many of whom lost most of their retirement savings) who trusted the financial statements issued by Enron and certified by Arthur Andersen. In addition, Arthur Andersen, once one of the five largest accounting firms in the world, no longer exists.

A key criterion for an occupation to retain its professional status is whether society can trust those who comprise the group. The behaviors of accountants at Arthur Andersen and other accounting firms raise questions about whose interests are being served. Is it the interests of accountants and their firms, the companies that pay accounting companies huge salaries for consultation, or society? Moreover, professions must have the willingness and ability to self-regulate. This has not been evident. Subsequently, the accounting industry may be in danger of losing the professional status previously conferred on it by society.

Professional Recognition for Recreation and Leisure Services

As we have seen, a great deal of evidence suggests that recreation and leisure services is a profession, but the issue of professionalism still generates controversy in recreation and leisure studies. Students in the field are all too familiar with the puzzled, perhaps alarmed, looks of parents and the amusement of peers when they reveal that one can indeed get a degree in recreation. Disbelief grows when friends and family hear references to the leisure services field as a profession. Yet it is clear that many in the field regard their work as a professional occupation. Why do people react skeptically to the notion that providing leisure and recreation opportunities may be a profession?

Leisure researchers have advanced several reasons explaining why the idea of leisure services as a profession is questioned. One line of thought holds that it is the relative newness of leisure services as a field that prevents the public from recognizing its professional status. For example, surgery and dentistry were both practiced by barbers in the 1500s. The barbers' pole, with its red and white stripes, represented the practice of bloodletting performed commonly by barbers through the 1700s (www.brownshair.com/history.htm). As professional standards for medical services gradually improved and they became separate from barbering, the status of those occupations rose. Given that well-organized leisure services have only become common during the past century, it is perhaps not surprising that the professional status of leisure services is not as advanced as traditional professions, which have had a much longer time to develop their service practices. This evolutionary interpretation suggests that it might simply be a matter of time before people come to accept the provision of recreation as a professional occupation.

Leisure services may therefore be a soft profession, meaning it shares some of the characteristics of the nonprofessional occupations beneath it and some characteristics of the hard professions above it. This hierarchical explanation of status also helps account for different interpretations of the professionalism of leisure and recreation subfields. For example, therapeutic recreation is often cited as the most professional subfield

Learning Activity: Professionalism and Leisure Service Subfields

Another obstacle for the recognition of leisure services as a profession is that it sits midway on the status pyramid between traditional professions such as medicine, law, and teaching at the top and nonprofessional occupations that make up the base of the pyramid. This is even further complicated by the fact that the general term *leisure services* or even *parks and recreation* includes a diversity of subfields, including tourism, adventure recreation, community recreation, therapeutic recreation, and so on. Where would you place each of these subfields in the figure?

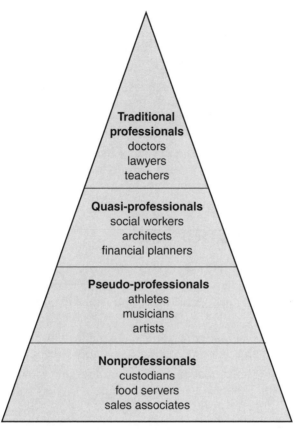

Pyramid of professional status.

because of its closeness to medicine, while tourism is seen as less professional because of its ties to commerce. Unlike the evolutionary model, the hierarchical model of professionalism suggests that the professional status of leisure services will always be somewhat ambiguous and depend on the particular subfield. In fact, while it may be convenient to talk about the professionalization of leisure services, it may not be particularly accurate or productive to do so.

Conclusion

Many fields, including leisure and recreation services, are striving to be recognized as professions. Being a profession carries both positive and negative components. Most notably, gaining authority and respect as a profession coincides with increased responsibility. This is not simply the responsibility to do more but to do what is good and right.

Industries striving for professionalism must carefully consider the ethical decisions and behaviors of their members. Proper conduct for individuals and groups cannot simply be left to chance. As Mark Twain once wrote, "Morals are an acquirement—like music, like a foreign language, like piety, poker, paralysis—no man is born with them" (1917).

Ultimately, it is not the industry that bestows professional status on itself. Leisure services cannot simply announce, "We are a profession." That status can only be conferred by society. And the criterion is service. If the field of leisure and recreation, with all of its subfields, can ethically and effectively deliver genuine benefits to individuals and to society, official professionalism won't be far behind.

QUESTIONS FOR DISCUSSION

1. Can you think of other fields that are attempting to gain professional status? What are they? How do you think their chances for recognition compare to the chances of leisure and recreation being recognized as a profession?

2. Has anyone ever questioned you about the legitimacy of the field or a particular subfield? If so, who was it and how did you respond?

3. How do the media treat the fields of leisure studies, parks, recreation, and tourism? What evidence do you have to support your answer?

4. What possible downsides are there to the professionalization of leisure and recreation?

5. Some leisure educators suggest that professionals in the field should teach and thus empower people with the ability to design and coordinate their own leisure activities rather than make them depend on an agency or business. Is this possible? If so, what would be the consequences?

ELEVEN

Wrapping Up and Moving On

For 10 years, Salvador Hernandez always came in an hour before everyone else. This quiet prelude, uninterrupted by CEOs, park district employees, and customers, was the perfect opportunity to mentally and emotionally prepare for the day. Serving as the go-to guy in a leisure service agency had been a dream of his since his sophomore year in college, and he truly believed that sitting at this desk—in this community on this day—was his destiny. Salvador had worked up through the ranks in other park districts, first as a sport program supervisor, then as a recreation coordinator, and for the last 3 years as an assistant director. Two weeks ago, he accepted the position of executive director of the Lamar Park District and now here he was on the second day of the job.

This park district had its share of problems. To be honest, it had *more* than its share of problems. Salvador had taken the position not because of pay or status, but because he thought he could make a difference in the lives of Lamar's citizens and in the community as a whole.

Another habit Salvador had developed over the years was writing down on a clean yellow pad the tasks he needed to get done and the issues he needed to address.

Tasks For Today

- Interview applicant for pool manager
- Talk to the police chief about security for next month's spring festival
- Meet with department heads
- Prepare presentation to the Kiwanis Club
- Go to newspaper for an interview
- Complete survey from local university

Things to Think About

- Location of new park and its effect on residents and the environment
- Building a new fitness facility and whether to accept a large donation from the local beer dealer
- Employee use of department copy machines and computers
- Department policy for youth employment
- Community assessment
- Budget for seniors trips

Some of these issues promised to be difficult. Whatever Salvadore did in most of these situations, someone would be unhappy, and in some cases someone might even be hurt. Although there was information about each issue and he could call some of his mentors for advice, it would ultimately come down to him.

Like Salvador Hernandez, most of you have already invested a great deal of money and effort preparing for your career and learning your job. Big or little, most of the decisions you make will have an ethical dimension, and they will affect more people than you ever imagined. While this responsibility may seem daunting now and will almost certainly seem overwhelming at times in the future, remember that you have a hefty toolbox full of valuable skills and knowledge to help you.

What Have We Learned?

Let's quickly review the contents of the book thus far. In chapter 1 we found that even though some may see leisure and recreation services as an idyllic field where everyone simply plays and has fun, ethical conundrums

What can be more fulfilling than enhancing the lives of individuals and helping to create a better society?

are rife. Every subfield struggles with common issues, and most of the subfields have ethical problems that are unique to them. Furthermore, it should be apparent that leisure and recreation services are not just fun and games. Leisure is vital to everyone, and the decisions we make influence people's lives in many ways.

We cannot simply rely on ourselves and others to automatically do what is good. Ethical behaviors don't happen on their own, and unethical acts are not limited to a few bad apples. History is replete with examples of average people acting in ways that shock others and themselves. At the same time, we're not doomed to thinking and acting unethically. As we learned in the second chapter, human beings develop morally. Although the growth is uneven and may even be arrested at an early stage in some individuals, most of us can attain the higher stages of moral and ethical awareness with some thought and diligence.

Chapter 3 introduced three approaches to determining ethical behavior. Each has its strengths and weaknesses. Consequence-based ethics considers what will happen as a result of our actions. We make decisions according to the effect they will have on others in the short- and long-term. Rule-based ethics focuses on the obligations people have to each other. People are granted certain rights and saddled with certain expectations based on their place in the world. Finally, virtue-based ethics focuses not on the individual's cognitive abilities to consider consequences and social obligations and rights but on the characteristics or virtues one should possess. Ethical actions are determined by the ideal characteristics found in persons who hold certain positions and take on specific roles.

The fourth chapter offered a three-stage model for systematic decision making. To aid in understanding the principles and application of the model, we compared it to the process of trying a criminal case in a court of law. While there are some obvious differences, there are also many similarities. The first step in the model is identifying the moral dilemma, just as in a criminal case, the police and attorneys collect facts and attempt to construct a picture of what happened. The second step is to address what is praiseworthy and blameworthy. In a court of law this is the analysis of the facts and the subsequent determination of guilt or innocence. The third and final step of the model consists of choosing a moral action plan. As in a criminal case, not only do we collect facts, analyze that information, and determine guilt or innocence, we also decide on an appropriate punishment.

The second part of the book discussed some of the more common ethical issues in the subfields of leisure services. While the particulars will be different for each person, the issues presented in these chapters promise to be around for quite some time. Management will struggle with sexual attitudes and behaviors in the workplace for years to come. Safety and conflicts of interest will always be a concern. And as long as there are competing values in the workplace, whistle-blowing will take place. The ethical issues related to the generation of profits in the commercial sector will most likely continue to cause problems in the future. Those who choose to go into therapeutic recreation will face situations involving paternalism, justice, confidentiality, and multiple roles. Outdoor recreation personnel will deal with a myriad of environmental issues, including rationing recreation resources and educating and leading others. Tourism by its very nature will have profound effects on cultures and the environment. Those in tourism will also face virtual reality with all of its promises and dangers.

In these chapters we also considered a few of the most common pitfalls in ethical decision making and acting. On the surface, legalism, complete reliance on codes of conduct, relativism, and ethical egoism appear to offer easy solutions to ethical dilemmas. It may also seem that the easiest way to deal with ethical problems is to refuse to even consider different points of view. But none of these options leads to sound ethical decision making and acting. Instead, they give us a false sense of security while leading us even farther away from good and right ways of doing and being.

In chapter 10, we discussed professionalism as it relates to leisure services. The race is on for every field, including leisure services, to become a profession. But professionalism is a complex, controversial concept laden with daunting responsibilities. Consequently, ethical decision making and acting are crucial to being a professional. Leisure services must carefully weigh the costs and benefits of professionalism.

Making a Difference in Recreation and Leisure

Whether you realize it or not, you are incredibly privileged. You have a chance to make a difference in the world. If you are reading this book, you're probably either already in leisure and recreation or you are considering or preparing for a career in this field. But with that privilege comes an awesome responsibility: We can make decisions based only our own wants and needs, we can continue as before without thinking about our actions, or we can be part of creating a better world by actively deciding what we will do.

As society slowly but surely recognizes the importance of leisure and recreation, even more authority will be granted to us and even more will be expected of us. In that respect, times have never been better or worse for our field. Much promise and many challenges await leisure services personnel in every imaginable setting. You will need to carefully weigh the consequences of your decisions and actions, consider the obligations and rights of all people, and strive to live a virtuous life both professionally and privately.

Now that we have laid out the basic philosophical foundations and techniques for ethical decision making and discussed several key issues in leisure services, it is time to consider some real-life dilemmas.

Case Studies

TWELVE

Classroom ethics instruction has some obvious limitations. Teachers and students are only able to talk about ethical situations rather than experience them. While discussion is valuable, it is also important to deal with real ethical dilemmas. At the same time, on-the-job learning is also problematic. As we have seen, poor ethical decisions can lead to disastrous losses for organizations and pain for the individuals involved. We've tried to reach a productive middle ground with these case studies—they're real, but not so real that people actually suffer during the learning process. The following scenarios are fairly detailed and provide an opportunity to engage with real problems.

The cases are designed to be read, contemplated, and then discussed. Don't just shoot from the hip, so to speak, with your solutions to the problem; apply the ethical theories and concepts that we have used throughout the book. Questions at the end of each case study should facilitate discussion. And remember, practice really does make better, if not perfect.

Funding Conflicts: Heads You Lose, Tails You Lose

Lately, they seemed to be watching you. It was especially unnerving the other night. You had a lot of paperwork to do so you returned in the evening when everyone else had gone home so you could work without interruption. Although it was dark and bitterly cold outside, it was warm and bright in your office in the new outdoor center.

As you labored over the budget for next year, you had heard a faint rustling of papers. You looked up and saw a small field mouse scamper behind the pinecone display. Then your gaze was drawn to the upper portion of the west wall of the visitors' center—looking down at you were 40 sets of eyeballs. Some were large and boldly intimidating, some were small and shrewd, and some were narrow and predatory. For just a moment, an irrational fear fell on you. Then, feeling incredibly silly and a little embarrassed, you forced yourself to remember what they were: glass—not even carbon-based. Actually, the eyes were more lifeless than the pencil in your hand.

© Human Kinetics

Some people are uncomfortable with wildlife mounts.

These wildlife mounts were the gifts of Mrs. McCaffrey, the widow of Ronald E. McCaffrey. Ron was an avid outdoorsman and hunter. Six years ago, he passed away. Because he and his wife had no children, Mrs. McCaffrey donated land and money to construct and maintain a nature center.

Mrs. McCaffrey had contacted you about a new nature center. Actually, it was a stretch to even call the old building a nature center, as it was hardly big enough to hold any exhibits and it was crowded with more than 10 people. On your first visit to the McCaffrey mansion to discuss the possibility of a gift, you noticed a few wildlife mounts and mentioned them to Mrs. McCaffrey. "Oh my," she explained, "Ronnie was so proud of these. And this isn't even half of them. There are twice as many in other rooms. They are important to me because I know what they meant to Ronnie."

Over the next 6 months an agreement was reached. The McCaffrey estate would donate $5 million and 50 acres of land for the nature center. It would be operated by your organization, and because Mrs. McCaffrey had known and trusted you from the start, you would continue as director. There was to be a plaque recognizing the donation and the McCaffreys' lifelong commitment to outdoor conservation. Early on Mrs. McCaffrey stated that she would like to have several of the wildlife mounts in the new building for people to view. You recalled telling her that it would be impossible to display all of them. She had responded, "Well honey, I'm sure you could at least save one wall for them. Couldn't you?"

"Yes," you agreed, "we can put several of them up in a prominent place when we get the center built."

She went on to say that her husband had been especially proud of several of the larger head mounts as they were in record books, and she would like to see them displayed. You had thought at the time that it was a mixed blessing. The heads might be a hassle to maintain but they did have some educational value and they were part of a deal that would benefit the entire community. There was certainly no other way a new nature center was going to happen.

The first 2 years of operation came off without a flaw, but there had been an increasing number of complaints about the mounts over the past year. Last week a family had stopped by the center and looked at the displays of animal tracks, discarded antlers, snake skins, and tree identifications. The mother and father complimented you on the nature center but asked about the appropriateness of displaying the heads of deer, elk, and other animals. You explained the educational value of the animal mounts. "Well, it just seems so contradictory to what the center is all about," the father answered. "How can you talk about caring for nature and educating people and then have a wall full of the heads of dead animals?"

(continued)

(continued)

The family stayed for another 20 minutes but you could tell they were disturbed. You sensed that this might be the last time you would see them at the nature center. If it had been just this one isolated incident, you might not have thought much about it, but complaints of this sort were becoming frequent. You decided to broach the subject of removing the mounts with Mrs. McCaffrey.

She greeted you warmly and after a few pleasantries, you carefully raised the subject. "You know, some visitors to the nature center don't seem to appreciate the game mounts we have on the walls. They think it's inconsistent with the nature center. I've explained to them that game can be harvested without any negative effect on the species overall. I tell them that it's actually good to allow hunters to harvest game because the dollars they spend on equipment and licenses pays for habitat protection and research. But they just don't seem to understand, and we're losing a lot of visitors and creating a fair amount of ill will." After a long, uncomfortable pause you continued, "What do you think about taking down the mounts? We could replace them with pictures or even self-operated videos on the animals."

You were a little surprised by the force of her response. "Young man, I like you and I think you're doing a fine job at the nature center. But those mounts need to stay. Ronnie was so proud of them and I'm proud to have them over there. We have an agreement. One wall was to be reserved for them. I even agreed not to put all of them up but the ones that are there need to stay."

"I understand, Mrs. McCaffrey, but I was just thinking that we could—"

She cut you off midsentence. "Now listen to me. If those animal heads go, so does the money to maintain and operate the building. Good day, young man."

That was pretty much the end of the discussion. Now you are sitting in your office contemplating next year's already tight budget and feeling those creepy eyes staring down at you. Without the money from the McCaffrey endowment, this place simply could not stay open. Families would not have a place to come and learn firsthand about nature. Schools would not be able to take field trips here, either. Over the past 3 years you developed relationships with several teachers and they regularly brought children out to the center. That definitely wouldn't happen anymore. What are you going to do?

General Questions

- What aspects of this case are merely symptoms of the real problem?
- What components of this case are technical and what components are ethical?
- At what point in the chain of problems and symptoms can you effectively intervene?
- What are your available options?

Consequence-Based Questions

- What are the consequences of displaying or not displaying the mounts (long- and short-term)?
- Who will benefit and who will suffer if the mounts are displayed (long- and short-term)?

Rule-Based Questions

- To whom do you owe an obligation in this situation?
- Do you owe equal obligations to all parties involved?
- What are you required by law to do?
- What are you prohibited by law from doing?
- What are the expectations for directors of nature centers?
- What have others done in similar situations?

Virtue-Based Questions

- What virtues are relevant in this situation?
- How have you acted in a situation similar to this one? What did you learn from that experience?
- What would the most ethical person you know (e.g., professional mentor, community leader, religious leader) do in a similar situation?

Final Questions

- What ethical theories are relevant in this situation?
- What ethical approach has the most potential for solving this dilemma?

Pool Problems: In Over Your Head?

You hung up the phone after speaking to the mayor; the reality of the situation had not yet sunk in. As the superintendent of a medium-sized municipal park and recreation department, for the past 5 years you had been trying to persuade the city council that Sommerset Pool, a public facility built in the 1950s, was inadequate. A referendum to replace the pool with a modern water park was narrowly defeated during the last election. While you were able to keep the pool functioning by increasing maintenance, you knew that at some point in the near future the pool would either have to undergo major renovations or be replaced by a new facility.

In a shocking conversation earlier in the week, the pool supervisor, John Smithers, revealed to you that on many occasions the water quality of the pool fell well below legal requirements despite the best efforts of the staff. John indicated that old pumping and filtration equipment simply was too unreliable to eliminate contaminants. As the pool was the only public facility of its kind in the area, he had been reluctant to close the pool when the equipment malfunctioned. Instead, he had the maintenance staff fix the equipment as quickly as possible and then falsified the water quality records to hide the

© Human Kinetics

Safety concerns can interfere with the desire for new facilities.

problem. Initially, this solution seemed to work. However, in the last few months there had been a rise in the number of breakdowns, and some of the parents were beginning to question the staff about the pool's water quality when they noticed that their children were contracting an unusual number of swimming-related illnesses. The possibility that some of the more vocal parents were going to take their complaints to the media spurred John to tell you the true extent of the problems at the pool.

When you expressed your shock and dismay that John would falsify the pool records, he became quite agitated and argued that he and his staff had done their best in a difficult situation. The pool needed a completely new filtration system, not to mention repairs to the deck, change rooms, and pool liner. He reminded you that he had pleaded with you repeatedly to secure funds from the city to renovate the existing pool.

However, you had not been able to convince the city council to appropriate more money, as the city budget was under considerable strain due to the recent downturn in the local economy and because many of the members on the council had run on a platform of not raising taxes. In addition, supporters of a defeated water park referendum had advised you not to seek too many improvements for the present pool, as they were planning to hold a new referendum for the water park when the next municipal elections rolled around. Since you would much rather have an entirely new facility, you agreed that it was unwise to invest too heavily in the old pool.

Little did you imagine that the lack of renovations at the old pool would lead to a situation where patrons were periodically being exposed to health hazards! You knew you had to act quickly to protect the public, and you ordered the pool closed until further notice. The local media, of course, caught wind of the situation, and you had to give an interview to explain that some equipment problems at the pool necessitated its closing. When queried by reporters as to how long the problem existed, you simply answered that you ordered the closing immediately upon learning of the problem.

What was a bad situation suddenly became worse when the mayor called to find out what was going on. She and other council members were getting angry phone calls from parents, some of whom were threatening to sue the city because their children had become ill after using the pool. Others were calling because they were upset that their children's swimming lessons had been abruptly cancelled and there was no indication when the pool would reopen.

As the phone conversation began, the mayor asked you how long the pool needed to be closed and how much it would cost to fix it. You replied that the entire filtration system required an expensive overhaul that would take several weeks to install even after a contractor was authorized to do the work.

(continued)

(continued)

Upon learning that the city would have to find substantial funds to repair a pool that would have to be shut down for an extended period of time, the mayor's tone became accusatory. She asked why you had not foreseen a major breakdown like this and had not taken corrective action before now. More ominously, the mayor also wanted to know how long you had known that the water quality at the pool was not meeting health standards. Without mentioning the fact that you had only recently become aware of the situation yourself, you answered that the water quality problem had been going on for about 3 months. The mayor then bluntly said, "Three months! What kind of ship are you running over there?" She told you that you had better have some good answers at tomorrow's council meeting as they would be dealing with the pool issue as the first item of business.

As you pondered the unpleasant prospect of being grilled about closing the pool, you wondered who was really to blame for this fiasco. Certainly, you felt that fingers were being pointed at you when there were several other people who made decisions that helped create the situation in the first place. You did not want to incriminate your staff, but you had to ask yourself whether you should report John Smithers' actions to the city council. Although you were shocked that he would falsify the pool records, you also knew that he was a loyal, long-time employee who always tried to do what he thought was best for the department. If you revealed his actions to the council, he might be fired just a few years before retirement. Not only that, John's wife had ongoing health problems and he would lose his medical benefits if he were terminated. In any case, was it fair to blame John when he was not given sufficient resources to keep the pool safe? What about the politicians who refused to raise taxes to pay for the proper maintenance and renovation of public facilities? What about the voters who chose to defeat the referendum to build a new pool? You wondered if you should bear the blame for the unsafe conditions at the pool, or if you should identify others who were responsible as well.

As you thought about what to say at the upcoming council meeting you buried your face in your hands and asked yourself how you could have ever thought that a career in recreation would be fun.

General Questions

- What aspects of this case are merely symptoms of the real problem?
- What components of this case are technical and what components are ethical?
- At what point in the chain of problems and symptoms can you effectively intervene?
- What are your available options?

Consequence-Based Questions

- What are the consequences of telling the council about John's actions (long- and short-term)?
- Who will benefit and who will suffer if John's actions are revealed (long- and short-term)?

Rule-Based Questions

- To whom do you owe an obligation in this situation?
- Do you owe equal obligations to all parties involved?
- What are you required by law to do?
- What are you prohibited by law from doing?
- What are the guidelines for superintendents of public park and recreation departments?
- What are the guidelines for pool managers?
- What have others done in similar situations?

Virtue-Based Questions

- What virtues are relevant in this situation?
- How have you acted in a situation similar to this one? What did you learn from that experience?
- What would the most ethical person you know (e.g., professional mentor, community leader, religious leader) do in a similar situation?

Final Questions

- What ethical theories are relevant in this situation?
- What ethical approach has the most potential for solving this dilemma?

River Use: Rough Waters Ahead

"Last month, a bunch of rafters and kayakers got on the Little Rocky River at Sparks Junction and headed down toward Bud's Takeout. About 2 miles down the river some landowners put up a fence across the water to stop people from using the river. One of the kayakers slipped through an opening in the gate, and that's when all hell broke loose. One of the landowners was there and forced some of the rafters and kayakers to stop. As it turns out, they were the lucky ones. A few others got past and rafted on down the river. They have since been named in a lawsuit as trespassers. It's a mess and I need you to help me out on this one."

That's what Tom Platt, the state attorney general and a long-time friend, told you a couple of days ago. He knew you wouldn't enter the investigation with too many preconceived ideas. "I want you to take 3 weeks and give me a recommendation. Hire a couple of students if you need to for research. Weigh the pros and cons of each option and give me a recommendation that I can pass on to the governor. You've been on our rivers as much as anyone in the state and you're also the owner of a nice piece of property up in the mountains, so I think you can understand both sides of the issue."

"Tom," you responded, "I don't know much about this but I did hear some rumblings about a group of white-water rafters not being able to float a particular stretch of the Little Rocky. I had no idea it had become such a hot issue."

"Let me tell you, this thing is huge. We can't afford to make the wrong decision, because it will

© Eyewire/Photodisc/Getty Images

Ethical dilemmas can occur when people want to use public property such as a river for different activities.

affect every river in the state and businesses that directly and indirectly make a living off the river. But it also affects property owners all over the state."

A couple of days later you asked two of the best students in the parks and recreation department, Sue and Arthur, if they would be interested in helping you with the project. You laid out what you knew about the situation.

Sue spoke up quickly. "People have been rafting this state's rivers for decades. Why is it a problem now? It seems like a no-brainer to me. Surely people ought to be able to raft or kayak on the rivers if they want to."

"Well," you replied, "there's the issue of property owners' rights. We can't just forget them."

Arthur added, "I think I see the point. There are two different groups involved here, and each group has rights. Whose rights will win out?"

"That's where we come into the picture. Collect as much information about the situation as possible. We'll get back together 3 weeks from now and discuss it."

Three weeks later you all gathered in your office to discuss the issue. In addition to Sue and Arthur, Jim Nelson, one of your colleagues, agreed to sit in and act as an objective third party. Although Jim would never dream of rafting a river and he owns no property, he is the smartest person you know.

You asked Sue what she found. "It's just as I thought. People have been rafting the rivers in this state for a century. They're like roads. The people of the state own the waters and they own the rivers. I have to admit that state law isn't too clear on this. The way it's been handled for a long time is that if rafters don't touch the bank or even walk on the bottom of the river, they haven't committed criminal trespass."

Then Arthur offered his findings. "The landowners actually have a pretty good case, too. Several own land on both sides of the river and rafters have really interfered in the use of their land. I talked to a couple from Westville who bought 20 acres on one side of the river, and their land goes right up to the edge of the water. They will both be retiring next year. For the last 20 years they have been dreaming of a peaceful place on the Little Rocky River. Last spring they built a porch on their cabin with a great overlook on the river. In May they began going out on the porch, but 7 days a week from 8:00 a.m. until 5:00 p.m. boaters float by in a never-ending parade of bright rafts full of people yelling and screaming and having a good time. They don't mind people having a good time, but they shouldn't have to put up with that every day all day long."

Jim asked, "Do the boaters get out and walk on their land?"

"Sometimes they do get out of their rafts and kayaks. This couple has had to put up with people taking a leak in plain sight and leaving trash everywhere. They have posted signs asking boaters not to stop and get out, but some still do it anyway. But even if they don't stop, they still make a lot of noise and

(continued)

ruin the peace that these landowners desire—and have paid a lot for. It is an intrusion on private property, and that's protected under law."

Sue chimed in. "I can understand that rafters and kayakers could disrupt the solitude of the river, but that's just part of the deal. They should have known there would be boaters when they bought the land. If they wanted to be alone, they should have bought land back in the foothills. It's not like they're losing money. If landowners can stop people from using the river, there will be a huge financial loss for a lot of people. Twenty rafting companies operate on the Little Rocky. They generate about $250,000 each summer. All of the communities along the river and the state benefit from this."

Arthur reported the rest of his research. "I talked to some people from the Little Rocky River Fishing Club. They own land on both sides of the river. Members pay to have the exclusive right to fish a mile of river. Five years ago it wasn't quite so bad, but now it's different. Each time one of those bright yellow rafts or kayaks comes floating by with a bunch of yelling and splashing people, the trout don't bite for 15 minutes. You can see the problem when you realize that boats or kayaks come by every 2 minutes. The fishing is pretty lousy and this private company—that I might add, also pays taxes—is going under.

"And as long as we're talking about taxes," Arthur continued, "those landowners who own property along the river pay taxes on all of their land. Each rock or patch of dirt, even if it's underwater, is calculated into their taxes. That's part of the reason they think they have the right to use the land as they see fit."

Sue thought for a minute and asked, "Couldn't they put up signs asking rafters and kayakers to be quiet while they ride the river in this particular stretch of river? If nothing else, I'm sure that if we just get the landowners, business owners, and boat leaders together to talk about this, we can find some type of solution. These are reasonable people."

Jim spoke up. "There's always the temptation to try to sidestep the issue in these dilemmas. But you really can't. A hard decision has to be made. Signs haven't worked and they aren't likely to work in the future. As far as having a neighborly meeting and coming up with a friendly compromise—well, each side has too much invested in this. Believe me, there won't be any compromises."

"Great," you thought to yourself. "I need to make that recommendation this afternoon and I haven't decided a single thing yet."

General Questions

- What aspects of this case are merely symptoms of the real problem?
- What components of this case are technical and what components are ethical?

- At what point in the chain of problems and symptoms can you effectively intervene?
- What are your available options?

Consequence-Based Questions

- What are the consequences of recommending against the landowners (long- and short-term)?
- Who will benefit and who will suffer if the boaters are allowed to use the river (long- and short-term)?

Rule-Based Questions

- To whom do you owe an obligation in this situation?
- Do you owe equal obligations to all parties involved?
- What are you required by law to do?
- What are you prohibited by law from doing?
- What have others done in similar situations?

Virtue-Based Questions

- What virtues are relevant in this situation?
- How have you acted in a situation similar to this one? What did you learn from that experience?
- What would the most ethical person you know (e.g., professional mentor, community leader, religious leader) do in a similar situation?

Final Questions

- What ethical theories are relevant in this situation?
- What ethical approach has the most potential for solving this dilemma?

The Last Lynching: Legitimate Display or Debacle?

The grainy old photographs were as disgusting and as frightening as any you had ever seen. Although faded by decades of neglect, the horror came through plainly. The least damaged picture showed approximately 20 white men and a few boys standing in the foreground. It appeared to be springtime because the redbuds were in bloom but several other trees were only beginning to leaf out. Perhaps it had rained in the last day or so because water lay in the trail and mud was splattered on the boots and pants of the men and boys. In the background, the lifeless body of a black man hung on a thick rope from a limb of a gnarled oak tree. In the bottom left corner of the photo, just as on the other four pictures, was the simple inscription, *S. Jones 1921.*

You have been haunted by this picture ever since you first saw it 16 months ago. Only this morning did you realize that it was the faces of the men and boys that you found so disturbing. Expressions of pride, joy, confidence, and comradeship repulsed at the first glance. The underlying expressions of sheer ignorance took a little longer to come through, but now they seemed to overwhelm everything else. The men's expressions displayed an ignorance

© Arthur S. Aubry/Getty Images

A picture can cause a big ethical dilemma.

of the consequences of racial hatred, a disdain for state and federal laws, and a complete disregard for human suffering.

As the chair of the county historical society and director of the local museum, you were struck by the importance of designing an exhibit of the event that this picture represents. At the same time, you felt that perhaps such an exhibit should not be made because of its potential to create problems. But a decision had to be made and it had to be made by you.

It had long been rumored that the last lynching of a black man in this country took place in your community. Whether rumor or dark secret, such talk was limited to the bars and bedrooms. The topic was simply too volatile for polite or even not-so-polite conversation. That changed about a year and a half ago when you went through some books and photographs recovered from a downtown building that was scheduled for demolition. The shocking pictures were at the bottom of a box that was to be taken to the landfill later that afternoon.

It took you only one afternoon to put the pieces of the story together. Samuel Jones was a black man accused of various petty crimes such as trespassing and disturbing the peace, and law enforcement was looking for him for questioning. Unfortunately, Jones never turned up. Most people thought that he had gotten word that he was a suspect and had left the state. Jones' family maintained that the initial crime and his subsequent disappearance were extremely unlikely and that he had been murdered. In the ensuing 75 years no additional evidence had turned up on the case.

Although you hesitated to make the discovery public, you gave the photographs to the local police department. After a short but thorough investigation, they determined that all of the participants who could be recognized in the photograph were deceased. They brought no charges and returned the pictures to the historical society.

The community learned of the pictures during the investigation, and everyone in the town and the surrounding communities was affected. Emotions ranged from shame and sorrow to an open recognition bordering on pride that this county had the last lynching. You received unsolicited input from a number of people about the possibility of a display based on this episode that occurred 70 years before. Two visits stood out in your mind.

Christine Alderson, the president of the local chamber of commerce, stopped by 4 weeks ago. "Obviously," she began, "this is a terrible discovery, but with some imagination and solid promotion we can turn this into a benefit to the community. I don't have to tell you about the economy around here. Over the past 2 years we've lost nearly 500 jobs. Our folks are hurting and this could be a shot in the arm for our town. You can bet that a bunch of people would come to see a display on the last lynching. And that means jobs in hotels, restaurants, and other businesses."

(continued)

"Christine," you explained, "I'm fully aware that we need more jobs around here. I have friends who have lost their jobs, and I know we're at risk of losing our schools if we don't get this town back on its feet. But I'm not sure this is the way to do it."

"Well, what other ideas do you have? We're losing residents every day. I shouldn't tell you this, but Jacobs Manufacturing will close its doors in 6 months. I'm not saying we should design a glitzy display that makes this lynching out to be anything other than what it is—a disgusting event in our country's history. But it happened. Let's not bury this. We can make the best of a bad situation. You know how to do this tastefully. Of course it would be educational, and we'll put it in the context of changing racial relationships in our country. What would be wrong with that?"

Shortly afterward, three other community members, Sarah Manatow, Adelle Jones, and Byron Horton, visited you at home. Byron spoke first. "We know that you're considering a museum display about the lynching of Samuel Jones. I represent a large number of the black residents in our community and we think the display is a bad idea. Blacks in this community think that a display will only get people stirred up about the racial issues in this community that we're finally making some progress on. We know blacks were lynched and we don't need to be constantly reminded of it. I'm not asking you to bury it, but we sure don't need to make a big deal of it, either. Let's not perpetuate the image that we're trying to change. We have to move on with the healing process and put this behind us."

Then Byron turned to Sarah and Adelle and introduced them as descendents of Samuel Jones. "Ladies, would you share with the director what we discussed last evening?"

"Sir, we're asking you not to develop a display about the last lynching in the United States. Samuel Jones was our great grandfather. Other people in this town are related to him as well. This has been an emotional period for all of us. It is very painful to know that a family member was lynched by men who have great grandchildren still living right here today. We know that you're a decent person and would make every effort to keep a display of this awful act from becoming a spectacle. But we also know that marketers and others in this community wouldn't be so conscientious. Please, don't do it."

In the last 2 weeks you've pondered the issue. Should you develop a display about the lynching of Samuel Jones, the last lynching in the country? It happened and there can be no disputing the facts. A well-conceived display could remind people of the hatred that was directed toward black Americans. On the other hand, a display, regardless of how well it was done, could cause anguish for individuals and reopen community wounds that needed to heal.

General Questions

- What aspects of this case are merely symptoms of the real problem?
- What components of this case are technical and what components are ethical?
- At what point in the chain of problems and symptoms can you effectively intervene?
- What are your available options?

Consequence-Based Questions

- What are the consequences of creating or not creating the display (long- and short-term)?
- Who will benefit and who will suffer if a display is created (long- and short-term)?

Rule-Based Questions

- To whom do you owe an obligation in this situation?
- Do you owe equal obligations to all parties involved?
- What are you required by law to do?
- What are you prohibited by law from doing?
- What are the expectations for museum curators?
- What have others done in similar situations?
- The Auschwitz concentration camp in Germany has been turned into a museum. Is this right?

Virtue-Based Questions

- What virtues are relevant in this situation?
- How have you acted in a situation similar to this one? What did you learn from that experience?
- What would the most ethical person you know (e.g., professional mentor, community leader, religious leader) do in a similar situation?
- Is it always best to tell the whole truth?

Final Questions

- What ethical theories are relevant in this situation?
- What ethical approach has the most potential for solving this dilemma?

Athlete Conduct: Runner Stripped From Team

Wanda Nielson, the athletic director, asked you to give her your decision on the Linda Grabeck situation by this afternoon. This would not be an easy decision, but as the track coach at Carver State University you were obligated to do your best in matters like this. You had kicked athletes off the team before and it was never enjoyable, but sometimes it just had to be done.

Maybe it would have been better if you hadn't heard the news about one of the young women on the track team. But you did and now you had to exercise your judgment and decide what was best for the university, track team, Linda, and yourself. Making tough decisions was one of the things the university paid you to do.

You knew you would base your decision primarily on the facts. However, you were not so naive as to believe that values—yours and many others'—wouldn't play a part in this. One thing was certain, you couldn't afford to get carried away by the emotional elements of the case. The first thing to do was to review all of the available information.

© Human Kinetics

Student athletes have a responsibility to conduct themselves in such a way that does not reflect poorly on their team.

About a month ago, you heard by way of a couple of the university's baseball players that one of the runners on the women's track team was working as a stripper at the Flamingo Club, an all-nude nightclub in Pittsburg. After a little research you found that Linda Grabeck had indeed been employed as an exotic dancer at the club for a few months.

Although you didn't know Linda well, she seemed to be a nice young person. She was always friendly and you had not encountered any problems with her. You did recall that she had been raised in a tough environment and that

216

she was the first one in her family to go to college. She was married but didn't have children.

Linda Grabeck did not have an athletic scholarship; there simply weren't enough scholarships to go around. Until the NCAA relaxed the rules and allowed you to come up with more scholarships, that was the way it had to be.

When you spoke to Linda about your concerns, she was very open about her part-time job. She indicated that, of course, college was very expensive. Tuition and fees were high and the cost of books and other materials grew more expensive each year. Certainly jobs were available such as working at one of the many burger joints in the area. But Linda told you that she could make as much in a single night of nude dancing as she could make in a whole week of flipping burgers. She asked how people knew that she was a Carver State athlete because she never wore any clothing at the club to connect her to the university or the track team.

You assured her that these things had a way of getting around, and that some of the school's baseball players had been in the club and noticed her. Linda said it seemed unfair that the ballplayers had worn their Carver State caps and sweatshirts to the establishment and she was the one getting called in on the carpet. You said that may be true, but that was a different issue that someone else would have to deal with.

So that was her side of the story. Linda Grabeck was an exotic dancer but she was not trying to use her position as a member of the track team in any way to her advantage. She saw it as a simple case of economics. She needed the money for school and this was the best way to make it. Besides, as she commented, "A lot of college students do this." She went on to say that her job was part of her private life and on her own time. She was not an 18-year-old freshman. She was a young adult who was capable of weighing the advantages and disadvantages of working in an all-nude club. Furthermore, Linda suggested that there might be a double standard at the school if it was acceptable for male athletes to visit a strip club but not acceptable for female athletes to work there.

However, there were other serious issues that you could not ignore. Not only did you have a responsibility to Linda, you had a responsibility to the university, other members of the track team, and yourself. Carver State had a particular image that it had earned over the years. This was an institution that cared about its students. Parents liked the idea of sending their sons and daughters to a school that was reasonably conservative and fairly safe. That image would be harmed if people knew that the school's athletes were working as strippers in the local bars. You wondered how you would respond to the parents of a young woman you were recruiting if they asked about a member of the track team who worked as a stripper. You knew that some potential

(continued)

athletes would, probably with their parents' input, opt for another university. This was a competitive conference and you were evaluated and retained by the product you put on the field. The bottom line in this job was that you had to win. You had done pretty well so far as evidenced in the number of dual meet victories, high team finishes in tournaments, and place winners in conference and national competitions, but that could easily change without enough talent on the team.

People needed to remember that representing Carver State University as a student athlete was a privilege, not a right. As a coach you had the right to recruit and keep the track athletes you thought would do the best for the team regardless of how that was defined. You also recalled that you cut dozens of people in the past for a variety of reasons. Most were dropped because of poor sport performance, some were dismissed because of trouble in the classroom, and a few were asked to leave because they had gotten into trouble with local law enforcement.

The other members of the track team had a right to expect certain behavior from you and their teammates. Did this include keeping an adult entertainer on the team? Ever since you had been here and for several years before your arrival, the university had an athletic code of conduct. Each athlete had to read and sign the code. Linda Grabeck had signed the code when she made the decision to become part of the track team. As a matter of fact, you knew that the code of conduct was designed by the athletes themselves some time ago, so it certainly reflected their wishes. It clearly stated that athletes must conduct themselves in a manner that positively reflects on the athletic department both on and off the field. You knew you had the support of the athletic director and the university if you decided to ask Linda to either quit her job or leave the team.

Finally, you thought about your personal values on the issue. Yes, Linda was a nice young lady who worked hard on the track. She must be a reasonably good student, as you had never heard of her having any difficulties in the classroom. A college education was expensive and many students worked to pay the bills and not get too deeply into debt. But the vast majority did not work in all-nude nightclubs, and you were certainly not aware of any other athletes at the university who were adult entertainers. You had seen several Carver State students and student athletes working at the local McDonalds and you knew that some of your other runners held part-time jobs that paid minimum wage. They probably made a fifth of what an exotic dancer made. Was it really fair to them? In addition, unfortunately, people paint with broad brushes. Would Linda Grabeck's actions reflect negatively on the other athletes?

You had to make the decision. Would Linda have to choose between being on the track team and holding her job, or would you allow her to continue to work as a stripper and stay on the team?

General Questions

- What aspects of this case are merely symptoms of the real problem?
- What components of this case are technical and what components are ethical?
- At what point in the chain of problems and symptoms can you effectively intervene?
- What are your available options?

Consequence-Based Questions

- What are the consequences of allowing Ms. Grabeck to be on the track team while she works as a stripper (long- and short-term)?
- Who will benefit and who will suffer if Ms. Grabeck cannot be on the team and continue her chosen employment (long- and short-term)?

Rule-Based Questions

- To whom do you owe an obligation in this situation?
- Do you owe equal obligations to all parties involved?
- What are you required by law to do?
- What are you prohibited by law from doing?
- What are the expectations for college coaches?
- What have others done in similar situations?

Virtue-Based Questions

- What virtues are relevant in this situation?
- How have you acted in a situation similar to this one? What did you learn from that experience?
- What would the most ethical person you know (e.g., professional mentor, community leader, religious leader) do in a similar situation?

Final Questions

- What ethical theories are relevant in this situation?
- What ethical approach has the most potential for solving this dilemma?

Vacation: Granted or Not?

"No problem. I know what to do. I'll just look at our code of ethics. I'm glad I thought of that. For a minute, I thought I'd have to struggle over this dilemma for the next couple of days." That's what you said to yourself yesterday, but now that you had the code on your desk you were beginning to think that maybe instant answers from a code of ethics were a myth more than anything else.

A couple of days ago, your boss, Arlo Elliot, told you and a couple of other employees about the great time he and his wife had while skiing in Vail, Colorado. The snow conditions had been perfect and the days bright and sunny. But even more interesting were Arlo's stories about the place they

© Photodisc

Dilemmas occur when employees aren't completely honest in their requests for reimbursements for business travel.

stayed in Vail and the meals and nightly entertainment. It sounded like they had spared no expense. You went home wondering how people were able to afford vacations like that. The Elliots seemed to take such trips five or six times each year.

The vacations didn't seem to cut into Arlo's work at the New Horizons Therapeutic Center. He was the agency director and things had never been better for the agency and its clients. Arlo seemed capable of writing a successful grant a proposal like it was nothing. When you came on board as recreation director a year ago, a parent of one of the agency's clients had commented, "You're a lucky young lady. This is a solid outfit. You know, other places are having a tough time making it through these past 2 years. But not Horizons. It's Arlo. That guy has a gift for getting grant money. For us and for a lot of other folks, he's the best thing that has happened for a long time."

You reflected on the agency's wonderful recreation program. You had been the recreation director in previous facilities and no place had the activities and the facilities you had here. But a couple of weeks ago when you needed to retrieve some reimbursement forms you had filed, you noticed Arlo's reimbursement forms. A causal glance at the paperwork turned into a longer look. It seemed curious that Arlo had requested reimbursement for training that had supposedly taken place in San Francisco on the same dates that he and his wife had spent in Vail. As you did some quick calculations, it became obvious that Arlo and his wife had gone to San Francisco for only a day. Then they had flown to Vail for a week of skiing and the high life. There it was—a request for reimbursement for $3,528. Perhaps $1,500 went toward legitimate training, and the remaining $2,000 paid for a week's vacation for the Elliots. Two nights later an hour's investigative work turned up nearly $18,000 for Arlo Elliot's travel and lodging for training and meetings. You guessed that nearly $12,000 of that had gone into personal vacations for Arlo and his wife.

After a few days of internal debate, you decided to speak to Arlo about your discovery. After a few pleasantries, you got right to the point. "I've been checking some of the paperwork for training reimbursement and it looks like you've spent a lot of grant money on personal vacations. That money was designated for your training and the training of staff. Only some of your reimbursement was legitimately used for training."

Arlo confessed, "You're right. I used some of the money for a personal vacation. Not much but some. But let me tell you a few other things. Do you know what disabled people in this community did 15 years ago? Nothing. They sat, and if they were lucky they were able to watch TV. Most of them were from poor families and their parents couldn't afford to do anything for them. That is, assuming their families weren't too ashamed of them to even let people know they had a disabled person in their home. I saw that and I decided to do something about it. For the first 10 years here, I arranged work

(continued)

(continued)

opportunities, supervised the workshop, ran the assisted living program, and essentially begged for money from anyone who would listen to me.

"You know, I look back on those years and wonder how I ever survived. I worked 70 hours a week, 52 weeks a year. No vacations and no holidays. I didn't draw many paychecks for the first 3 years. There were a lot of months when there wasn't any money left over after I paid the people who worked for me. After that I got paid, but it was hardly anything at all. I qualified to get food stamps until 5 years ago. That's when I decided that if this place was going to survive, things would have to change. So I wrote grant proposals, and I got pretty good at it. We're doing very well. While other places are closing their doors and sending the disabled out on the streets, we're still going strong. I'm not boasting, but it's because of me. You haven't invested your money and yourself in this agency like I have. Yeah, I've taken a couple of vacations on grant money, but that's minor stuff compared to what I've done for our clients over the past 15 years.

"I suppose you can bring this to light. It wouldn't look good, and I would get fired. But the most important thing is what it will do to the people we work for—no employment opportunities and certainly no recreation opportunities. Go on home and think about what you're going to do. I'll see you tomorrow."

Should you tell Arlo that you can't just ignore what's been happening? Maybe you should tell him that nothing good can come of dishonest practices regardless of how beneficial they seem on the surface. Or maybe you should grow up and realize that this is the way the world works. Other people do it. As a matter of fact, it happens quite often, maybe not to the same extent, but certainly a lot of vacations are taken on company time. Should you focus on the big picture or the details?

General Questions

- What aspects of this case are merely symptoms of the real problem?
- What components of this case are technical and what components are ethical?
- At what point in the chain of problems and symptoms can you effectively intervene?
- What are your available options?

Consequence-Based Questions

- What are the consequences of exposing Arlo's vacations on grant funds (long- and short-term)?
- Who will benefit and who will suffer if Arlo is no longer with the agency (long- and short-term)?

Rule-Based Questions

- To whom do you owe an obligation in this situation?
- Do you owe equal obligations to all parties involved?
- What are you required by law to do?
- What are you prohibited by law from doing?
- What are the expectations for recreation directors in facilities for disabled people?
- What have others done in similar situations?

Virtue-Based Questions

- What virtues are relevant in this situation?
- How have you acted in a situation similar to this one? What did you learn from that experience?
- What would the most ethical person you know (e.g., professional mentor, community leader, religious leader) do in a similar situation?

Final Questions

- What ethical theories are relevant in this situation?
- What ethical approach has the most potential for solving this dilemma?

Resource Rationing: Happy Trails to You

You were really getting a dose of reality in this internship. The first 13 weeks of your internship at the Granada Park District were great. Most of the people you worked with were wonderful. Mr. Driskill, your immediate supervisor, told you a few weeks ago that a position would be opening up soon. He mentioned that the job could be yours if you continued to do a good job in the internship. It is the position you have been working toward for 6 years.

Then Mr. Driskill added, "You know, we have a real mess over at Citizens' Park. Everyone wants to use all of the trails in the park. Maybe they should be able to, because they all pay taxes. But bicyclists, walkers, and horse riders don't exactly mix. Get back to me after you've had a chance to look it over and let me know what you think we should do with those trails. Those folks don't seem to get along any better in an office than they do on a trail. I tried to sit down with them to see if we could smooth things out last spring. I thought they were going to kill each other." After a pause, he said quietly, "By the way, I happen to know that if you make a good decision on this one, you're in as far as the job goes. If you blow it . . ." His voice trailed off, but you could figure out what he meant.

You stammered, "Thanks, Mr. Driskill. That would be great. I would love to get that job. Do you have any ideas where I might start on this trail thing?"

© Human Kinetics

Too many users of an outdoor resource can create conflict and environmental damage.

"You should probably start by looking at our mission statement. Any solution you come up with has to fit with that statement. Then I would suggest that you speak to some of the key players for each of the interested parties."

It had not taken you long to find the agency's mission statement: *It is the mission of the Granada Park District to offer all of its citizens quality recreation opportunities regardless of age, gender, race, or ability.* The mission addressed differences in age, gender, race, and ability but it didn't say anything about providing recreation for people with different interests. Since the mission statement wasn't very helpful, your next move was to find out about the trails and Citizens' Park.

Citizens' Park, nearly 1,000 acres of rolling hills and valleys, was the most popular park in your agency. Like most public areas, it didn't just happen. The park was the result of years of hard work and sacrifice by many community groups and individuals. Although the park was used all year long, the spring and fall were the busiest times. As a matter of fact, it appeared to you that the park had either reached or exceeded its carrying capacity. Because of this, you could not afford to make a decision that would adversely affect the park and its trails.

When you spoke to Buck Jones, the president of the saddle-riding group, he was adamant about the group's right to ride their horses on the trail. "We have no other place to ride except Citizens' Park. It has wonderful trails, which, by the way, we helped build a few years ago. The park district asked for groups to help build new trails and fix the old ones. A bunch of us showed up and worked for more than a month in the evenings and on the weekends. That's a lot of time to give up. Besides, we pay the same property taxes as anyone else in town, and we deserve to use that park. And not just a few hours a week, either. We want to use the park's trails during the prime times. I know that some people have complained that they're frightened by the horses. But I have to remind you that those darned bikes scare the hell out of our horses."

Ann Stires, an informal spokesperson for the bikers, was equally intense when you spoke to her regarding the park usage. "Bikes don't do the kind of damage that horses do. Maybe we leave a rut or two, but for the past few years we've done quite a bit of trail maintenance. Without our annual work days at the park and financial contributions, I don't believe you folks could keep the park and its trails in as good of shape as they're in right now. You know those nice signs along the trails? One of our members makes those at home. He doesn't get a dime for it. If you're looking for the bike riders to just roll over and leave the trails to walkers and horses, you can forget it. It's not going to happen."

While there was no organized group for trail walkers, it was obvious that more people used the trails for walking than biking or horseback riding combined. They were the silent majority that weren't often heard but had some legitimate concerns about the condition and safety of the park trails. Some walkers had complained about nearly getting run over by "crazy riders on

(continued)

bikes," and others had commented on the damage done by horses on muddy trails.

It was obvious that things could not go on much longer as they were. Trail usage was increasing, and with that increase came deterioration. It was inevitable that there would be collisions between horses, bikes, and walkers. Something had to change.

General Questions

- What aspects of this case are merely symptoms of the real problem?
- What components of this case are technical and what components are ethical?
- At what point in the chain of problems and symptoms can you effectively intervene?
- What are your available options?

Consequence-Based Questions

- What are the consequences of leaving things the way they are (long- and short-term)?
- Who will benefit and who will suffer if nothing is done (long- and short-term)?

Rule-Based Questions

- To whom do you owe an obligation in this situation?
- Do you owe equal obligations to all parties involved?
- What are you required by law to do?
- What are you prohibited by law from doing?
- What are the expectations for interns?
- What have others done in similar situations?
- Is this a wonderful opportunity or an unsolvable quandary?

Virtue-Based Questions

- What virtues are relevant in this situation?
- How have you acted in a situation similar to this one? What did you learn from that experience?
- What would the most ethical person you know (e.g., professional mentor, community leader, religious leader) do in a similar situation?

Final Questions

- What ethical theories are relevant in this situation?
- What ethical approach has the most potential for solving this dilemma?

Sponsorship Versus Personal Beliefs: Little League, Big Problem

The Little League sponsorship problem had been on your mind for several weeks, and as you sat in the Russeltown Little League Board of Directors' meeting, you realized it was crunch time. Ever since you became aware of the situation, you were certain of the course of action the Little League should take. Unfortunately, your "certainty" vacillated from one option to another. Being open-minded and willing to listen to the different sides of the issue, you heard a lot of discussion about sponsorship and you were not yet convinced of the right course of action. Although initially it may have seemed like a minor problem, many people in the community were upset. Everyone had an opinion. A few times you wondered if it was such a great idea to agree to serve on the Little League board. But you made a commitment last year and you were going to honor it, which meant making the best decisions you could make.

For the hundredth time, you reviewed the events that led to tonight's board meeting. You first heard about the sponsorship issue at the beginning of the

© Human Kinetics

Team sponsorship can cause problems when some team members object to the sponsor.

(continued)

(continued)

season from one of the coaches in the league. After the game, the coach mentioned that a player on an opposing team had been taping over the name of the sponsor on the back of her jersey. The officials let her play the games up to that point, but they said that a decision on her action would have to be made for the rest of the season. The coach mentioned this could be trouble. You shrugged it off, expecting the coaches and officials to deal with it. The participants in the league—coaches, officials, and players—knew the league's rules prohibiting the altering of jerseys, and you expected that this situation would be readily resolved.

Boy, were you wrong! When you turned on the radio a few mornings later you were surprised that the topic of discussion was the Little League player who refused to wear a shirt bearing the name of a tavern. More shocking than the topic, however, was the intensity of the discussion. The calls seemed evenly divided: Some people thought the player should be admired for standing up for her principles, while others thought it was just a publicity stunt that would embarrass the league and the community.

Over the next week you learned that the player at the center of the controversy was Karen Newton, an above-average player who had been in the league for 7 years. Karen played on the team sponsored by the Drop-Inn Tavern and, as far as you were aware, she had never been involved in any problems during that time. Players were expected to wear their jerseys for the games. Occasionally, players were unable to wear their jerseys because they forgot them or they were in the wash. Those explanations were accepted as long as they didn't happen too often. However, the current circumstances were different. Karen wore the shirt but put tape over the sponsor's name on the back of the shirt. She had been asked to remove the tape and had refused. Having never encountered a situation like this before, the coach of the Drop-Inn team and the game officials didn't know what to do.

The Drop-Inn, a faithful sponsor of Russeltown Little League teams for over 20 years, was a well-known restaurant and tavern in the community. The owners had children of their own who had played in the league, and they had come forward to do their civic duty. In addition, the Drop-Inn had helped other community sport programs in many ways. While you weren't close friends with the owners of the business, you believed them to be decent people who were genuinely interested in Russeltown's young people. Currently, they were sponsoring two teams at a cost of $500.00.

At the beginning of tonight's meeting, Michael Lippner, the chair of the board, gave you and the rest of the board members the details as he knew them. He had spoken to the Drop-Inn Tavern's managers, Karen Newton, Karen's mother, and representatives in the national Little League office, and he had a good understanding of the situation. Michael indicated this would be a difficult decision, as there were convincing arguments on both sides of the issue.

One certainly had to admire a young person for standing up for what she believed. It would have been easier for her to just wear the shirt and not say anything. But Karen would have had to live with that, just as we all must live with the decisions we make. Karen had stated that she learned in school that the use of alcohol was not good for kids. As a matter of fact, a local doctor had talked about the health dangers of drinking alcohol and an officer from the police department had spoken about why it was illegal for young people to use alcohol. It seemed to Karen and her mother that an outlet for liquor might be using kids as walking billboards for a product that could ruin lives and even cause death.

Karen's mother had asked if an exception could be made, as youngsters in other youth ball programs had been granted waivers on uniforms. In one case, a young player's religion required a high level of modesty and the shorts that were part of the official uniform were considered offensive. The parents had requested and been given permission for their child to wear long pants for the games. In another case, a Jewish boy had to wear his yarmulke during the game, and a waiver was granted in that instance as well. If something similar could not be arranged, Karen's mother offered to contribute $250 to sponsor the team. Or maybe, she suggested, her daughter could be moved to another team. As you listened, you agreed that the girl and her mother had some good arguments.

"On the other hand," Michael said, "there are good reasons for not allowing exceptions to the rules." He pointed out that exceptions should always be considered carefully. They set precedence and increase the chance that others will choose to defy rules in the future. Other players and families could make the same request and defeat the purpose of even having game uniforms. Someone commented that the shirt didn't actually have the word *alcohol* on it. Did that make a difference?

One board member asked, "Where do we draw the line? Grocery stores, pizza places, and other restaurants that sponsor teams sell alcohol. Will we need to ban them? And what if someone objected to another advertiser for personal reasons? What then?"

Another board member said, "Hey, this is a little town. Our programs depend on the good will of its people and organizations. We can't afford to cave in to this request. If we kick out the Drop-Inn Tavern, we'll scare away other sponsors and you all know we can't run the program without sponsors. Each year we sit down and try to make the money go as far as possible. We can't charge kids who want to play any more than we already do. This is a good program and we aren't going to lose it over one person."

Finally, an older gentleman stated, "I've been involved with this ball program for 25 years. There were times when we didn't know how we were going to make it. I remember, and I am sure some of you can too, that the owners

(continued)

of the Drop-Inn and other folks like them saved this league. If you don't allow them to help now, you'll be slapping them in the face."

The board president added, "The national office has no bans on advertisements like this—they leave it up to us. So, we aren't going to get any help from them. And before someone suggests it, moving the young lady to another team is not a solution. We can't move her because the season is half over, and even if we could, it's only a temporary solution. Besides, do we really want to set the precedent of moving kids from team to team every time someone doesn't want to follow a rule?"

"Well," Michael said, "it's time to make a decision. It's pretty obvious that we don't have any 'bad guys' in this situation. We have a young lady who wants to play softball but has strong convictions about the use and promotion of alcohol. At the same time, the folks who own and operate the Drop-Inn are just trying to support the program and the community. It looks like whatever we do, we'll have some upset people. I believe the best way to do this is to go around the table and ask each member of the board if we should or should not make an exception to our rule of not altering the team uniforms."

"Please start us off," says Michael, gesturing toward you. "What do you think?"

General Questions

- What aspects of this case are merely symptoms of the real problem?
- What components of this case are technical and what components are ethical?
- At what point in the chain of problems and symptoms can you effectively intervene?
- What are your available options?

Consequence-Based Questions

- What are the consequences of making an exception to the rule (long- and short-term)?
- Who will benefit and who will suffer if there is no exception to the rule (long- and short-term)?

Rule-Based Questions

- To whom do you owe an obligation in this situation?
- Do you owe equal obligations to all parties involved?
- What are you required by law to do?
- What are you prohibited by law from doing?
- What are the guidelines for volunteer board members?
- What have others done in similar situations?

Virtue-Based Questions

- What virtues are relevant in this situation?
- How have you acted in a situation similar to this one? What did you learn from that experience?
- What would the most ethical person you know (e.g., professional mentor, community leader, religious leader) do in a similar situation?

Final Questions

- What ethical theories are relevant in this situation?
- What ethical approach has the most potential for solving this dilemma?

Appendix: Codes of Ethics

To help readers better understand the value and the limitations of codes of ethics, we're providing two of them in this appendix. The following pages contain the code of ethics for the American Therapeutic Recreation Association and the code of ethics for the National Therapeutic Recreation Society. Readers would benefit from examining both codes for similarities and differences.

In addition, we're including a link to the Web site of the National Recreation and Park Association/American Association for Leisure and Recreation (NRPA/AALR) Council on Accreditation: www.nrpa.org/content/default.aspx?documentId=1037. The site offers a valuable overview of the accreditation process, along with the 2004 Council on Accreditation standards. A careful reading of the standards will show that studying and understanding the contents of this book will partially contribute to the meeting of several standards.

The authors wish to thank the American Therapeutic Recreation Association and the National Therapeutic Recreation Society for permission to reprint their codes of ethics.

National Therapeutic Recreation Society Code of Ethics (approved, 1990) and Interpretive Guidelines (approved, 1994)

A special publication of the National Therapeutic Recreation Society

National Recreation and Park Association
22377 Belmont Ridge Road
Ashburn, VA 20148-4501
703-858-0784
Fax: 703-858-0794

e-mail: NTRSNRPA@nrpa.org
Copyright © 1994
Second Printing: April, 1998
Revision, October, 2001
All rights reserved

For more information on the use and intention of the Code, visit the Web site at www.nrpa.org/content/default.aspx?documentId=867.

Preamble

Leisure, recreation, and play are inherent aspects of the human experience, and are essential to health and well-being. All people, therefore, have an inalienable right to leisure and the opportunities it affords for play and recreation. Some human beings have disabilities, illnesses, or social conditions which may limit their participation in the normative structure of society. These persons have the same need for and right to leisure, recreation, and play.

Accordingly, the purpose of therapeutic recreation is to facilitate leisure, recreation and play for persons with physical, mental, emotional or social limitations in order to promote their health and well-being. This goal is accomplished through professional services delivered in clinical and community meetings. Services are intended to develop skills and knowledge, to foster values and attitudes, and to maximize independence by decreasing barriers and by increasing ability and opportunity.

The National Therapeutic Recreation Society exists to promote the development of therapeutic recreation in order to ensure quality services and to protect and promote the rights of persons receiving services. The National Therapeutic Recreation Society and its members are morally obligated to contribute to the health and well-being of the people they serve. In order to meet this important social responsibility, the National Therapeutic Recreation Society and its members endorse and practice the following ethical principles.

The Preamble to the Code of Ethics presents the central values and ideals of the Society which express the commitment of the profession to the common good. The professions differ from commercial enterprises because of the altruistic values which shape their relationship to society. These values are fundamental to an understanding of therapeutic recreation. Since the purpose of the profession is to serve the public interest, issues of personal advancement, or even the advancement of the profession are secondary to the purpose of the Society indicated in the Preamble.

In order to fulfill its obligations to promote leisure values in society, and to facilitate the leisure, recreation, and play for persons with limitations, members of the National Therapeutic Recreation Society obligate themselves to be bound by specific ethical principles.

I. The Obligation of Professional Virtue

Professionals possess and practice the virtues of integrity, honesty, fairness, competence, diligence, and self-awareness.

A. Integrity

Professionals act in ways that protect, preserve and promote the soundness and completeness of their commitment to service. Professionals do not forsake nor arbitrarily compromise their principles. They strive for unity, firmness, and consistency of character. Professionals exhibit personal and professional qualities conducive to the highest ideals of human service.

The virtue of integrity creates moral coherence. As its name suggests, it is the ability to integrate multiple moral obligations and commitments into a balanced whole. For example, commitment to the advancement of the profession would not outweigh concern for the leisure needs of deprived groups within the population, or specific duties to clients. A professional of integrity is characterized by wholeness, a consistent incorporation of all parts of practice into a moral totality.

Although the private practice of virtue is a personal matter, in the fulfillment of professional responsibilities, members of the Society are required to maintain the highest standards of personal conduct. Each member should distinguish clearly between statements and actions made as a private citizen and those made as a representative of the profession or member of NTRS. Therapeutic recreation professionals should be alert to and resist any pressures that interfere with the exercise of professional discretion and impartial judgment in carrying out professional functions. They should likewise avoid any actions which may reduce the public trust in the profession. It is not an objective of NTRS to achieve growth in the number of members at the expense of professional standards, but rather to encourage more qualified individuals to meet the high standards which have always characterized the Society.

B. Honesty

Professionals are truthful. They do not misrepresent themselves, their knowledge, their abilities, or their profession. Their communications are sufficiently complete, accurate, and clear in order for individuals to understand the intent and implications of services.

Therapeutic recreation professionals shall not engage in any act or omission of a dishonest, deceitful or fraudulent nature. They should neither misrepresent nor conceal a fact or information which is material to determining the suitability, efficacy, scope, or limitations of service.

Far from misrepresenting qualifications, the members of the Society make every effort to be accurate and objective in describing the scope and limits of their professional service, affiliations, and functions. They base any public statements about services and outcomes on scientifically acceptable findings and techniques, with full recognition of the limits and uncertainties of such evidence. Practitioners accept the obligation to correct those who misrepresent the qualifications and functions of therapeutic recreation professionals. Since the general public will have difficulty distinguishing between NTRS and ATRA, it may become increasingly necessary to explain the differences between them.

C. Fairness

Professionals are just. They do not place individuals at unwarranted advantage or disadvantage. They distribute resources and services according to principles of equity.

The principle of justice requires professionals to treat equitably all those with whom they are involved—clients, colleagues, agencies and any other associates. In times of economic austerity, this ethical principle can be extremely demanding. For example, while the good of the client clearly requires that all professions operate in a spirit of cooperation, economic constraints can generate a spirit of interdisciplinary competition which works against the fair and equitable distribution of available resources.

Affirmative action guidelines in hiring and promotion of staff, as well as in selection and treatment of clients, are not simply legal issues. Meeting minimal standards set by law may not suffice for ethical practice, which looks beyond the sanction of law to a spirit of justice in providing access equally to all. Thus, it is not enough not to refuse a minority applicant a position, or a promotion; we must actively recruit a pool of minority candidates, and once they are hired, we must provide them with the professional development opportunities which will enable them to meet promotion standards.

Competing claims among clients, both individuals and groups, pose many an ethical dilemma for the therapeutic recreation professional seeking to serve conscientiously. Cuts in funding and in personnel mean that staff are asked to do more with less; at times an impossible task, where quality of service is sometimes pitted against quantity of clients served. For example, in times of fiscal austerity, therapeutic recreation staff may be required to cut back on some of their more specialized programs which seem to be very effective with selected groups of clients, in order to offer general programs serving larger groups.

Those in administrative positions have a special responsibility to ensure that staff are treated fairly in the allocation of resources, including opportunities for development and training. Furthermore, supervisors need to be alert to the possibility that some staff are asked to bear more of the burdens of stress and burn-out which result from reduction in resources.

D. Competence

Professionals function to the best of their knowledge and skill. They only render services and employ techniques of which they are qualified by training and experience. They recognize their limitations, and seek to reduce them by expanding their expertise. Professionals continuously enhance their knowledge and skills through education and by remaining informed of professional and social trends, issues and developments.

Every member has the obligation to grow in knowledge and in capacity to respond to the specific societal needs served by the profession. This means much more than learning new skills, techniques, or programs of intervention, important as those are. It suggests, too, that practitioners have the obligation to wrestle with philosophical questions which shape decisions made by the profession as it grows in response to changes in the world around it.

The concept of continuing education reaches far beyond the narrow counting of points gathered as a means of compliance; rather, the ideal ethical practice requires that the professional be on the cutting edge of discovery, eager to learn more about client groups being served, about new ways of contributing to leisure, alert for possibilities of enhancing the general quality of life through leisure.

When the increasing complexity of human service delivery places professionals in a situation which may exceed their level of competence, they must exercise judgment in accepting responsibilities, seeking appropriate consultation, and assigning responsibilities to other therapeutic recreation practitioners. Similarly, professionals who find that they lack the competence or experience necessary to perform functions assigned them have the obligation to refuse such assignments, for the client's protection and their own. Thus, for example, an inexperienced therapeutic recreation worker who is asked to fill in on a unit with severely incapacitated clients must make it clear that she or he is not prepared to deal with such clients without very close supervision, and, if pressed, must refuse the assignment.

E. Diligence

Professionals are earnest and conscientious. Their time, energy and professional resources are efficiently used to meet the needs of the persons they serve.

The public has a right to expect of a professional not only competence, in the sense of abilities, but also diligent performance, in the sense of consistently applying those abilities in serving their clients. Furthermore, professionals are obligated to support efforts to effect such improvements in procedure as will benefit the client and increase the overall efficiency of therapeutic recreation service.

Sometimes connotations generated around the concept of leisure lead others to perceive the profession as one which does not take seriously responsibilities of the workplace. Indeed, the element of the "non-serious" can give the profession a distinct advantage in working with some clients, particularly in clinical settings. It would be a mistake, however, for therapeutic recreation professionals to fail to see themselves as seriously committed to their work—to the clients, and to the agencies, whom they serve. Particularly in times of budgetary restrictions, every profession has the duty to demonstrate careful stewardship of resources, so that optimal service gains may be preserved.

It is important to note, in this context, that diligent effort is not equated with a stressful over-extension; indeed, prudence would suggest that diligent effort has more to do with consistent, well-organized allocation of energies, than with frantic efforts to make up for periods of negligence. An abiding sense of accountability will lead to efficient and effective utilization of available resources for maximum client benefit.

F. Awareness

Professionals are aware of how their personal needs, desires, values, and interests may influence their professional actions. They are especially cognizant of where their personal needs may interfere with the needs of the persons they serve.

Since the therapeutic relationship plays an important role in treatment, all professionals have the obligation to take the measure of their own strengths, and of those areas in themselves which need strengthening. The therapist holds a position of power. In order that power be used to help and not to harm clients, professionals need to assess carefully and honestly that power, and their reaction to it. Emotional maturity, patience, the ability to be open to many different kinds of persons, give and receive constructive suggestions—these qualities are sometimes taken for granted until tested in a demanding work scene.

An important attribute required of the helping professional is the ability to leave personal problems outside the therapeutic relationship. Without this quality of congruence, the professional runs the risk of using clients to meet personal needs, something which is contrary to the ethical principle of respect for persons.

II. The Obligation of the Professional to the Individual

A. Well-Being

Professionals' foremost concern is the well-being of the people they serve. They do everything reasonable in their power and within the scope of professional practice to benefit them. Above all, professionals cause no harm.

Therapeutic recreation professionals enter into or continue professional relationships based on their ability to meet the needs of clients appropriately. Similarly, they terminate service and professional relationships which are no longer required or which cease to serve the client's best interests. Recognizing that the private and personal nature of the therapeutic relationship may unrealistically intensify clients' feelings toward them, they take special efforts to maintain professional objectivity. They are careful to avoid, and do not initiate, personal relationships or dual roles with clients.

Appropriate settings are chosen for one-on-one interactions, in order to protect both the client and the professional from actual or imputed physical or mental harm.

When the client's condition indicates that there is clear and imminent danger to the client or others, the therapeutic recreation professional must take reasonable personal action or inform responsible authorities. Consultation with other professionals must be used where possible. The assumption of responsibility for the client's behavior must be taken only after careful deliberation.

A professional who knows that he or she has an infectious disease, which if contracted by another would pose a significant risk, should not engage in any activity which creates a risk of transmission of that disease to any others with whom he or she would come in contact. The precautions taken to prevent the transmission of a contagious disease to others should be appropriate to the seriousness of the disease and must be particularly stringent in the case of a disease that is potentially fatal.

B. Loyalty

Professionals' first loyalty is to the well-being of the individuals they serve. In instances of multiple loyalties, professionals make the nature and the priority of their loyalties explicit to everyone concerned, especially where they may be in question or in conflict.

Professionals serving in group settings may sometimes find themselves expected to balance a number of competing loyalties—to a large number of residents/patients, to family members or surrogates, to the administrators of the service facility, to the funding source, to the accrediting agency. They are careful to clarify, first to themselves, then to all parties involved, the primacy of their loyalty to patients/residents, while at the same time honoring obligations to other claimants.

When serving individuals with diminished competence, who are represented by surrogates, the professional is careful to honor the interests and concerns of the client, insofar as these can be determined, above those of the surrogate. It happens sometimes that family members and surrogates have their own agendas which do not necessarily match those which the client has evidenced in the past.

When procedures mandated by regulating agencies seem not to be in the best interests of clients, professionals have the obligation to make this known, and to make every effort to facilitate appropriate changes in the regulation.

C. Respect

Professionals respect the people they serve. They show regard for their intrinsic worth and for their potential to grow and change. The following areas of respect merit special attention:

1. **Freedom, Autonomy, and Self-Determination:** Professionals respect the ability of people to make, execute, and take responsibility for their own choices. Individuals are given adequate opportunity for self-determination in the least restrictive environment possible. Individuals have the right of informed consent. They may refuse participation in any program except where their welfare is clearly and immediately threatened and where they are unable to make rational decisions on their own due to temporary or permanent incapacity. Professionals promote independence and interdependence as appropriate for each individual. They avoid fostering dependence and other behaviors that manipulatively control individuals against their will or best interests. In particular, sexual relations with clients is expressly unethical.

   Professionals recognize the obligation to do good for their clients, but the question of who decides what is in the client's best interests is not so easily answered. Precisely because of their knowledge and competence, and because they want to do good, many professionals find themselves slipping into an attitude of paternalism toward clients. Fostering independence, self-determination, and autonomy is sometimes a labor-intensive process. It is much easier and quicker to make choices for a client whose processes may be slower, or whose confidence may be faltering. Sometimes too, in response to their limiting condition, clients develop a relationship of dependency which the professional who lacks insight may find flattering. Such attitudes and behaviors are not ethically acceptable in any profession, but in therapeutic recreation they are especially to be avoided, since the heart of play, leisure, and recreation is freedom.

In every treatment plan, the client should be closely involved, and in fact, as far as is reasonably possible, should play the primary role in determining treatment goals. Because the profession tends to follow a medical model—a model which has publicly acknowledged the need to correct its own paternalistic approach—there is often an attempt to prescribe recreation for clients. Respect for client autonomy would suggest that this be done only in those very rare situations where clients are not able to make their own choices.

There are, indeed, very few clients who are not able to participate at any time, in any way, in decisions regarding their treatment. Professionals sometimes engage in labeling clients as incompetent on the basis of superficial assessments or incorrect diagnoses. Labeling, whether spoken, written, or thought, can be very harmful to clients, either because the client internalizes the label and acts in accordance with it, or because the professional reduces quality of life expectations for the labeled client, and thus does not engage in serious rehabilitative efforts which might, in fact, improve client functioning.

In some cases, the nature and extent of impairment may be so severe as to justify imposition of the professional's judgment on a client. Discernment is needed in such cases, and in making a judgment of this sort, priority should always be given to the possibility that the client's decision-making capacity is operational.

One facet of respect for personal autonomy is the provision of information necessary to consent to treatment. Legally, this process can be reduced to a routine signing of a standard form, but ethical practice requires full explanation of treatment procedures, expected outcomes, and options, including the option of refusing treatment.

The continuum of service delivery followed in therapeutic recreation ranges from programs for clients with serious limitations (assuming that these are genuine, and not the result of incorrect labeling) to those for clients with only mild limits to functioning. Ethical practice would encourage clients, whenever possible, to move along the treatment continuum until they are able to manage their own leisure. Freeing clients from the need for professional intervention is the goal of every profession. To the extent that clients require treatment, the professional must provide it thoroughly, but always with the underlying objective of client empowerment.

Professionals need to recognize and carefully protect boundaries between themselves and their clients, as well as those between client and client. In cases where the limiting condition of clients may be centered precisely in the ability to set and maintain appropriate boundaries, professionals have the obligation to exercise special care, lest their communication of respect and support be misinterpreted by the client.

Any sexual exchange between professional and client is clearly unethical, as the Code notes. However, sexual needs of clients, even those with severe limitations, are very real, and need to be recognized. Special precautions must be taken when working with those who are not fully capable of making decisions about the exercise of their sexuality. Staff need to be fully aware of their responsibility in this area, and must be educated thoroughly in this, as in other aspects of client background. In other cases, the right to sexual expression between consenting adult clients is not always respected by professionals in some service settings. In fact, at times clients who choose to engage in appropriate sexual relations with other clients are treated with ridicule by staff who are not emotionally mature enough to deal with this choice, or whose personal value system might not support such behavior. This very delicate area of personal choice can be particularly problematic in the institutional setting, and requires very sensitive handling by professionals.

Although the need for scientific research in the field is recognized, clients may not be pressed into participation, either by coercion or persuasion. Legislation on the rights of human subjects attempts to protect against such abuses of authority, especially with vulnerable populations, but ethical practice requires, further, that professionals not exploit their special relationship with clients for the purpose of gaining knowledge, however valuable, let alone for personal prestige.

2. **Cultural Beliefs and Practices:** Professionals respect cultural diversity and provide services that are responsive to the cultural backgrounds and needs of clients. They use "person-first" language to acknowledge and honor individual uniqueness above any disability, illness, impairment, or condition.

3. **Privacy:** Professionals respect the privacy of individuals. Communications are kept confidential except with the explicit consent of the individual or where the welfare of the individual or others is clearly imperiled. Individuals are informed of the nature and the scope of confidentiality.

   The value placed on privacy varies greatly among people of different personality type, family background, and ethnic group. This does not usually present serious ethical problems in dealings among peers; but in the therapeutic setting, professionals hold power over clients, and are in a position to impose their values. They thus have the obligation to be cognizant of the many different ways of viewing privacy and to carefully guard the spatial and informational privacy of those they serve. Since much information of a very private nature is needed in order to offer effective treatment, great pains must be taken to share that information only with other professionals, and then on a need-to-know basis. Although the law protects confidentiality of patient information, ethical practice requires that such information be held in a spirit of reverence.

   Interviews, which often deal with confidential matters, are to be conducted in places where not only is the information safeguarded, but the sense of respect is communicated to clients. This is not always easy in institutional settings which sometimes fail to provide for the privacy needs of residents. Where the institution is clearly deficient in this matter, professionals have the obligation to contribute to rectifying the deficiency. Indeed, most institutions find it impossible to grant residents the full measure of privacy which they desire. For this very reason, professionals in institutional settings have the obligation to be on their guard against a spirit of easily disregarding residents' privacy.

   In view of the extensive data storage and processing capacities of the computer, the professional must ensure that data maintained on the computer is limited to information that is necessary to service delivery, destroyed when it is no longer necessary for service provision, and restricted in access by using appropriate computer security methods. The informal nature of recreation can add to this problem, and thus requires careful watchfulness.

D. Professional Practices

Professionals provide quality services based on the highest professional standards. Professionals abide by standards set by the profession, deviating only when justified by the needs of the individual. Care is used in administering tests and other measurement instruments. They are used only for their express purposes. Instruments should conform to accepted psychometric standards. The nature of all practices, including tests and measurements are explained to individuals. Individuals are also debriefed on the results and the implications of professional practices. All professional practices are conducted with the safety and well-being of the individual in mind.

In order to provide service based on the highest professional standards, therapeutic recreation practitioners have the obligation to thoroughly understand those standards and their implications. In a field such as therapeutic recreation, which is characterized not only by its own existing complexities, but also by rapid changes in the many environments in which it functions, individual practitioners must continue studying throughout their working lives. Indeed, like members of all professions, they must consider themselves lifelong learners. Their study should not be confined to their own profession solely, but should include knowledge about specific client groups which they serve, and those aspects of related fields which touch upon the practice of therapeutic recreation.

Tests and instruments of measurement should be used only by fully qualified persons; they should not be selected lightly, nor should results be taken absolutely, especially where validity and reliability are doubtful. Projective and other indirect methods of testing which rely strongly on interpretation should be used with caution. Consent, in writing, should be obtained from individuals being tested, or from their authorized representatives. Professionals must recognize the effects of socioeconomic, ethnic, and cultural factors on test performance. It must be remembered that test results constitute only one of a variety of pertinent sources of information to be used in professional service. Ethical practice mandates the avoidance and prevention of the misuse of test results which have become obsolete.

To the professional standards which govern the practice of therapeutic recreation, NTRS members must also add other standards governing service in particular settings or to specific client groups. They practice their profession in compliance with legal standards, and do not participate in arrangements undermining the law. Indeed, obedience to and respect for law and regulatory authority should be viewed as an absolute minimum standard of professional conduct below which no therapeutic recreation professional should fall. The potential consequences of violating this admonition extend beyond those which may fall upon the person of a violator, since one member of NTRS may indeed bring discredit upon the profession by violating laws or regulations which govern the conduct of therapeutic recreation service.

III. The Obligation of the Professional to Other Individuals and to Society

A. General Welfare

Professionals make certain that their actions do not harm others. They also seek to promote the general welfare of society by advocating the importance of leisure, recreation, and play.

In their efforts to promote leisure values, therapeutic recreation professionals are not seeking their own narrow self interest or that of their own profession. While it is clear that in the long run, both they as individuals, and the profession as a whole, will gain by the promotion of leisure values, the primary focus of the profession is to others. It is this altruistic value system which sets the professions apart. Professions differ from commercial enterprises precisely by their special social role, the promise they make, implicitly and explicitly, to contribute to the common good.

B. Fairness

Professionals are fair to other individuals and to the general public. They seek to balance the needs of the individuals they serve with the needs of other persons according to principles of equity.

Professionals recognize that the burdens and benefits of living and working in any group must be distributed fairly. In bidding for the resources needed to deliver therapeutic recreation services, they will be mindful that other services also need funding. Similarly, when cutbacks are called for, they will accept their fair share of these, not seeking special exceptions.

Any professional who has acquired a unified body of knowledge is necessarily indebted to predecessors and contemporaries who have shared freely their knowledge, skills, and understanding of the profession. In fairness, the professional is bound to repay that debt by sharing freely with contemporaries, and, thus, future generations, the fruits of his or her experience and insights. A corollary of this principle is that professionals are required to share in the burden of research activities which will enable them to make a fair contribution to knowledge of the discipline, and thus manifest their genuine concern for the public good.

IV. The Obligation of the Professional to Colleagues

A. Respect

Professionals show respect for colleagues and their respective professions. They take no action that undermines the integrity of their colleagues.

In order to act with due regard for the needs, special competencies, and obligations of their colleagues, professionals need to know and take into account the traditions and practices of related professions. The absence of formal relationships with other professional workers does not relieve the therapeutic recreation practitioner of the obligation to exercise foresight, diligence, and tact in obtaining assistance from other professional colleagues which could be beneficial to their own clients.

B. Cooperation and Support

Professionals cooperate with and support their colleagues for the benefit of the persons they serve. Professionals demand the highest professional and moral conduct of each other. They approach and offer help to colleagues who require assistance with an ethical problem. Professionals take appropriate action toward colleagues who behave unethically.

The therapeutic milieu profits greatly when there is a spirit of cooperation among the different service professions. It would be particularly reprehensible to attempt to involve clients in any competitive strife or personal animosities which might arise between professionals, or to exploit a dispute between a colleague and employers to obtain a position or otherwise advance one's own interests. The professional should seek arbitration or mediation when conflicts require resolution for compelling professional reasons.

The spirit of collegiality is fostered when professionals represent accurately and fairly the qualifications, views, and findings of colleagues and use appropriate channels to express judgments on these matters. Sharing of resources is essential for the successful functioning of the interdisciplinary team.

The professional should create and maintain conditions of practice that facilitate ethical and competent professional performance by colleagues. When he or she becomes aware, however, of inappropriate or questionable practice in the provision of care, concern should be expressed to the person carrying out the questionable practice, and attention called to the possible detrimental effect upon client welfare. If necessary, the questionable conduct should be reported to the appropriate authority both within the service delivery institution, and to the worker's professional organization. There should be an established process for the reporting and handling of incompetent, unethical, or illegal practice within the employment setting, so that such reporting can go through established channels without fear of reprisal. The therapeutic recreation professional needs to be informed about the process of reporting questionable practice and be prepared to use it if necessary.

In order to deal effectively with ethical dilemmas, it is helpful to have in the service setting an established Ethics Committee, composed of representatives of all the professional disciplines serving in the facility. Therapeutic recreation professionals should take their place on the Ethics Committee, and, if there be no such committee in their place of service, should take the leadership in establishing one.

V. The Obligation of the Professional to the Profession

A. Knowledge

Professionals work to increase and improve the profession's body of knowledge by supporting and/or by conducting research. Research is practiced according to accepted canons and ethics of scientific inquiry. Where subjects are involved, their welfare is paramount. Prior permission is gained from subjects to participate in research. They are informed of the general nature of the research and any specific risks that may be involved. Subjects are debriefed at the conclusion of the research, and are provided with results of the study on request.

The professional is obliged not only to keep up with the growing body of knowledge, but also contributes to it. Being involved in research is the duty of every professional. For those engaged in a therapeutic intervention it is imperative that the evaluation of processes and outcomes be shared with the professional community.

In the conduct of research they establish with research participants, prior to the research, a clear disclosure of all aspects of the research that might reasonably be expected to influence willingness to participate. Research with children, or with those whose impairments might limit understanding, requires special safeguarding procedures. The same is true of those studies in which the use of some measure of concealment or deception is necessary.

After the data are gathered, the researcher debriefs the participant, and in the process attempts to clear up any misconceptions about the study. The researcher has responsibility for any harm, physical or emotional, which participants may experience during the research process.

Individuals and groups participating in research have the right to be informed about the results. The researcher is scrupulously honest in every aspect of presenting research findings, not only in discussion of results, both disappointing and encouraging, but also in acknowledging the use of sources.

B. Respect

Professionals treat the profession with critical respect. They strive to protect, preserve, and promote the integrity of the profession and its commitment to pubic service.

Knowledge of the history of the profession is a prerequisite for preserving the integrity of its goals and ideals. Participation in the democratic process of selecting officers of the Society is a duty of all members. They are, furthermore, obligated to contribute to the shaping of professional policy by participating in discussions, communications, or surveys at local, state, and national levels. They are careful to offer constructive suggestions for the improvement of the Society, or, when necessary, for restoring its traditional prioritization among values.

Members must carefully distinguish between promoting the integrity of the profession, which the Code requires, and promoting the profession for gain. It is especially important to avoid degenerating into mere special interest groups engaged in a struggle for privilege, power, and position.

C. Reform

Professionals are committed to regular and continuous evaluation of the profession. Changes are implemented that improve the profession's ability to serve society.

Evaluation of the profession can only be done on the basis of a philosophical consensus. When such consensus is lacking, the members have the obligation to work collaboratively toward establishing or re-establishing it, in a spirit of collegiality and honesty.

Once philosophical consensus is established, the members must engage in on-going dialogue in order to see that the values of the Society are applied in the developing circumstances in which they must practice. It is quite usual in the development of professions that controversies arise about directions and policies. Ethical practice indicates that such controversies not be exploited for the gain of individuals or sub-groups within the membership. Rather, therapeutic recreation professionals will strive to perceive differences of opinion as opportunities of growth for the Society, and will endeavor to work through to decisions which will best serve the common good.

VI. The Obligation of the Profession to Society

A. Service

The profession exists to serve society. All of its activities and resources are devoted to the principle of service.

In order to render appropriate service, the members must be familiar with changes in society which suggest new ways for the profession to exercise its mission to the common good. For example, it is the obligation of the profession to seek out new groups within the population, who do not have adequate access to leisure, and to generate public policy to address the leisure needs of such groups.

Furthermore, therapeutic recreation professionals should do their utmost to assist in minimizing the costs of their service, without compromising the quality of benefits they provide, not only by helping to improve the operational efficiency of therapeutic recreation programs, but also by contributing to the solution of economic, legal, political, and social problems which demonstrably increase the cost of health care services. The therapeutic recreation practitioner should not neglect his or her personal duty, as a good citizen and a professional, to become actively involved in the search for underlying causes of and long-run solutions to such problems.

B. Equality

The profession is committed to equality of opportunity. No person shall be refused service because of race, gender, religion, social status, ethnic background, religious preference or sexual orientation. Therapeutic recreation specialists support affordable health care services to persons currently without coverage or the means to pay for services. Additionally, they are committed to pro bono work that offers some relief for those unable to pay.

Since the profession exists to serve society, the members must be on guard about their manner of selecting clients. A profession does not serve society simply by selecting from it a small group whom it is profitable to serve. Following the medical model of service too closely, for example, might lead to practice that is elitist, too easily conscious of prestige or monetary gains. Selecting clients whom it is in the profession's financial interest to serve is tantamount to using the clients, something that is ethically unacceptable. Furthermore, selecting clients on the basis of diagnoses which are advantageous for the profession, whether in terms of monetary reward, or presumed prestige, amounts to a kind of discrimination.

Clients with contagious diseases are not to be refused treatment, although due precautions are to be exercised in the settings where they are served. In order to correct misinformation about such clients, professionals need to be fully informed about all facets of their conditions.

Members do not condone or engage in sexual harassment, which is defined as deliberate or repeated comments, gestures, or physical contacts of a sexual nature.

C. Advocacy

The profession advocates for the people it is entrusted to serve. It protects and promotes their health and well-being and their inalienable right to leisure, recreation, and play in clinical and community settings.

Therapeutic recreation must be faithful to the values of play, leisure, and recreation—the primary focus of the profession which in some service situations can sometimes be relegated to a secondary position behind measurable clinical gains, and perhaps neglected altogether.

Members of NTRS recognize responsibility not only to their own clients, but also to society. The public duties of the profession include playing a part in the formation of social philosophy and policies, a part which goes far beyond providing technical expertise, to making a contribution to addressing society's underlying problems and needs.

In order to fulfill their public duties, professionals must strengthen their commitment to the concept of the common good, thus helping society to resist the influence of self-interested values which pose a threat to the common good. The special contribution which therapeutic recreation professionals can make to the development of a public philosophy is through their presentation of the relation between leisure/play/recreation and the quality of individual and community life in a just social order. By nurturing the value of leisure in society, NTRS members can shape our cultural heritage and way of life.

Reprinted, by permission, from the National Therapeutic Recreation Society, a branch of the National Recreation and Park Association.

American Therapeutic Recreation Association Code of Ethics

ATRA
1414 Prince Street, Suite 204
Alexandria, Virginia 22314
703-683-9420
Fax: 703-683-9431
www.atra-tr.org

ATRA Definition Statement

Therapeutic Recreation is the provision of treatment services and the provision of recreation services to persons with illnesses or disabling conditions. The primary purposes of treatment services which are often referred to as Recreational Therapy, are to restore, remediate or rehabilitate in order to improve functioning, and independence, as well as reduce or eliminate the effects of illness or disability. The primary purposes of recreational services are to provide recreation resources and opportunities in order to improve health and well-being. Therapeutic Recreation is provided by professionals who are trained and certified, registered and/or licensed to provide Therapeutic Recreation.

The American Therapeutic Recreation Association's Code of Ethics is to be used as a guide for promoting and maintaining the highest standards of ethical behavior. The Code applies to all Therapeutic Recreation personnel. The term Therapeutic Recreation personnel includes Certified Therapeutic Recreation Specialists (CTRS), therapeutic recreation assistants and therapeutic recreation students. Acceptance of membership in the American Therapeutic Recreation Association commits a member to adherence to these principles.

Principle 1: Beneficence/Non-Maleficence

Therapeutic Recreation personnel shall treat persons in an ethical manner not only by respecting their decisions and protecting them from harm but also by actively making efforts to secure their well-being. Personnel strive to maximize possible benefits, and minimize possible harms. This serves as the guiding principle for the professional. The term "persons" includes not only persons served but colleagues, agencies and the profession.

Principle 2: Autonomy

Therapeutic Recreation personnel have a duty to preserve and protect the right of each individual to make his/her own choices. Each individual is to be given the opportunity to determine his/her own course of action in accordance with a plan freely chosen.

Principle 3: Justice

Therapeutic Recreation personnel are responsible for ensuring that individuals are served fairly and that there is equity in the distribution of services. Individuals receive service without regard to race, color, creed, gender, sexual orientation, age, disability/disease, social and financial status.

Principle 4: Fidelity

Therapeutic Recreation personnel have an obligation to be loyal, faithful and meet commitments made to persons receiving services, colleagues, agencies and the profession.

Principle 5: Veracity/Informed Consent

Therapeutic recreation personnel shall be truthful and honest. Therapeutic Recreation personnel are responsible for providing each individual receiving service with information regarding the service and the professional's training and credentials; benefits, outcomes, length of treatment, expected activities, risks, limitations. Each individual receiving service has the right to know what is likely to take place during and as a result of professional intervention. Informed consent is obtained when information is provided by the professional.

Principle 6: Confidentiality and Privacy

Therapeutic Recreation personnel are responsible for safeguarding information about individuals served. Individuals served have the right to control information about themselves. When a situation arises that requires disclosure of confidential information about an individual to protect the individual's welfare or the interest of others, the Therapeutic Recreation professional has the responsibility/obligation to inform the individual served of the circumstances in which confidentiality was broken.

Principle 7: Competence

Therapeutic Recreation personnel have the responsibility to continually seek to expand one's knowledge base related to Therapeutic Recreation practice. The professional is responsible for keeping a record of participation in training activities. The professional has the responsibility for contributing to advancement of the profession through activities such as research, dissemination of information through publications and professional presentations, and through active involvement in professional organizations.

Principle 8: Compliance With Laws and Regulations

Therapeutic Recreation personnel are responsible for complying with local, state and federal laws and ATRA policies governing the profession of Therapeutic Recreation.

March 1990/Revised June 2001

American Therapeutic Association Code of Ethics (2001).

Glossary

3S tourism—Type of tourism in idyllic settings that include sun, sand, and sea. Along with adventure tourism and consumptive and captive tourism, it is particularly harmful to the environment.

absolutism—Theory that there is always one indisputably correct perspective.

adventure tourism—Type of tourism that involves adventurous activities such as white-water rafting, skydiving, wilderness hiking, sea kayaking, mountain climbing, caving, and orienteering. Along with 3S tourism and consumptive and captive tourism, it is particularly harmful to the environment.

altruism—Unselfish regard for the well-being of others.

anthropocentrism—Theory that all natural objects exist for the sake of human beings.

autonomy—Self-governance.

biocentrism—Theory that all living things have moral standing, not just human beings.

bribe—Something given to persuade or induce an action. In business reciprocity, bribes are generally illegal.

consequence-based ethics—Moral justification that appeals to consequences.

consumptive and captive tourism—Type of tourism dependent on the environment and including recreation activities such as hunting and fishing (consumptive) and zoological parks (captive). Along with adventure tourism and 3S tourism, they are particularly harmful to the environment.

Defining Issues Test (DIT)—Test developed by psychologist James Rest to measure an individual's level of moral development.

deontological ethics—Ethical theory that focuses on the obligations of human beings to each other.

distributive justice—Type of justice in which social goods are made available to those who are deemed worthy of receiving them.

ecocentrism—Theory that natural nonliving things such as ecological systems have moral standing.

ecotourism—Type of tourism in which the natural environment is the main attraction and preservation and enhancement are primary concerns for promoters and tourists.

ethical egoism—Philosophy that individuals should always act purely in their own best interests.

ethical relativism—Theory that truth and moral values are not absolute but are relative to the persons or groups holding them.

ethical sensitivity—The ability to recognize significant ethical quandaries.

ethos—The guiding beliefs of a person, group, or institution.

fiduciary duty—The responsibility of middle and upper management to oversee the effective and efficient use of an organization's money.

future market—Market that will be available in the future, such as today's children who will be tomorrow's adult consumers.

gift—Something given without an expectation of return.

influence market—Target market that influences actual buyers, such as children who influence their parents' choice of products.

kickback—An illegal rebate from a previous exchange.

Kohlberg's theory of moral development—Psychologist Lawrence Kohlberg's theory that, as people mature, their ability to reason has the potential to become more sophisticated, ascending six stages of complexity in moral reasoning.

moral standing—Term used to designate worthiness of ethical consideration.

naive legalism—Deferring moral responsibility for ethical behavior to the legal system.

negative rights—Rights based on the idea that one has an obligation to refrain from doing certain things to another person.

paternalism—Doing something to or for another person, which is believed to be in the person's best interest, without that person's consent.

positive rights—Rights based on the idea that other people have an obligation to others to do certain things.

primary market—The population at which most marketing efforts are directed.

professionalism—The conduct, aims, or qualities that characterize or mark a profession or a professional person.

psychological egoism—Theory that individuals can only behave in their own best interests.

rationing—The planned allocation of resources, services, and opportunities often used in outdoor recreation resource management.

reciprocity—Relationship between people involving the exchange of goods, services, favors, or obligations. Business reciprocity includes gifts, bribes, and kickbacks.

rule-based ethics—Ethical theory that focuses on the obligations of human beings to each other.

self-dealing—Behavior in which a person places his or her own pecuniary interests over those of an organization in such a way that the organization is harmed.

soft law—Codes that provide guidance for dealing with difficult ethical issues in a profession.

speciesism—Discrimination against animals, suggesting that conventional treatment of animals is similar to the discriminatory treatment previously accorded to women (sexism) and to people of color (racism).

tautology—An empty or vacuous statement composed of simpler statements in a fashion that makes it logically true regardless of whether the simpler statements are factually true or false.

theocentrism—The belief that God is the central fact of existence.

transference—Phenomenon in which patients, clients, or even students view their therapists or professors excessively positively, thereby increasing their own vulnerability.

uncontestable positions—Rigid, dogmatic beliefs that cannot even be discussed.

utilitarianism—Ethical theory that the consequences of our actions should be judged by how much good is produced for others, with the goal of attaining the greatest good for the greatest number.

virtue-based ethics—Ethical theory that focuses on character rather than cognitive abilities; according to virtue ethics, resolving moral dilemmas depends on the type of person one is or the role one plays.

References

Abbott, A. 1988. *The systems of professions.* London: University of Chicago Press.

Abbott, D.A., S.L. Cramer, and S.D. Sherrets. 1995. Pathological gambling and the family: Practice implications. *Families in Society* 76(4): 213-217.

Allen, J. 2000. *Without sanctuary: Lynching photography in America.* Santa Fe, NM: Twin Palms.

Alm, R. 1996. Taking a chance on boats. *Kansas City Star Magazine,* June 30, 9.

American Academy of Pediatrics. 1995. Children, adolescents and advertising. *Pediatrics* 95(2): 295-297.

American Gaming Association. 1996. *Economic impacts of casino gaming in the United States, Volume 1: Macro study.* Washington, D.C.: American Gaming Association.

American Gaming Association. 2004. *2004 State of the States: The AGA survey of casino entertainment.* Washington, D.C.: American Gaming Association.

An outline of the Anita Hill and Clarence Thomas controversy. History 122. http://chnm.gmu.edu/courses/122/hill/hillframe.htm (accessed January 2005).

Arctic National Wildlife Refuge. Wild lands. http://arctic.fws.gov/seismic.htm (accessed January 2005).

Arendt, H. 1963. *Eichmann in Jerusalem: A report on the banality of evil.* New York: Viking Press.

Berman, E. 1986. *In Africa with Schweitzer.* Far Hills, NJ: New Horizon Press.

Blackburn, S. 2001. *Being good: An introduction to ethics.* Oxford, UK: Oxford University Press.

Blanco, W. 1992. *Herodotus: The histories.* New York: W.W. Norton and Co.

Bouma-Prediger, S. 2001. *For the beauty of the earth: A Christian vision for creation care.* Grand Rapids, MI: Baker Academic.

Browne, D.J., D.O. Kaldenberg, and B.A. Browne. 1992. Socio-economic status and playing the lotteries. *Sociology and Social Research* 76(3): 161-167.

Bryce, J. 2001. The technological transformation of leisure. *Social Science Computer Review* 19(1): 7-16.

Campbell, A., and K.C. Glass. 2001. The legal status of clinical and ethics policies, codes, and guidelines in medical practice and research. *McGill Law Journal* 46(2): 473-489.

Canada West Foundation. 2002. *Canadian gambling behavior and attitudes: Summary report.* Calgary: Canada West Foundation.

Canadian whistleblower laws. Canadian Law Site. www.canadianlawsite.com/whistle-blower.htm#b (accessed January 2005).

Clarke, M., and J. Stewart. 1986. Local government and the public service orientation. *Local Government Studies* 12(3): 28-32.

Cleek, M.A., and S.L. Leonard. 1998. Can corporate codes of ethics influence behavior? *Journal of Business Ethics* 17(6): 619-630.

Coalter, F. 1990. The politics of professionalism: Consumers or citizens? *Leisure Studies* 9:107-119.

Cross, G. 1990. *A social history of leisure since 1600.* State College, PA: Venture.

Crossley, J.C., and L.M. Jamieson. 1993. *Introduction to commercial and entrepreneurial recreation.* 2nd ed. Champaign, IL: Sagamore.

Cruz-Neira, C., D.J. Sandin, T.A. DeFantini, R. Kenyon, and J.C. Hart. 1992, June. The CAVE Audiovisual Experience automatic virtual environment. *Communications of the ACM,* 64-72.

D'Angelo, R. 2001. *The American civil rights movement: Readings and interpretations.* New York: McGraw-Hill/Dushkin.

Dandekar, N. 1991. Can whistleblowing be fully legitimated? A theoretical discussion. *Business and Professional Ethics Journal* 10(1): 89-108.

Deck, M. 1997. *Business ethics survey report.* KPMG.

Defenders of Wildlife. America votes "Yes!" for wolves. www.defenders.org/wildlife/wolf/yeswolf.html (accessed January 2005).

Duffy, R. 2000. Shadow players: Ecotourism development, corruption and state politics in Belize. *Third World Quarterly* 21(3): 549-565.

Dustin, D.L., L.H. McAvoy, and J.H. Schultz. 2002. *Stewards of access, custodians of choice: A philosophical foundation for the park and recreation profession.* 3rd ed. Champaign, IL: Sagamore.

Edelman, V. 1996. Touch goes high-tech. *Psychology Today* 29(1): 59-63.

Edgington, C.R., D.J. Jordan, D.G. DeGraaf, and D.R. Edgington. 1995. *Leisure and life satisfaction: Foundational perspectives.* Madison, IA: Brown and Benchmark.

Fetto, J. 2002. Off the map. *American Demographics* 24(8): 72.

Field Jr., T.G. 2004. Copyright on the Internet. Franklin Pierce Law Center. www.fplc.edu/tfield/copynet.htm (accessed February 2005).

Finnis, J. 1998. *Aquinas: Moral, political, and legal theory.* New York: Oxford University Press.

Fish and Wildlife Research Institute. 2000. *Puffer fish in Florida.* www.floridamarine.org/features/view_article.asp?id=15773 (accessed January 2005).

FloridaTravelUSA. 2004. Sea World: What's old and what's new. *Florida Travel Magazine.* www.floridatravelusa.com/articlesnew/seaworldmay04p036.html (accessed January 2005).

Foreman, D. 1993. Putting the earth first. In *Environmental ethics: Divergence and convergence,* ed. S. Armstrong and R. Botzler, 422-429. New York: McGraw-Hill.

Freidson, E. 1994. *Professionalism reborn: Theory, prophecy, and policy.* Chicago: University of Chicago Press.

Futrell, A. 1997. *Blood in the arena: The spectacle of Roman power.* Austin: University of Texas Press.

Gazel, R.C., W.N. Thompson, and J.T. Brunner. 1996. *Casino gamblers in Illinois: Who are they?* Leesburg, VA: National Coalition Against Casino Gambling.

Gilligan, C. 1993. *In a different voice: Psychological theory and women's development.* Cambridge, MA: Harvard University Press.

Glazer, M., and P. Glazer. 1989. *The whistleblower: Exposing corruption in government and industry.* New York: Basic.

Grappling with rock climbing. 1993. *Environment* 35(10): 39-43.

GreenPACK. 2004. Tourism. http://greenpack.rec.org/tourism/tourism_growth/index.shtml (accessed January 2005).

Grinols, E.L., and J.D. Omorov. 1995. *Development or dreamfield illusions? Assessing casino gambling's costs and benefits.* Champaign, IL: University of Illinois Department of Economics.

Guber, S.S, and J. Barry. 1993. *Marketing to and through kids.* New York: McGraw-Hill.

Hamilton, E., and H. Cairns, eds. 1961. *The collected dialogues of Plato.* Princeton, NJ: Princeton University Press.

Harrison, D. 1994. Tourism and prostitution: Sleeping with the enemy? *Tourism Management* 15: 435-443.

Hayhurst, C. 2001. Pay to play. *E: The Environmental Magazine* 12(1): 20-22.

Hemingway, J. 1988. Leisure and civility: Reflections on a Greek ideal. *Leisure Sciences* 10: 179-191.

Herring, M., and T. Bledsoe. 1994. A model of lottery participation: Demographics, context and attitudes. *Policies Studies Journal* 22(3): 245-257.

Hoig, S. 1961. *The Sand Creek massacre.* Norman, OK: University of Oklahoma Press.

Hostetler, J.A. 1993. *Amish society.* 4th ed. Baltimore: John Hopkins University Press.

Houghton, J. 2002. *Curriculum catalog: Recreation and park education, 2002-2003.* Ashburn, VA: Society of Park and Recreation Educators.

Ilies, R., N. Hauserman, S. Schochau, and J. Stibal. 2003. Reported incidence rates of work-related sexual harassment in the United States: Using meta-analysis to explain reported rate disparities. *Personnel Psychology* 56(3): 607-631.

Iso-Ahola, S.E. 1980. *The social psychology of leisure and recreation.* Dubuque, IA: William C. Brown.

IUIC Red List of Threatened Species. Summary statistics. www.redlist.org/info/tables.html (accessed January 2005).

Jackson, K.M. 1993. *Walt Disney: A bio-bibliography.* Westport, CT: Greenwood Press.

Jubb, P. 1999. Whistleblowing: A restrictive definition and interpretation. *Journal of Business Ethics* 21(1): 77-94.

Kelly, J.R. 1987. *Freedom to be: A new sociology of leisure.* New York: MacMillan.

Kelly, J.R. 1996. *Leisure.* 3rd ed. Boston: Allyn and Bacon.

Kimball, B. 1992. *The "true professional ideal" in America: A history.* Cambridge, MA: Blackwell.

Knudson, D. 1984. *Outdoor recreation.* 2nd ed. New York: Macmillan.

Kohlberg, L. 1976. Moral stages and moralization: The cognitive-developmental approach. In *Moral development and behavior,* ed. T. Lickona, 31-53. New York: Holt, Rinehart and Winston.

Kohlberg, L. 1981. *Essays on moral development, vol. 1.* San Francisco: Harper & Row.

Kohlberg, L. 1984. *Essays on moral development, vol. 2.* San Francisco: Harper & Row.

Kraus, R.G., and J.E. Curtis. 2000. *Creative management in recreation, parks and leisure services.* 6th ed. Boston: McGraw-Hill.

Kraybill, D. 1989. *The riddle of Amish culture.* Baltimore: John Hopkins University Press.

Kuehn, M. 2001. *Kant: A bibliography.* New York: Cambridge University Press.

Kyle, D. 1998. *Spectacles of death in ancient Rome.* London: Routledge.

Lawton, L., and D. Weaver. 2000. Nature-based tourism and ecotourism. In *Tourism in the twenty-first century,* ed. B. Faulkner, G. Moscardo, and E. Laws, 34-48. London: Continuum.

Leitner, M.J., and S.F. Leitner. 2004. *Leisure enhancement.* 3rd ed. New York: Haworth Press.

Lord, J., P. Hutchison, and F. VanDerbeck. 1991. Narrowing the options: The power of professionals in daily life and leisure. In *Recreation and leisure: Issues in an era of change,* ed. T.L. Goodale and P.A. Witt, 247-261. State College, PA: Venture.

Lorenz, V. 1995. *The national impact of casino gambling proliferation.* Hearing before the Committee on Small Business, House of Representatives, 103rd Congress, 2nd session. Washington, D.C.

Maaga, M. 1998. *Hearing the voices of Jonestown.* Syracuse, NY: Syracuse University Press.

MacIntyre, A. 1984. *After virtue.* 2nd ed. Notre Dame, IN: University of Notre Dame Press.

Mathieson, A., and G. Wall. 1982. *Tourism: Economic, physical and social impacts.* London: Longman.

Maticka-Tyndale, E., E.S. Herold, and D. Mewhinney. 1998. Casual sex on spring break: Intentions and behaviors of Canadian students. *The Journal of Sex Research* 35(3): 254-264.

McBride, P. 1989. *Pioneers in leisure and recreation.* Reston, VA: American Alliance for Health, Education, Recreation and Dance.

McKeon, R. 2001. *The basic works of Aristotle.* New York: Modern Library.

McLaren, D. 2003. *Rethinking tourism and ecotravel.* 2nd ed. Bloomfield, CT: Kumarian Press.

McLean, D.J., and R.C.A. Johnson. 1993. The leisure service delivery dilemma: The professional versus the marketing model. *Journal of Applied Recreation Research* 18(4): 253-264.

McLean, D.J., and R.C.A. Johnson. 1997. Techniques for rationing public recreation services. *Journal of Park and Recreation Administration* 15(3): 76-92.

McNamee, M.J., H. Sheridan, and J. Buswell. 2000. Paternalism, professionalism and public sector leisure provision: The boundaries of a leisure profession. *Leisure Studies* 19(3): 199-209.

McNeil, J.U. 1992. *Kids as customers: A handbook for marketing to children.* New York: Lexington Books.

McNergney, R.F., E.R. Ducharme, and M.K. Ducharme. 1999. *Educating for democracy: Case method teaching and learning.* Mahwah, NJ: Erlbaum.

Mewhinney, D., E.S. Herold, and E. Maticka-Tyndale. 1995. Sexual scripts and risk-taking of Canadian university students on spring break in Daytona Beach, Florida. *The Canadian Journal of Human Sexuality* 4: 273-288.

Meyer, F.S. 1998. The twisted tree of liberty. In *Freedom and virtue: The conservative–libertarian debate,* ed. G.W. Carey, 13-19. Wilmington, DE: Intercollegiate Studies Institute.

Milgram, S. 1974. *Obedience to authority.* New York: Harper and Row.

More, T. 1999. A functionalist approach to user fees. *Journal of Leisure Research* 31(3): 227-244.

More, T., and T. Stevens. 2000. Do user fees exclude low-income people from resource-based recreation? *Journal of Leisure Research* 32(3): 341-357.

Muller, J.S. 1993. *Adam Smith in his time and ours.* Princeton, NJ: Princeton University Press.

Mullings, B. 1999. Globalization, tourism and the international sex trade. In *Sun, sex and gold: Tourism and sex work in the Caribbean,* ed. K. Kempadoo, 55-80. Lanham, MA: Bowman and Littlefield.

National Whistleblower Center. 2005. NIH whistleblower stripped of protection. www.whistleblowers.org/html/nih_drug_safety.htm (accessed February 2005).

Neville, K. 2000. *Internal affairs: The abuse of power, sexual harassment, and hypocrisy in the workplace.* New York: McGraw-Hill.

Newton, L. 1978. A professional ethic: A proposal in context. In *Matters of life and death,* ed. J.E. Thomas. Toronto: Samual Stevens Press.

Noonan, J.T. 1984. *Bribes.* New York: MacMillan.

O'Day, R. 2000. *The professions in early modern England, 1450-1800.* Harlow, UK: Pearson Education.

O'Sullivan, E.L. 1991. *Marketing for parks, recreation and leisure.* State College, PA: Venture.

Occultopedia. 2004. *Cannibalism.* www.occultopedia.com/c/cannibalism.htm (accessed January 2005).

Oppermann, M. 1999. Sex tourism. *Annals of Tourism Research* 26(2): 251-266.

Oppermann, M., S. McKinley, and K. Chon. 1998. Marketing sex and tourism destinations. *Sex, tourism and prostitution: Aspects of leisure, recreation and work,* ed. M. Oppermann, 20-29. New York: Cognizant Communication.

Pavalko, R. 1972. *Sociological perspectives on occupations.* Itasca, IL: F.E. Peacock.

Peters, F.E. 1967. *Greek philosophical terms: A historical lexicon.* New York: New York University Press.

Platz, L., and M. Millar. 2001. Gambling in the context of other recreation activity: A quantitative comparison of casual and pathological student gamblers. *Journal of Leisure Research* 33(4): 383-395.

Polanyi, K. 1944. *The great transformation.* New York: Pearson Books.

Priest, S. 1990. The semantics of adventure education. In *Adventure education,* ed. J.C. Miles and S. Priest, 113-117. State College, PA: Venture.

Punch, M. 1986. *The politics and ethics of fieldwork.* Beverly Hills, CA: Sage.

Putnam, R.D. 2000. *Bowling alone: The collapse and revival of American community.* New York: Simon and Schuster.

Rawls, J. 1971. *A theory of justice.* Cambridge, MA: Harvard University Press.

Regan, T. 1983. *The case for animal rights.* Berkeley, CA: University of California Press.

Reid, T.R. 2003. The Sherpas. *National Geographic Magazine* 203(5): 42-71.

Rest, J.R. 1994. Background: Theory and research. In *Moral development in the professions: Psychology and applied ethics,* ed. J.R. Rest and D. Narvaez, 1-26. Hillsdale, NJ: Erlbaum.

Rest, J.R., and D. Narvaez, eds. 1994. *Moral development in the professions.* Hillsdale, NJ: Erlbaum.

Rest, J.R., D. Narvaez, M. Bebeau, and S. Thoma. 1999. *Postconventional moral thinking: A Neo-Kohlbergian approach.* Mahwah, NJ: Erlbaum.

Rosenstand, N. 1997. *The moral of the story: An introduction to ethics.* 2nd ed. Mountain View, CA: Mayfield.

Saletan, W. 2002. Wok the dog. *Slate,* http://slate.msn.com/id/2060840/ (accessed January 2005).

Schneider, J., and R. Weiss. 2001. *Cybersex exposed: Simple fantasy or obsession?* Center City, MN: Hazelden Publishing and Educational Services.

Schwartz, M. 2001. The nature and relationship between corporate codes of ethics and behavior. *Journal of Business Ethics* 32(3): 247-262.

Sessoms, H.D. 1991. The professionalization of parks and recreation: A necessity? In *Recreation and leisure: Issues in an era of change,* ed. T.L. Goodale and P.A. Witt, 247-261. State College, PA: Venture.

Shapiro, J.P. 1996. America's gambling fever. *U.S. News and World Report,* January 15, 58, 60.

Singer, P. 1990. *Animal liberation.* 2nd ed. New York: New York Review of Books.

Skinner, S.J. 1990. *Marketing.* Boston: Houghton Mifflin.

Slater, L. 2004. *Opening Skinner's box: Great psychological experiments of the twentieth century.* New York: W.W. Norton and Company.

Smith, A. 1776. *An inquiry into the nature and causes of the wealth of nations.* London: Penguin Books.

Steidlmeier, P. 1999. Gift giving, bribery and corruption: Ethical management of business relationships in China. *Journal of Business Ethics* 20: 121-132.

Stevens, E. 1979. *Business ethics.* New York: Paulist Press.

Sylvester, C., J.E. Voelkle, and G.D. Ellis. 2001. *Therapeutic recreation programming: Theory and practice.* State College, PA: Venture.

Thomas, M., and Ostiguy, L. 1998. Therapeutic recreation: Profession at a crossroads. *Journal of Leisurability* 25(2): 26-36.

Thornton, M. 1991. *The economics of Prohibition.* Salt Lake City: University of Utah Press.

Twain, M. 1917. *Mark Twain calendar.* New York: Sully and Kleinteich.

Twardzik, L.F. 1984. A case for the study of ethics in professional education and practice. *Leisure Sciences* 6(3): 375-385.

USA Today. 2004. Utah, other states mulls how to handle search-and-rescue costs. June 20, www.usatoday.com/news/nation/2004-06-20-funding-searches_x.htm (accessed January 2005).

U.S. Attorney General. 1986. *Attorney General's commission on pornography report,* 933. Washington, D.C.: UGO.

U.S. Census Bureau. 2000. Household and family statistics. Washington, D.C.: UGO.

U.S.-Parks. National park fees. U.S.-Parks.com. www.us-parks.com/misc/National_Park_fees/park_fees.shtml (accessed January 2005).

U.S. Water News Online. 2002, November. Michigan health department orders Amish to install septic tanks. www.uswaternews.com/archives/arcpolicy/2micheall.html (accessed February 2005).

VanDeVeer, D. 1986. *Paternalistic intervention: The moral bounds of benevolence.* Princeton, NJ: Princeton University Press.

Vielba, C. 1986. Marketing and local government: A contradiction in terms? *Local Government Studies* 12(6): 14-19.

Waterman, L., and G. Waterman. 1979. *Backwoods ethics: Environmental concerns for hikers and campers.* Washington, D.C.: Stonewall Press.

Whistleblower. Recognizing retaliation: The risks and costs of whistleblowing. www.whistleblower.org/article.php?did=34&scid=72 (accessed January 2005).

White, N. 2003. Say neigh to that. *Casper Star-Tribune,* January 1.

Williams, S. 1985. *Conflict of interest: The ethical dilemma in politics.* Brookfield, VT: Gower.

Wyllie, R. 2000. *Tourism and society: A guide to problems and issues.* State College, PA: Venture.

Index

About the Authors

Donald J. McLean, PhD, is an associate professor in the department of recreation, park, and tourism administration at Western Illinois University–Quad Cities in Moline, Illinois. He has been teaching ethics classes since 1989. His interest in this area was spurred by practical experience gained through 12 years of coaching competitive rowing and founding rowing programs and clubs at the varsity, campus recreation, and community levels. He has presented papers on applied ethics at national conferences and served as guest editor for a special applied ethics issue of the *Journal of Applied Recreation Research.* In his own leisure time, he enjoys golfing, traveling, and boating.

Daniel G. Yoder, PhD, provided most of the case studies in this book from his experiences. Yoder is a professor in the department of recreation, park, and tourism administration at Western Illinois University in Macomb, Illinois. He has taught at the university level for 12 years and has also worked in the leisure services field for 12 years. He is a member of the National Park and Recreation Association and of the Illinois Park and Recreation Association (IPRA), having served in a number of positions with the IPRA. He is also involved in a variety of nonprofit organizations dealing with recreation and youth in his community. Yoder has served on various university judicial boards, hearing cases involving students' alleged misconduct. Besides his teaching and community involvement, he is a husband, father, part-time farmer, full-time conservationist, and avid beekeeper.

*You'll find
other outstanding
recreation resources at*

www.HumanKinetics.com

In the U.S. call

1-800-747-4457

Australia.............................. 08 8277 1555
Canada 1-800-465-7301
Europe......................+44 (0) 113 255 5665
New Zealand.................. 0064 9 448 1207

HUMAN KINETICS
The Information Leader in Physical Activity
P.O. Box 5076 • Champaign, IL 61825-5076 USA